3.00

REMODEL, DON'T MOVE

How to Change Your Home
to Fit Your Lifestyle

Remodel, Don't Move

HOW TO CHANGE YOUR HOME TO FIT YOUR LIFESTYLE

by WILLIAM E. HAGUE

DOUBLEDAY & COMPANY, INC.
Garden City, New York

Library of Congress Cataloging in Publication Data

Hague, William E.
    Remodel, don't move.

    Includes index.
    1. Dwellings—Remodeling. I. Title.
TH4816.H285   1981   690'.837'0286
ISBN: 0-385-15910-2
Library of Congress Catalog Card Number 80–498

CONTENTS

Part Three   SPECIAL AREAS

INTRODUCTION

CHANGED LIFESTYLES: HOW THEY AFFECT YOUR HOME

Rapidly changing lifestyles have prompted families all over the country to adopt a whole new, vastly different approach to their homes. In the past, families tended to keep their home "as is" with little regard to different living requirements. The home became a kind of sacred cow and people went on making-do with cramped quarters, uncomfortable master bedrooms, inadequate storage, poorly equipped kitchens, and a host of other inconveniences. When major upheavals came about, they were handled in terms of the living space that existed. If the situation finally became unbearable, the house was apt to be sold and everyone moved to a different and often only marginally better residence. When a husband's position improved and his income increased appreciably, a family's first thought was to sell and go to a more prestigious neighborhood. There was little or no thought given to modifying the existing house to fit a changed situation, to make it more comfortable, or to give it a look commensurate with new prosperity.

Today fast-changing lifestyles have forced new thinking. In fact, at no time in the recent American past have living patterns changed as rapidly and as drastically. Men and women are taking early retirement to travel, develop personal interests, and enjoy leisure. Teenage children are demanding greater independence, with sleeping and social quarters apart from close parental supervision, yet under the parental roof. Divorced daughters and sons are returning to their parents' home, sometimes with a child, always with the need for privacy with understanding. Two men and two women often join forces to make a home for each other with the needs for shared yet independent living. Young couples sometimes must accept in-laws and other relatives and make their home accommodate two family units. Then, there is the family moving up the economic ladder who wants its home to reflect its changed status. Perhaps they want to entertain more and need a larger, more important living room or dining room. Another family may become sports-minded and want to develop outdoor space to include a swimming pool or tennis court. Still another changed lifestyle might result when a wife and/or husband becomes interested in gourmet cooking and needs a larger, better-equipped kitchen.

Lately, more and more homeowners are taking a long, hard look at the property they have. When a husband retires, rather than rattling around in a too-big house for a while, then selling it and moving to Florida or some sunny climate, he and his wife are more apt to consider turning the too-big house into sensibly sized quarters for themselves, plus one or two income-producing apartments, with the tax advantages that accrue plus the security advantage of having someone to keep an eye on the property while they winter in the sun. A young family that must accommodate in-laws finds a way of rearranging the house so the two families are not in each other's pockets. Perhaps the carport can be turned into a pleasant bed-sitting room and bath or maybe that big playroom at the rear of the garage could become a second, private world under the same roof. If a husband longs for a dressing room and bath of his own, he takes a new look at the small, unused bedroom adjacent to the master bedroom and sees that space in a new light. His wife, meanwhile, may be thinking of ways to create a kitchen more suited to her needs, perhaps by incorporating the unused back porch next to it.

THE QUESTION: TO MOVE OR STAY AND REMODEL?

What all these hypothetical situations add up to is that each family must make a decision about their living: they must either sell the house they have or remodel it to respond to new living demands. This can be a difficult decision and this book has been designed to help them make the decision and guide them through the process of evaluation and into the nitty-gritty of remodeling. Obviously, our basic premise is that in most cases today it is more practical, economical, and all-around desirable to "stay put" and remodel, but we recognize that there can be no hard-and-fast rules about anything as personal as family living. When it comes to moving or staying, each family must weigh the pluses and minuses.

On the plus side of selling and moving, you might just find a house exactly suited to your basic needs. There is also the adventure of exploring a new neighborhood and starting afresh in a whole different environment. All this is tempered by some minuses. First, there is the price tag you will find on for-sale homes. Today's home buyers are usually shocked at the inflated cost of real estate in good and even not-so-good neighborhoods. Another shocker is soaring interest rates on new home mortgages. Then there will be new assessment and real estate taxes based on the new, inflated prices. There is the tiresome but important task of searching for a new home, with all the attendant study of neighborhoods, reading newspaper advertisements and working with real estate salespeople. Also comes the realization, as you look at possibilities to buy, that no new house ever "fits" completely; it always needs some redecoration—new paint, drapery, carpet here and there, perhaps one or two new appliances. Last but not least is the agony of sorting out the accumulated belongings of years, getting rid of some, packing up the rest and moving, a dreadful chore in itself. Finally, once in the new place, there is the long-term business of getting settled in a new, unfamiliar neighborhood.

The Pluses In Staying Where You Are

There are a lot of advantages in keeping the house you have and remodeling it. First, there is the equity you have built up in your home. Perhaps the mortgage is paid off or substantially paid off and the interest is at the original low rate which is favorable to the rate currently offered by banks. Taxes may be modest because of an existing low assessment and they may include a homeowner's exemption. Location is in a known neighborhood with shops you know and like, near church and medical facilities, close to old friends and neighbors. Also on the plus side is the possibility that with remodeling you'll arrive at the house you've always wanted, tailor-made to your own special brand of living. On the minus side of staying and renovating are the time, effort and expense it will require to improve it to what you need. There is also the inconvenience of living with the mess if the work goes on while you're in residence.

The House You Have Holds the Answer

As you weigh the above and look for an answer—to move or to stay—remember that it is your present house which is one of the decisive factors. The physical structure of the home you own will reveal whether it can be remodeled to respond to your new living requirements. If it is a house that was a compromise from the start, one you never really liked but just tolerated, if the neighborhood has deteriorated and holds few redeeming qualities, then of course the answer is to sell and move. On the other hand, if you have an affection for "the old place," and feel it has a lot more good living to offer, then it must be thoroughly explored for its remodeling potential. You must look beyond existing walls, room dimensions, and lot boundaries. You must exercise your imagination to the fullest to discover latent possibilities. In this, our book can be of great help, with room-by-room renovating ideas, including tips on special planning for each. If you feel that your untrained eye cannot see the full potential, and you need to call on a professional architect or designer, you will find tips in these pages on how to employ them, with the least amount of friction and misunderstanding.

Make It a Stimulating Experience

As you get into your remodeling project, use it as an adventure for the whole family, rather than a difficult chore you somehow have to get through. As your house changes and expands, you can change and grow along with it. When you dig into ways to improve your surroundings, you will also get a new, objective look at your own brand of living: new housekeeping ideas will emerge; outmoded equipment for preparing meals will be replaced by new equipment; new storage space will free you from tedious reshuffling. At the same time you can also be learning a lot about what goes into a house, what makes it tick, as it were. Too many homeowners tend to regard the structure they live in as something to be understood only by a contractor, plumber, or some other professional mechanic. Not so. There is nothing mysterious about the inner workings of a house, nothing you cannot learn for yourself. This book will teach you a lot and you can learn from many other sources, too: the operation manuals that come with new appliances, free booklets offered by manufacturers of all kinds of building materials and equipment, special magazines, friends who have undergone the experience—to name but a few. So that at the finish of your project, you will have not only a better house, but one which you understand better. However, the main thing to remember in all this is that remodeling is the chance of a lifetime to have the kind of lifestyle you've always dreamed of.

This is the quest in millions of homes everywhere, owned by families in all economic brackets and social situations. The aim of this book is to help as many of you as possible attain your goal. We will present space solutions applicable to a variety of house sizes and styles that are found in most areas of the country. Of course, we realize it's not possible to anticipate the exact requirements of any given family, but it is hoped that by taking an idea here and a solution there, you will be able to create a new, more comfortable and convenient mode of living in the house you have. And remember, in addition to the tangible factors of convenience and comfort in the newly renovated home, families may also experience a kind of rebirth themselves, because as their home takes on new life, so do they. Remodeling their home becomes a tonic to their spirit. We hope this happens to you. So go into your project with an open mind, a will to learn, great patience, and above all, with excitement and a sense of adventure!

PART ONE

The Beginning Basics

CHAPTER ONE

EVALUATION

How to Know Whether Your House Is Worth It

All remodeling projects, no matter how small or large, can be expensive. They can also be time-consuming and aggravating, so it is wise to know what you're getting into before you start. Because once you start, it is difficult and inconvenient to turn back, so if you don't want to live with a mess, be as certain as possible that what you have in mind is feasible from the standpoint of the house you have. The project must be evaluated before you begin, and evaluation is a blend of investigation, professional advice, and personal opinion.

Presumably you have decided that you like the neighborhood and the house itself enough to want to stay, so the first question becomes: Can the structure be remodeled to give you the new livability you want at a price that is sensible from the standpoint of the home's worth? In other words, if you put X thousands of dollars into creating a separate apartment in the basement or turning the garage into a new living room, will the house gain in intrinsic value? Or will it be priced out of a realistic comparison with other homes in your neighborhood? Would you be able to get the cost of the proposed project plus the value of the house before remodeling, if and when you might want to sell? And secondly, can you afford to carry the project to completion? In other words, if you get a firm figure, does it put the whole scheme within the limits of your budget?

Investigation

You can do a great deal on your own in this evaluation process. Start reading the real estate ads in your newspaper to get an idea of the going prices of homes in your area. If there are open houses, go and inspect the properties and compare them with your own place. You'll likely find a real estate salesman on hand who will give you a specification sheet with the price and description of the property. Talk to the salesman about values in your area, then go to a real estate office in another part of the city and find out what they think. Do they feel that homes like yours are gaining in value? Ask if a broker would come to your house and give you an appraisal. Talk to neighbors and friends in your area and see what they think: Are they contented to stay; do they feel the neighborhood is improving; what do they think their own house is worth? If you have a mortgage with a bank or savings and loan association, go to them and ask for an appraisal to consider refinancing. (That may not be a bad idea, because you may want them to refinance to pay for the remodeling, so you'll be that much ahead.) Now you have three sources to compare: the real estate broker, your friends, and the bank. This should give you a realistic approximate dollar figure to start from.

PROFESSIONAL ADVICE

The next step is to get the opinion of a remodeling contractor and/or an architect about three things: the present condition of the house, its ability to take the project you have planned for it, and the approximate cost of that project. If you have to pay a nominal fee for this inspection, it is well worth it. Many contractors and architects have an inspection fee or will work on an hourly basis. Explain in as specific terms as you can what you want to do and tell them that if it turns out to be structurally feasible, you'll have exact plans drawn up at a later date. Meanwhile, order a complete house inspection—roof, foundations, windows; electrical, plumbing, and heating systems. See what needs to be done to bring the basic structure up to par and what it will cost. The professional will be able to give you an idea of how the various house systems—heating, plumbing, electrical—can be extended to include the new areas, and whether the foundations are adequate to take the remodeling or will have to be reinforced. Then get a ball-park figure on what it will cost to add the wing, finish the basement, create an apartment in the attic or whatever you have in mind. Add this figure to the present value of the house and you have another step toward the evaluation of your project.

PERSONAL OPINION

All the discussions about cost, budget balancing, and candid advice from professionals must be balanced by personal opinion. A home is an intangible thing; it cannot be adequately measured only in terms of dollars and cents and structural practicality. Get all your facts together and then have a round-table discussion with the members of the family. Present your facts and then get opinions. If everyone likes the present house and the neighborhood, that is important. Remember, anything can be done in remodeling. It's just a matter of time and money. Every family slices its economic pie differently; you may be willing to give up some other part of your life—an expensive vacation, a new car, clothes—to afford this new kind of living.

Only you can decide this, not a contractor or a bank or an architect. As long as your plan is legally possible—zoning will permit a new wing on your lot or building codes will allow that rental unit in the attic—then there is nothing to stand in your way. Foundations can be shored up, the structure can be raised to create an additional floor, the house can be moved on the property. Anything is possible; it becomes a matter of economics.

As you and your family consider the project, don't be short-sighted; think of the future and future needs. Remodeling can be done in stages. Once you have a master plan, it doesn't have to be done all at once. You can complete certain areas you need right away and anticipate others with plumbing and electrical and other utilities roughed in for future reference. That's one of the good things about remodeling: you can make it long-term and finish it part by part as time and money permit. And that's a special advantage in remodeling a house you have over one you might buy and remodel: you already own it; you're living there; you can renovate it whenever and however you please. There are no necessary deadlines and no instant demands for money. It can be a phased project. This is where personal opinion—common sense, if you like—can come into play in your over-all evaluation.

CHAPTER TWO

FINANCING

ONCE you have decided exactly what you want to do with your house, and have a good guesstimate on what it's going to cost, you're ready for the next step. And that is, paying for it. How are you going to finance this project, which may run into thousands of dollars? For those who prefer to pay as they go, the answer is to take money out of existing savings, or to sell something—a car, jewelry, stocks. If this is impossible or you prefer to borrow the money and deduct the interest as a tax advantage, there are possibilities. First, do you have a life insurance policy? If so, and it is a whole life policy—that is, until death—you can always borrow up to the cash value of that policy, for any purpose according to its terms. On old policies the rate of interest is low, 5 per cent or 6 per cent; on newer policies it is higher. You are free to pay back what you borrow, but if you don't, the amount borrowed is simply deducted from what is ultimately payable to your beneficiary. If you own stock, you can borrow on it from most banks, which will give you up to a certain percentage of the current value of the stock. Interest rates are high and loans are short term, a year or two. The certificates representing the stock shares are kept by the bank until repayment and, should the stock drop heavily in value, the borrower can be called on for additional money to bring the bank's holding up to the minimum percentage of current value.

BANKS AND SAVINGS AND LOAN ASSOCIATIONS

In recent years these lending institutions discovered that home improvement is a major industry and a good source of income. They welcome customers who seek long-term home remodeling loans. If you own your own home, you are a good candidate for such a loan.

Before you go to a bank or savings and loan, be sure to have your facts and figures in order. Have an accurate estimate of costs and if the plan calls for carpentry, plus heating, plumbing and wiring, provide a schematic plan detailed to give over-all cost. Your contractor and/or architect can draw up such a plan, but if you're contracting the job yourself, the bank can give you an idea of what they require and you can draw it up yourself. Securing a loan will be determined by certain factors: Does your house presently have a mortgage, large or small? Has it been greatly reduced over the years or is it a long way from being paid off? Are your mortgage and any other loan commitments—car, personal, and other indebtedness—low enough so that you won't be paralyzed by monthly payments? The lending institution will have to protect its investment by not letting you get in over your head. In that regard, the bank will investigate to be sure you aren't overimproving your home as compared to other homes in your neighborhood. If, for example, most houses in your area are in the $65,000 class, the bank would be concerned if you planned to invest $100,000 in your property.

SAVINGS-AND-LOAN FINANCING

Savings and loan associations all over the country offer home-improvement financing in two different ways. First, where state rules and regulations permit, the S & L can give a second mortgage, or second deed of trust as it is called in some states, for the purpose of home improvement. These mortgage loans are given at the prevailing rate of interest. For a fifteen-year term, the usual minimum is $10,000; for a smaller amount, say $5,000, the term might be eight years and would seldom exceed ten years. It is not necessary to have your basic first mortgage with the same S & L from which you seek a home-improvement loan. You may have your first mortgage with a bank and want to shop around among S & Ls for the most favorable rate on your remodeling loan. The second approach to home-improvement financing with a S & L is, if you have your first mortgage with that S & L, to have it rewritten and increased to give you the additional funds you need. In which case it would be revised to include interest at the prevailing rate.

And here is where an important decision must be made. If your mortgage is rewritten, the prevailing rate may be at a much higher rate than in your original mortgage, which may have been written years ago at, say, 6 or 7 per cent. However, the term for the new rewritten mortgage will be for thirty years, so while you are paying a higher rate of interest, the monthly payments may be lower than if you keep the original mortgage and go for a second for a shorter period of time. That's because if you go the latter route, you'll have two monthly payments—the original one plus the one for the remodeling which will cover a loan at a higher rate of interest and a shorter term. The borrower must compare total monthly payments of these two different ways and make a decision.

Financing Through a Bank

If a bank holds a first mortgage on your home, it is the best place to start looking for a home-improvement loan. As with a savings and loan, the bank can handle it either of two ways. The bank can rewrite your mortgage to include the new money you need, and this mortgage may be at a higher rate of interest than your original mortgage. It will, however, be for thirty years and you will have a unified monthly payment. The other approach is for the bank to take a second mortgage or deed of trust. Generally, banks will lend a minimum of $5,000 for a fifteen-year term at the prevailing rate of interest. Amounts lower than that would be for a shorter term. Theoretically, there is no limit to the amount the bank will lend, depending on their appraisal of the property. However, many banks do not wish to give a home-improvement loan over and above a total evaluation of, say, $125,000, which would include the current value of the house and the total estimated cost of improvement. However, circumstances alter cases and a desirable property in the best residential area appraised at $200,000 could warrant a much larger home-improvement loan, depending on the borrower's credit status and the bank's belief that he can handle all his obligations plus the payments on a new, sizable loan. The bank will send an appraiser to evaluate your property and then do a credit check on you. If findings are favorable, there is every likelihood you will get the loan you want.

As with a savings-and-loan transaction, you must decide whether it is better for your pocketbook to rewrite the mortgage to include the loan and pay a higher rate of interest for a thirty-year term, or keep your existing mortgage at a lower rate and take a second mortgage for the loan at the prevailing, high rate for a fifteen-year term. Only you can decide whether you want to have two payments or one each month. Remember, too, it is important to shop around for your remodeling loan. Go to your bank first, but go to a savings and loan and to other banks, also. Bank approaches vary and there is always the personal element over and above the property appraisal, credit investigation, and all the rest.

Open-end Mortgages

If you have what is called an "open-end" clause in your existing mortgage, the first place to go for home-improvement financing is to the bank or other lending organization which holds that mortgage. An open-end clause permits you to borrow part or all of the equity— the amount to which you have reduced the original mortgage—that has accumulated in the property. For example, if your original loan was $30,000 and you have reduced it to $20,000, you should be able to borrow the $10,000 difference, without having to go through the expense of a new loan. In certain states the open-end clause permits the repayment schedule to be extended over a longer period. And the interest rate is apt to be considerably lower than for a personal loan or a regular home-improvement loan.

Government Help in Financing

The federal department of Housing and Urban Development, HUD, is the central authority for financing help. The original Federal Housing Authority has been absorbed into HUD, but FHA-backed loans are still available through some banks under FHA's housing act of 1961, specifically under Provision 203(k). This provides for loans up to $12,000 for twenty years at the current FHA interest rate. Of course, the loans must always be secured by the property and must cover property outside certified urban-renewal areas. In order for a home under ten years old to qualify under 203(k), the improvement must be a major structural change. Specifications and drawings must be presented by the borrower or his contractor to the lender, either a bank or savings and loan, and to the regional HUD office. New loans are processed similarly to a new home mortgage. There are three inspections required: first, before construction; second, during construction; and third, on completion. Borrowers must be good credit risks and a credit investigation is conducted by the bank in the same thorough way as with a first mortgage or other home loan.

Another part of the HUD home-improvement financing is the so-called 312 Loan Program. There are certain federal moneys, called entitlement amounts, funneled through HUD to cities all over the country for urban rehabilitation. The city certifies a certain section as a special housing area, the purpose being to upgrade a deteriorating part of the community. The HUD-backed loans are available to low- and moderate-income families who own homes in these designated areas. An office is set up with funds from HUD in the area, and potential homeowner/borrowers can seek loans there. A Community Development staffer will visit and evaluate the property and if he sees fit, will approve the loan. Loans are available up to $27,000 at a low, favorable interest for twenty years. There are no extra charges and no prepayment penalties; the loans are not transferable. HUD issues the funds directly to an escrow account.

City involvement is merely one of designating the deteriorating area, doing certain local improvement—street paving, tree-planting, parks, etc.—plus giving its over-all blessing to the project. To find out whether you qualify for an FHA-backed home improvement or whether your home is in a certified urban renewal area and is qualified for a loan under the 312 Program, call your local Housing and Urban Development office. They can give you further information, including current interest rates.

In addition to federal financing help for home improvement, there are also state funds available for areas designed as Concentrated Rehabilitation Areas. A State Housing Financing Agency is set up to handle this program, and homeowners can make inquiries to that agency to find out if they are in such a Concentrated Rehabilitation Area and if they qualify for a loan under their state's program.

CHAPTER THREE

CONTRACTING THE JOB

THERE ARE two approaches to this: hiring a general contractor or contracting the work yourself and hiring carpenter, plumber, electrician, etc., and supervising them. There are pros and cons with each approach, so let's start with the general contractor.

HOW TO CHOOSE A CONTRACTOR

Skilled, reputable, efficient contractors are usually scarce and very busy. They usually employ union workers and deal with subcontractors who use union workers and so their services are expensive. The best way to find one is to talk to friends who have had home-improvement work done which you have seen and admired. They will be candid and you can expect some criticism of their contractor's work along with some praise, rather than over-all rave reviews. If your friends are satisfied and tell you that working relations were smooth and that the company stood behind their work, then that is an adequate recommendation. If you can get a lead on reputable contractors from two or three groups of friends, you have a good list to draw from.

As you interview a prospective contractor, listen carefully. Beware of special deals, prices, offers, and exaggerated claims. Remember, something for nothing is a myth. Be cautious about references the contractor gives you: he's not apt to refer you to a dissatisfied customer. But do telephone clients he suggests; if possible make an appointment and talk to them and see the work. You can also check him out through his bank or through your bank or lending institution. If a bank or savings and loan is financing your remodeling, it will want to be as sure as possible that you are using a reputable contractor. The local Better Business Bureau or Chamber of Commerce should be able to give you an opinion about the firm, since they will know of complaints registered against a specific contractor. Find out from the contractor if he is a member of a trade association. In areas where such associations exist, they can be a good lead, because they have been formed by a group of contractors to uphold honest, ethical trade practices. If possible, line up two or three likely contractors and get bids. Choose what seems like the best deal and you are ready to get to the specifics of a contract.

CONTRACT DETAILS

The biggest cause of trouble in working with a contractor results from lack of understanding between him and the homeowner. So be sure from the outset that you have a meeting of the minds on all the details of the job. Get everything spelled out in advance and try not to change your mind after that. Don't let the contractor draw up a contract until you are certain of what you want. That way, you'll avoid delays and wasted time with all that means in terms of extra costs. A top contractor will submit sketches and include specifications along with his contract (you'll need these when securing loans). Many contracting firms retain architects or architectural designers and include their services in a contract, and their professional plans and sketches are important to have. When it comes to specifications in a contract, insist on brand names of materials and avoid "or equal" references that will permit the contractor to substitute an inferior product. Insist on serial numbers of appliances to be used, and be sure of specified quantities. If there are to be three baths in the house, make sure three toilets are mentioned. The contract should include a time schedule, so that you can check along the way to be sure he's not going to be late with completion. Be sure the contract covers his liability insurance and other necessary insurance including workman's compensation. Insist, too, on a clause that will permit you to cancel the contract if you change your mind at an early stage before work has been done or money has changed hands. Last but not least, set up the fee schedule.

Contractors work in several different financial ways. Most prefer to work on a cost-plus basis, charging the total of materials, subcontractor's bills, etc., plus their fee, either a fixed fee or percentage of the cost which can vary from 10 to 25 per cent. A fixed fee is the most advantageous for you because it cuts out the possibility of the contractor gouging you on cost overruns. A contract will specify the amount of a deposit at the outset plus fixed payments at various stages of the work progress. Final payment should be at least thirty days after completion of the work to provide time for remedying mistakes and correcting items not to your satisfaction. Study the contract carefully before signing it or paying anything and have your lawyer check the contract, especially if it is on a printed form supplied by the contractor. Remember, if you make a deposit, it seals the contract legally and binds you. Few reputable contractors today will give you a fixed cost for the whole job, simply because the prices of so many materials change rapidly in an inflationary period. In practical terms, a fixed cost contract doesn't mean much anyway, because the contractor is almost sure to go over estimated cost and then come threatened lawsuits and unpleasantness with all the attendant aggravation. Far better to have a cost of material-plus-labor contract.

How to Work With a Contractor

Once the contract is signed and work begins, there is a definite modus operandi you should observe in dealings with the contractor. First of all, some one person—husband, wife or whoever—should have the sole responsibility of dealing with the contractor. He or she should not haunt the site and get in the way of the workers with a million questions. He should talk only to the general contractor who in turn will deal with the plumbing or the electrical contractor involved in the matter at hand. Workers have a quite proprietary interest in the structure they're working on. In a sense, until the work is finished, it is theirs and they resent interference. Problems are bound to arise; there will be arguments—even violent ones—but if only one person is the communicator it will be easier on everybody. If you choose a contractor you trust—and for heaven's sake don't choose any other kind if you can help it—then rely on him to straighten out things that you think may be wrong. Don't question his integrity or engage in nit-picking and generally aggravate him if you want to keep a smooth relationship. You've got to proceed on the assumption that if you treat him fairly, he will treat you similarly. By all means, make the required payments on schedule. He has a payroll and other obligations connected with your project.

Don't expect him to follow the contract to the letter if you don't. If a certain amout is due to be paid the fifteenth of August, don't ask him to stretch it to the twentieth or the thirtieth. And as mentioned before, keep changes from the original agreement to a minimum.

There are bound to be details that come up where change is not only desirable from the standpoint of living efficiency on your part but for a better construction method on his part. Such changes should be included as addenda to the contract indicating the extra charge, if any, and initialed by both parties. All these tips will add up to a more pleasant climate during the period of construction and at the end of the project.

Do You Need An Architect?

If your contractor doesn't provide design services in your agreement and it is a large, complicated project, it is well to hire the services of an architect. An architect can work for you in two ways: he can draw up plans and specifications for an hourly fee and turn over his work to you for transmittal to your contractor. Or he can be hired as supervising architect for a percentage of the total cost of the project. This will include not only the initial plans and specifications and his consultation with you, but also day-to-day follow-up with the contractor at the site until the job is done, making sure that the details specified in the contract are executed as agreed. He can, in a sense, be the communicator for you and your family, the one who deals with the contractor. You can find a good architect through friends who have used one, or the nearest chapter of the American Institute of Architects will be able to recommend several to choose from. Interview each until you find the one who seems most understanding of the style you want to predominate in your project. (If an architect is known for work that is breathlessly contemporary and you want a French country look, he is not your man.) Also be certain, if you are looking for a supervising architect, that he or she is personally compatible with you, because you are going to be seeing a lot of each other. Designing living quarters is an intimate business and it is well to be working with someone who is not only qualified professionally, but is pleasant and understanding to deal with. Incidentally, the American Institute of Architects office has contract forms (A101 and A201) for use with both a contractor and an architect.

Should You Contract the Project Yourself?

The answer to this depends on several factors: How much time can you devote to the project? If it is a large remodeling, running into thousands of dollars, contracting it can be a full-time job. You have to be at the job site consistently to answer questions as they arise, to see that deliveries of materials arrive on time for the various phases of the project, and to see that work progresses so that the efforts of one trade follow another logically. For example, the electrician and the plumber cannot rough in their work until the carpenters have put up the studs for new walls. Once the studding is installed, then you must decide whether plumber and electrician will be in each other's way and if so decide which to schedule first. In most cases, the different trades are used to working around each other with minimum friction, but there has to be coordination.

Another factor is your experience in remodeling. If you have been involved in home renovation before, you are apt to know some of the perils and pitfalls. You know something about how to deal with the various mechanical trades. This is important, because an efficient, economical project must be organized. A lot of money is being spent and time is money. Good carpenters today range anywhere from nine dollars an hour to thirty; plumbers from twenty to thirty-six, and electricians from twenty to thirty-five, and these hourly fees are going up all the time. And the charges are mostly portal-to-portal— that is, the plumber's time clock starts to run from the minute he leaves his shop, so it is costly for you if he arrives and you aren't ready for him to do his part of the work. If he returns to his shop, you are charged; if he stands around waiting for the preliminaries to his work to be done, you are charged. It has to be organized.

How to Organize a Contract-It-Yourself Project

The first step is to get your ideas on paper. Once you and your family have agreed on what is to be done, take exact measurements of the areas to be remodeled. Then buy graph paper at the stationery store (quarter-inch scale is the best) and with ruler and pencil draw up a "before" plan of the existing space, marking in doors, windows, and other architectural features. It is easiest to have one foot of space equal a quarter inch on the graph. After that, start redesigning the space on another sheet of paper. You may have to make several drawings before you get the "after" plan you want. If you find this is beyond your skill, then as mentioned before, get an architect or architectural designer to step in and make the drawings for you. There may be structural considerations that only an architect or structural engineer is qualified to handle and in that case you have to call in a professional. In any case, whatever you have put to paper, rough as it may be, will be helpful in conveying your requirements to the architect. He will furnish you with blue line drawings which you can take to the bank, for a loan, and to the local building department for permission to do the work, if that is required in your area.

Dealing with the City Building Department

There is no mystery in dealing with a city building department. Don't be afraid to ask questions and get help. As a homeowner you are within your right to take out a building permit. While the man at the information desk is more used to dealing with professional contractors, he has undoubtedly dealt with the homeowner-turned-contractor, too. You will be asked to fill out an application for a building permit and pay a fee. At that time they will take your proposed plans and most often will accept your graph paper "before" and "after" drawings for uncomplicated remodelings. If they need additional drawings from an architect or structural engineer, they'll ask for them. You will have to give a rough estimate of the cost of the project on the application. (This will go to the tax office so that your property can be re-evaluated for real estate tax purposes.) If they question a too-low estimate, the building inspector will probably revise it higher. You will receive notification to come down and pick up your permit when it is ready, which could be weeks or months from the time you file. On the theory that the squeaky hinge gets the oil, it is wise to telephone if you haven't heard anything in two weeks. There will be a number on your copy of the application to refer to in asking the status of your project. In some cities, the building departments require proof of workman's compensation and you may have to get proof of this or other liability insurance from your subcontractors.

Building Codes

Except, perhaps, for certain very rural areas, all parts of the country have building codes designed to keep uniformity and safety in building practices. In some cases these codes may seem arbitrary and unnecessary, but you have to work within them so you might as well familiarize yourself with them. As you go over proposed plans with carpenter, plumber, and electrician, they will usually be able to point out any details of your plans that do not conform to the local codes so that by the time you get to the building department for a permit, what you propose will be legal. However, the information desk at the city building department will spot disallowed elements of planning and will ask that these be changed at the outset. Code no-nos can be as simple as that it is forbidden to have a door to a bathroom open onto a kitchen, in which case you'll have to rework your plan for separate access to both rooms. The building department will have available a published brochure that you can check if you have doubts about the legality of any detail in your plan. It is important to have a meeting of the minds with the building inspector on any questionable detail, well in advance, because you won't want to go to the expense and heartache of having to tear out something that has been built. Some details of your house you want to retain in your new plan may not conform to present-day codes, but most often they will be passed as "existing" and allowed to be kept. Except for dangerous wiring and plumbing, these "existing" conditions will not have to be replaced. In other words, you don't have to worry that the building inspector is going to make you change areas of your home not part of your remodeling plans.

ZONING

While you're at the city building department and filling out your building permit application, you'll likely find a place on the form to indicate how your property is zoned. If you don't know, the information desk can likely tell you or direct you to the city planning department or other bureau in charge of zoning. Sections of cities are zoned for various property uses—commerical, residential, mixed, etc. For example, an area zoned R-1 would indicate residential use, with the limit of one single-family residence, while R-3 would mean that a lot was zoned for a structure to accommodate three apartments, etc. Some areas will be mixed, primarily, say, for residential use but with provisions for certain kinds of commercial use—food stores and other convenience commerce, but excluding industrial or other heavy commerical uses. It is important for you to know the purposes for which your property can be used, especially if you are thinking in terms of adding a rental unit to your home.

Zoning may also include restrictions on how much of the land you may cover with structure: there will be square foot percentages of land use specified for various zones. For example, in one area you may be permitted to have your structure cover 55 per cent of the land, while in another the allowed percentage might be 40 per cent.

If your house already covers more than the allowed percentage, it will be classified as existing and you have no problem. But it is important for you to know the allowance if you plan to create an addition which will occupy more of your land. If you wish either to do something to your property not allowable under zoning—to add an apartment in an area zoned R-1 or to extend your structure beyond the allowable percentage of your land, you can apply for a variance and go before a board and plead your case. However, the boards are usually strict, because degree of density is a sensitive matter, especially in cities where more and more people want to live in convenient areas. Chances of approval are more favorable in outlying suburban sections where spaces are apt to be more open with less housing per square mile.

Your Building Inspector

It is well to get acquainted with the building inspector who is assigned to your section of the city. If the permit is slow in coming and he knows what you plan to do, he is apt to give his tacit approval for you to start even before you get the final permit, especially if the first stages of the project are simple and uncomplicated. In any event, call and make an appointment for him to come out and see your property and go over what you intend to do. This is usually the inspector for the general construction or carpentry involved in the project. There will be an electrical and plumbing inspector, too, in most cases. However, the plumber and electrician you hire will usually be involved directly with them. On your application, you will be asked to indicate whether plumbing and electrical work is also to be done and that will automatically alert those city departments. Your subcontractors will then work with them until completion and sign-off of the project. You will be given a permit marked approved which will have to be kept in evidence at the job site until the project is done and the building inspector has signed your project off his books as completed to satisfaction.

The Beginning Phases

First you've got to locate reputable firms to do the three basic parts of your remodeling—carpentry, plumbing, and electricity. These can be found much in the same way as with a general contractor or architect. Ask friends, check the Better Business Bureau, get references

and follow them up. A top-grade carpenter is basic to a successful
project. A small, tightly knit group—a father and his sons, or a
young, strong head man and his one or two helpers—are good
choices. While hourly rate is not always an indication of excellence,
you can judge pretty much how the men classify themselves. If they
evaluate their services at the prevailing rate or somewhat above, you
can be fairly sure of competence. Beware of those two nice young
men a neighbor recommends who charge only five dollars an hour instead of fifteen and are oh so good. They may also be oh so slow and
drive you up the wall, working with primitive tools, a truck that is
broken down half the time, and erratic working hours and habits. Far
better to hire a team at a much higher hourly rate who arrive with a
table saw, a pneumatic hammer, and all the latest electric tools, because they're apt to work quickly, do a professional job, and meet
your deadline. In the end you will have paid about what the slow-
pokes charge and end up with your sanity and a better job.

The same goes for plumbers and electricians. There are a lot of
men around in these fields who moonlight at lower than prevailing
hourly rates. They may be licensed, but do the same or other types
of work by day and will come to you weekends and evenings to earn
extra money. Some of these men are qualified but may arrive of an
evening exhausted from already doing a day's work and will give you
less than their best. And there will be weekends they have social
plans and can't come to you, which makes it difficult to organize
your project. You will do better in the long run to hire firms that
work during regular hours along with other trades who work regular
hours. Remember, remodeling at its worst is a trying, frustrating
business and there's no sense asking for extra trouble. If you go the
route of professionals all the way, you're apt to arrive at a successful
project.

Once you have your main trades chosen and contracts signed with
them and you have your building permit, if one is required, you are
ready to begin.

Now comes the demolition, the tearing down of unnecessary walls,
floors, and whatever. This is messy and a lot of trash will accrue. If
the amount is not large, perhaps your carpenter can take it to the city
dump in his pickup truck, or you can have it carted away by your
refuse service company. If there is a lot, order a debris box from the
yellow pages in your telephone directory. And make some arrangement to have the mess removed from inside the premises on a regular
basis. Nothing impedes efficiency like workmen tripping over hunks

of plaster and dismantled lumber. You will probably not want carpenters and other mechanics who earn a high hourly rate to clean up at the end of each day, so plan to keep the job site tidy yourself or with the help of family members. The workmen will usually be on hand from eight in the morning until four in the afternoon. After that, you and your family can clean up and toss the debris into the box. Have a good broom and dustpan handy; the carpenters will have to do some sweeping as they go along. If you plan to be on hand during all the working hours (a good idea to keep an eye on things and make sure details are done as you want), you can clean up as work is done, being careful not to get in the workmen's way.

You'll want to be on hand, too, for the building inspector's visits, to get his opinion on the work done and review future work. It is helpful to have your car handy, so that if the carpenter, plumber, or electrician needs something right away, you can drive to the building materials dealer, electric supply store or whatever and get it, that way speeding up the work. You will have to settle at the outset what supplies the carpenter, electrician, and plumber will provide and what you'll have to get. Usually, they'll get everything for the basic construction; you'll want to specify to them or order yourself the plumbing fixtures, chandeliers and other electrical fixtures, and the decorative hardware for doors, windows, cabinets, etc. The various trades can show you catalogs with pictures of electric fixtures, etc., or can send you to supply stores where you can pick out what you want. The important thing is to have ordered them in advance or have gotten them yourself and have them ready to be installed when the time comes, so as not to hold up work. That way you'll avoid aggravation and save money.

THE FINAL PHASES

After the major trades leave and the carpentry, plumbing, and electrical work are completed and all inspections have been passed, you are ready to tackle a new group of subcontractors—namely, plasterers, painters, and flooring contractors. Today the usual method of construction for walls and ceilings is to remodel using gypsum board, or "Sheetrock" to cite one brand name. After these modular panels are nailed by the carpenter over existing bad plaster or to new studs, they must be taped and seamed. Most good carpenters can do this, but there are plasterers who specialize in this work, called tapers, and often you're better off using them. They will come in after the carpenters leave and go through all the rooms quickly and thoroughly. It is a messy business, especially the last step—the sanding—so having it all done at once, and cleaning it all up at once is better and in the final analysis about the same cost as having the carpenters do it. Once the tapers are through, and their plaster has dried, you are ready for the painters. These may very well be you and members of your family. If you have the time and patience, as amateurs you can do an adequate job. However, if you want a professional job, contact several painters and get estimates, making sure they specify the type of paint you prefer—oil base or water base—the number of coats, the method of payment, completion date, etc. There will be more information in a later chapter about the kinds of paint to use for various areas.

Floor covering is a very competitive business, so it pays to shop around for carpet, sheet vinyl, tile, or whatever material you prefer. There will be full information later about this aspect of remodeling. Suffice it to say here that it is wise to go with brand-name products and get the best price you can. Be sure you have a contract, specifying type of floor covering and brand, type of underlayment, if any, exactly what rooms are involved, and at what cost.

PART TWO

The Project

CHAPTER FOUR

PRELIMINARIES

To RECAPITULATE, you've made the decision to stay and remodel; you have lined up your general contractor or subs, if you're contracting yourself; you have your plans, specifications and materials lists from a contractor or architect, or you have developed them yourself; you have your financing all set, you have your permit. You are ready to move on the project.

SHOULD YOU MOVE OUT WHILE WORK GOES ON?

That depends on the scope of the project. If you're really changing the whole house, yes, it would be wiser to rent a temporary apartment, preferably one nearby, or go with friends or relatives and put your furniture in temporary storage. If you're planning a new look in the remodeled house, have a garage sale in advance and get rid of what you know you won't want. No sense paying storage on things you won't use anyway.

HOW TO LIVE AT HOME DURING THE REMODELING

Living at home during remodeling can be an awful mess. However, it can be done, and millions of homeowners have survived. Here are some tips on how to have a successful remodeling and survive without too much damage to yourself and your family. First, set aside a bedroom or bedrooms and turn them into compact living-sleeping rooms with TV, the necessary furniture, etc. Keep one bath and the kitchen operative. If these rooms are part of the whole scheme, plan to have them remodeled last. Store all other furniture in the garage, basement, or some area out of the way and cover everything securely with sheets, a big tarpaulin or whatever. Clear the decks as much as possible. You don't want workmen tripping over furniture, worrying about damaging something, and you don't want to be worrying yourself over Aunt Emma's Victorian sofa.

Big sheets of polyethylene plastic can be useful, too. One family who did over their entire upstairs, lived in relative comfort downstairs, simply by funneling all work traffic through the front hall to upstairs and closing off the entry into the downstairs areas by hanging polyethylene over the archway into the living room. They lived, ate, slept and used the powder room downstairs for the two months it took to complete the work. And they had relatively little mess from sawdust, plaster dust and all the inevitable debris of renovation. Incidentally, on the subject of plaster dust, nothing takes it up like a good vacuum cleaner. This applicance has become a basic remodeling tool. If you're doing the cleanup each night after the workmen leave, be sure they leave you an active electrical plug in the project area. Get up the heavy debris with broom and shovel, but vacuum up the rest. That will keep down the pollution in the air, keep the plaster and sawdust from filtering down or up or into the areas where you are living.

By all means, keep your clothes in a tightly closed closet. Nothing frays tempers like not finding fresh linen, towels, suits, and dresses when husband or wife has to be groomed and ready to go out in the morning to work or out in the evening for a bit of relaxation away from the mess. If you are putting an addition onto the living room, the carpenter can put up a temporary partition of plywood so that you can use the old part of the room while they work on a new segment beyond the false wall. Seal the cracks between plywood panels at the floor and ceiling with wide masking tape to keep out mess. When it finally comes time to work on the kitchen, you can still survive by converting the bath into a temporary kitchen, with hotplate, electric coffee maker and other electric appliances. Determine the minimum number of pots and pans, dishes and glasses you'll need and form an emergency kit. You'll have to wash dishes in the bathroom sink for a while, but if you plan carefully, it can be done. Meanwhile, the refrigerator can be moved into your temporary living-sleeping room. If you have only one bath, when it comes time for work there, you may have to move to a motel a night or two or wash your face in your newly remodeled kitchen and rely on the hospitality of neighbors for toilet and shower facilities. Inconvenient, yes, but the money so saved can go into the project.

THE SEARCH FOR SPACE

New living space is the name of the game in remodeling. So the first way to make the most of the house you have is to analyze its space potential. Make a checklist of possibilities.

The basement

Is there a cellar used for nothing more than the furnace, water heater and as a repository for cast-off furniture and assorted trash you can't bring yourself to get rid of? If it is dry and concrete-floored, it's a good candidate for that extra living room the teen-age children need, or it can be a hobby room for the whole family, with a worktable for Dad's spare-time carpentry projects, a wall for a daughter's record collection, turntable, and speakers, a darkroom in the corner where the old laundry tubs can be converted for use in your son's photography pursuits, a corner for Mother's sewing machine and all the paraphernalia for her hobby. If you're lucky enough to have a house on a sloping lot and the rear of the basement has windows opening onto a yard, there is the possibility of a new guest suite, a master bedroom suite with new bath, sleeping and sitting room plus loads of closets. Or a second living room for informal family life, opening onto a deck. If a little extra income would be welcome, perhaps a rental apartment can be created in this space, or a separate apartment for in-laws, adult children, or guests.

The attic

Most homes built before 1920 had them, and they constitute a gold mine under the eaves of your house. Granted it may be a hike to get up there, but it's worth it. With insulation to keep out summer heat and winter cold, with the extension of plumbing and drain lines from a lower-floor bath, for a new top-floor bath, and even a small kitchen on the upper floor, you can make a whole new living and sleeping world for your children, who won't mind the stair climb at all. For young apartment-seekers in congested urban areas, there is a special romance about an attic apartment, and they are good candidates for extra income if you need it. The attic also has great potential as the location for a home office, a quiet spot away from the hubbub of family activity, for a guest suite or a hobby center for everyone in the family. Perhaps there's a view and a small deck can be created

Before: Attic bedroom was just that, with sloping ceiling and walls angling in all directions. However, it offered sizable space which designer Ethel Samuels used to create something of a private apartment at the top of the house.

leading from a dormer window. If the existing attic is unfloored, by all means put down blanket insulation between the joists to cut down sound transmission to the floor below. If there is a floor, have small holes drilled in the boards and have cellulosic fiber or other insulation blown into the spaces between the joists. And carpet over the floor boards or plywood in any case for extra sound deadening.

The garage

For the average-sized home, a car or cars may be taking a disproportionate amount of space that could be used for living. Look at it a moment from the standpoint of dollars and cents. A single-car garage measures a minimum of ten by twenty feet or two hundred square

After: The window wall was visually and functionally improved by building a storage compartment for bedding under the window, treating the window with folding shutters, and illuminating the alcove with fluorescent tubes hidden from view. Masonite brand paneling with a textured surface was used to cover ceiling and window wall.

After: The opposite end of the big room was "straightened out" by building a storage wall of open shelves and a walk-in closet. The same Masonite woodgrain paneling was used and contrasts nicely with the textured white ceiling paneling. Husband's desk fits into this corner; wife has a makeup-writing-sitting area in another part of the room.

feet of space. At today's cost of at least thirty dollars a square foot, your automobile is costing you six thousand dollars to store. If it is a two-car garage, double that amount. Can you afford that cost? If not, think in terms of building an open carport somewhere on the property which you could do for, say, ten dollars a square foot and then think of what you could do with the garage space. You've got one whole wall, the garage door, which can be fitted with windows. You've got a concrete floor that can be carpeted or covered in some kind of resilient flooring, and you have stud walls and open ceiling that can take any kind of decorative treatment you wish. Think of a terrace protected with a privacy fence in the area just outside the old garage entrance, and you can begin to see many possibilities.

Car storage space can give way to a new master bedroom suite, a family room, a living room with fireplace and its own adjacent patio, a rental studio apartment—all of these are possible in single-car garage space. As you plan the new area, notice if there is a bath or kitchen on the other side of a garage wall; if so, that is the logical place for an apartment kitchen and bath, a wet bar for the new family room. You may be lucky enough to have a laundry in the garage, in which case you already have hot and cold water lines plus drainage. At least one sidewall can be opened up for additional fenestration and you also have a door into the main house that can be sealed off if you're thinking in terms of a rental unit, or retained as the entry from the house into the new living space.

The carport

Here is a roofed area of at least two hundred square feet that your local zoning ordinances already permit. So you won't be taking an extra amount of your lot to form new living space. Granted you'll have to build sidewalls and, if there is only a gravel floor, you'll have to have a concrete slab poured for the new floor, but it will be worth it. The nice thing about a carport is that it is already an open space. You can design windows and doors to suit yourself. Another advantage is that, since it is usually in the front of the house, it can sometimes be incorporated with the existing living room to give you a larger space. It can be a good location, too, for a new, bigger kitchen since it is near the street for service deliveries and for bringing in cooking supplies conveniently. It can also be floored with decking and given privacy trellis or some other style of fencing to form a protected patio. Its location in relation to the house structure and its orientation to the sun, to the street and to the rest of your property will be determining factors in what best use you can make of it.

Extra-large rooms

In your search for space, don't overlook huge rooms in older homes. Turn-of-the-century houses often had cavernous kitchens, dining rooms larger than the living rooms, and immense baths, because building costs were low and life was expansive, so space was easy to achieve. Today, as we all know, it is an expensive luxury, what with new building costs anywhere from thirty dollars a square foot up. That big, old-fashioned kitchen can yield a new compact, efficient cooking area plus a family room with dining space. The big bathroom can give way to two baths, back-to-back or a compartmented arrangement with dual use in privacy. A big bedroom can become a sleeping area of adequate size plus a dressing room and even a bath. The old dining room can be the new living room, with the old living room becoming a downstairs bedroom and bath for an elderly relative who shouldn't climb the stairs. There are many, many possibilities in a big, old house and that is one of the reasons why young families are buying and remodeling them into efficient and handsome present-day living quarters.

Large areas mean extra cost in renovation, but they are worth it. An old home may require a new heating system, new insulation wherever possible, and likely new kitchen and baths, but if you think of such houses in terms of the replacement cost of the total square footage at today's prices, you begin to see that these elderly structures are a gold mine. In many cities, zoning permits old mansions to be made into apartments, so that a family can have sizable living for themselves and rental income, too. If you have such a house, don't overlook any of these possibilities.

Front porches

Big, old houses were apt to have large porches, too, and these can be turned into living space. Of course, this will require relocating the main entrance, since the former entry was almost always from the front porch, but considering the fact that you already have a floor, roof, and sidewalls, a porch offers an economical way to increase the use and value of a home. By adding windows to the open sides and continuing electrical, plumbing, and heating systems to service the

Before: A waterside cottage had a screened porch that was little used. The owners found that they could take better advantage of this space and get as much comfort and enjoyment of the view by turning it into enclosed living space.

After: The result: a sunny sitting room, quite easily created by installing Andersen *Perma-Shield* windows—fixed windows above, opening awning-type windows below. Old porch floor was given an underlayment and carpet. Traverse drapery gives snug look at night.

new area, you can economically include all necessary conveniences. If the original house had a huge, useless entrance hall, by changing the location of the main entrance, say, to the side of the house, you can turn part of the old hallway into a room. Most often, porches were open to the ground underneath, so you'll want to have blanket insulation installed between the joists for warmth. If the original board floor is in good condition and relatively flat, you can simply add underlayment and carpet to create a new floor.

REMODELING BY ADDITION

In your search for space, don't overlook your lot. When you look out a window to green grass, see instead green dollars in potential new living areas. A wing added onto your present home may give you the extra space you need and an opportunity to live in your house with relatively little mess while the work is being done. Also the proximity to the new construction lets you keep close tabs on work in progress, important if you are contracting the job yourself. There is economy, too, in this kind of new space planning: you will only have to build three new walls, since one will be the side of your present home. Other advantages include access to existing plumbing, heating, and electrical lines, efficient receipt of materials delivery, and economical foundation work in the form of a concrete slab and footings.

The first step toward implementing this kind of remodeling is to find out what local ordinances will permit. Usually zoning specifies the percentage of land that can be covered with structure—55 per cent house, 45 per cent of the lot to be left open, for example. If your projected plan will keep the structure within this limit, you will have no problem and it becomes a matter of applying for a building permit. If it almost fits the requirement, you will likely be able to get a variance from the building or city planning department. Visit the planning department and ascertain the requirements and get an idea of your chances for a variance.

If you get a green light and can go ahead with an addition, then you must consider the best location. You'll want to plan the new wing in relation to the sun, prevailing winds, established planting, street traffic, privacy from neighbors, and noise sources. If it's to be a living room or some other area used primarily in daytime, sunshine is important. If it is a bedroom, sun is not as important. If there are large shrubs and trees on one part of your lot, you may want to place the new wing where they will not be disturbed or you may be able to design the new living room around an existing tree. Many stunning garden rooms have a tree as their focal point. If you live in a warm climate, orientation to take advantage of prevailing winds is important, especially in the light of new energy-saving efforts, as air conditioning is expensive and energy-consuming. Conversely, cold winters may rule out north or northwest exposures, from the standpoint of heating.

The best way to attain privacy from neighbors is to create your addition so that a solid wall faces that boundary. If that isn't desirable from the standpoints of sun and wind, then consider high privacy windows on that wall, with diffused instead of clear glass in the sash. A privacy fence, raised to the full legal height will also give a measure of privacy from neighbors. There is no legal height limit to trees

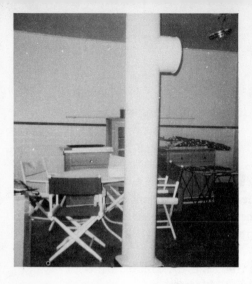

PLATE 1

Photographer: Henry Bowles, Jr.

PLATE 1

Before: Large basement room, once part of the garage, was used as a family recreation area and auxiliary kitchen for service to the rear terrace and picnic-style family dinners. Pipe for exhaust of furnace and gas range upstairs was in the middle of the area.

After: Space, roughly 24 by 18 feet, was partitioned to form a separate apartment with small entry foyer off garage, kitchen, bed-sitting room and dressing room—bath, the latter created from space borrowed from the garage. Existing cabineted sink was left in place; range was moved and vented into the pipe, now painted bright orange as a decorative accent. Secondhand cabinets were grouped in a corner arrangement with new white laminate counter.

After: Door at the rear of the sitting room leads to new bath, carpeted and equipped with blue fixtures, including a fiber-glass combination one-piece tub-shower. Sliding-door closet is next to built-in chest of drawers, making a complete dressing room, too.

After: Highlight of the sleeping-sitting room is a unitized bay window, wood-framed, double-glazed for insulation and with factory-installed weather-stripping. Window seat overlooks the garden and terrace. Flooring and pillows restate the green garden look. See Chapter Seven for floor plans.

PLATE 2

Before: Families in the search for space often cast an eye on the garage, frequently empty by day, sometimes merely a repository for cast-offs. One-car garage of this ranch-style house gave way to a combination family-utility-laundry area.

After: Glass panels now fill space of old garage door and look onto trellis design that gives street-side privacy. Another large window was included on the side wall and juts out to form a colorful window seat. Concrete floor was carpeted; walls and ceiling were finished off with rough-sawn plywood. Corner fireplace is a cheery note. The former 21 by 24-foot garage space is now a 12 by 18-foot dining-lounging area with a 6 by 12-foot utility area tucked in back. *Architect: J. Donald Bowman.*

PLATE 2

PLATE 3

PLATE 4

PLATE 5

PLATE 6

PLATE 7

BEFORE

AFTER

Floor Plan By Thomas L. Bastianon

PLATE 3

After: Proving that there's gold under the eaves that can be mined in terms of valuable new living space, this remodeled attic is a bright, functional sitting and hobby room. Gable-end wall was surfaced in a plaid vinyl wallcovering, with shutters for the new, enlarged window covered in the same pattern. Spaces between the ceiling joists were in-filled with striped and solid vinyl. Monticello carpet of Anso nylon was used not only as floor covering, but also for castored cubes and banquettes, made of two-by-fours and plywood. *Vinyl wallcoverings by Comark.*

PLATE 4

Before: Part of vanished America: the garage building with chauffeur's quarters above offered a space bonanza for the family who owned the property. The lower floor could house three cars, while the upper, granted its exposed radiators, vaulted ceiling, and awkward closet and entry doors, could comprise a studio apartment.

After: Designer G. Allen Scruggs turned the space bonanza into a lively apartment, chock-full of do-it-yourself touches, light, airy outdoor furniture, and vivid red carpet. This color extended to painted window and door frames, kitchen and dining-counter tops. Ceiling accent is a whimsical, kitelike lamp. Built-in platform bed is a sofa by day. *Carpet by Masland is of Anso nylon.*

PLATE 5

Before: The owners of this old house found it comfortable inside, but felt that a small, unattractive, added-on porch spoiled its exterior. Here was another example of potential living space going to waste.

After: Remodeling gave the house new character and added a cheery, livable enclosed sunroom in erstwhile porch space. Focal points are the wood window "walls," fixed windows over tall casements to bring in maximum light. The view of lovely trees and yard is another bonus.

PLATE 6

Before: Many a garage is destined to house, not a car, but family cast-offs. This half of a two-car garage had deteriorated into just such a repository. However, certain features—an unusual beamed ceiling and a clerestory—suggested that it could make interesting living space.

After: Rehabilitation turned the area into a pleasant retreat for all family members. Sliding glass doors opened the rear wall to the garden; grooved plywood panels surfaced the exposed stud walls; partition wall goes only to partial height, leaving storage space for seasonal sports gear. Original beams were left exposed and painted in contrasting tones. Ribbed carpet was cemented down over concrete subfloor, adding needed insulation. *Carpet by Monticello of Anso-X nylon.*

PLATE 7

After: A cigar maker's cottage in Key West, Florida, built about 1890, though remodeled several times over the years, still remained a narrow 14 by 35-foot structure until a recent owner saw possibilities for expansion into a side yard. An addition of roughly the same dimensions was designed, with the same roof pitch, the same clapboard look, although the new wing is in vinyl clapboard. Open-beamed ceiling in the new wing permitted glass gable ends as a nod to contemporary style. Plan shows how a sizable living room was arrived at by a transverse arrangement which partakes of both old and new wings. Highlight of the white-painted room is a floor of Italian tile in a blue and white pattern. Vertical venetian blinds control light and air, traverse across two walls. Master bedroom suite is an open arrangement of sleeping area, bath, and dressing-laundry area. Open-beamed ceiling with old-fashioned electric fan gives an airy feeling. *Photographer: Louis Reens*

After: Three examples of how to build storage into a room. A bedroom was given closet space plus a French country feeling with Masonite brand paneling used for walls and closet door facing. Window wall was built out 18 inches, creating a niche for the window which was enhanced with a shade in a textured fabric that gives glare-free light control. Flexibility within the closets is attained with a system of standards and brackets commonly used for bookshelves. Shelves can be any length, can be rearranged to handle any items.

and hedges, so these may give you better protection. A fence is also a good baffle against street traffic and its attendant noise. It is important to point out, however, that even a solid wood fence is of little value as far as sound-deadening is concerned, when it comes to traffic noise. The same can be said of high hedges and thick trees. There is some reduction of noise by absorption, but not much. Some sounds will bounce off a solid fence, but the main thrust of the noise will carry over top of it, so you can't count on significant noise control. However, you can get a great measure of visual privacy from the sidewalk or street with hedges or fencing.

Another matter to consider when planning your addition is its relationship to services inside the existing house. For example, if there are water and drain lines—a bath, a kitchen or a laundry—along a wall, that may be a good location for a wing, as you will save money by being able to use these services. If you plan a bath in the wing,

After: Another solution for extra storage, this time for a bed-sitting room. Designer Helen Masoner sized the two new closets to accommodate a daybed between. Walls were surfaced in Masonite brand paneling, applied vertically. For contrast the bed niche uses the same paneling on the diagonal. Crown molding ties all walls and jogs together. Closet doors have chicken-wire screening with shirred fabric above, panels below.

After: A different look, same general treatment: here a floral chintz pattern in fabric for upholstery and pillow covers, in wallpaper for closet-door panels gives a very feminine feeling in contrast to the texture of the Masonite brand panels used for walls.

and there is a bath on the opposite wall, you can likely use the exist-ing vent stack, saving more money. If the main electrical service with circuit breakers, etc., is near a planned addition, you'll also save money. In other words, any reduction in length of heating ducts, wiring, and piping will be economical.

You will want to consider the relationship of the new wing to the traffic pattern of the whole home. For example, you won't want to have to pass through the kitchen to get to a new master bedroom suite or living room. And it is not economical, either from the stand-point of space or cost, to create a new hall to arrive at the addition. On the other hand, a new family or dining room wing makes sense opening off an existing kitchen. A master bedroom and bath addition can be well located off a living room as it will then have privacy from other bedrooms and will give husband and wife the advantage of being able to use the living room as a private sitting room when it is not otherwise in use. If the living room has a fireplace, there is the possibility of a fireplace in the master bedroom by adding an addi-tional flue in the chimney. And a bedroom fireplace is the romantic dream of many a couple.

From the design standpoint, it is well to have an architect or designer plan the appearance of an addition, so that it is consonant with the rest of the house. New windows should line up with the existing ones and the roofline, roof pitch and surfacing should blend. If you want to sheathe the walls in a less expensive material, make sure that it is related in style with the walls of the main house. For ex-ample, if the house is stone or brick and traditional in style, you can add a wood-shingled or board-and-batten wing that would cost less and have a design precedent, as many eighteenth-century additions to brick structures were wood or shingles. If the main house is stucco, asbestos-cement shingles or clapboard it is well to continue that mate-rial in the addition. If the house is streamlined contemporary, you must repeat the same look. A skilled architect is worth his fee in this matter, because it is important that the wing look as though it were an original part of the structure. He will specify correct detailing— windows, doors and other woodwork—that blends with what you al-ready have.

CHAPTER FIVE

ROOM BY ROOM REMODELING

THE MOST REMODELED ROOM: THE KITCHEN

When it comes to room remodeling, the kitchen is far and away the most demanding room in the house and requires more careful planning than any other. After all, as the most mechanized room, it is the most expensive and, as the homemaker's work center, it is the place where many of the waking hours are spent. Because of both factors, it has been a room that some have approached with trepidation: many have an instinctive distrust of mechanical things, while many others have come to associate dreary hours of drudgery with kitchen work. On both points let today's homemaker be reassured. Kitchen-appliance manufacturers make as certain as humanly possible that mechanisms function with minimum understanding and attention. They have come to realize that service calls are not only costly to them, but also produce ill will on the part of the consumer. So today's appliances are engineered expressly to eliminate service problems. New appliances are also designed to take as much tedium as possible out of both food preparation and cleanup. In short, to make kitchen work a creative experience rather than a necessary chore.

The kitchen of today makes it possible for you to develop a whole new approach to food and homemaking. It offers a golden opportunity to attain a new lease on life, to review your existing work patterns and bring them up to date. To do this you must first realize that merely replacing new equipment for old doesn't give you the most efficiency and pleasure for your money. You must rethink your attitudes about patterns of food preparation and homemaking generally. You have probably worked in a kitchen or a series of kitchens which were far from totally efficient and in working around their inadequacies you now have an ingrained work pattern that is time-consuming and step-wasting. Now is the time to review this pattern critically and decide which kitchen arrangement you really want. You are at a crossroads: you are faced with X number of square feet to use and X number of dollars to spend and from both you can create either a masterpiece of personal efficiency and good looks or an inconvenient bore. The choice is up to you, and all the architects and kitchen planners in the world cannot design a workroom tailored expressly for you as well as you can design one for yourself, provided you have done your homework assiduously.

And homework is precisely the *raison d'être* of this chapter. It was planned as a primer to guide you in every phase of the kitchen-planning process. You will find a full discussion of the most popular and efficient kitchen arrangements. Following this comes an exhaustive examination of each major appliance, with special features, sizes, and advantages pointed out. Then finally, the frosting on the cake—decoration. This comes last because it is important to set the basic arrangement first and then, with cabinet style, color and pattern plus the myriad tools of decoration, make it a French Provincial, Early American, country kitchen, or whatever. An expert once said that a well-planned kitchen will look well, but this is only partially true. Efficiency can be there, but beauty being in the eye of the beholder, you may not be pleased unless your kitchen has a specific and unmistakable period style. And there is no reason why you shouldn't have the look you want, without compromise. Full efficiency comes in many guises and the array of choice in every kitchen component is so staggering that the most rarefied decorating preferences can be satisfied. Just don't put the cart before the horse: plan first and decorate second. Then you'll have the best of both worlds.

Basic planning

Today's properly planned and equipped kitchen is far more than a place for food preparation. It may be the communications center of the house, with an intercom at the home-planning desk that links the homemaker with the main entrance and to other rooms of the house, plus a telephone to make calls outside the home. It may include a secondary dining area—a sizable informal one, or simply a nook for breakfast. It may be the laundry center and it most certainly will act as the informal entry into the house, the secondary approach from the garage or carport for the convenient delivery of groceries and other household supplies. All of these extra kitchen duties must be taken into account.

Locating the kitchen

If the presence of plumbing and drain lines dictates that it is most sensible, economical and efficient to keep the kitchen where it is, all well and good. However, if there is some freedom in locating the kitchen, take the following considerations into account. For example, if there are small children in the family, their play will have to be supervised by their mother or housekeeper, who spends at least half her active day in the kitchen. So it makes sense to have the kitchen overlook the yard. If the house is in a warm climate or a temperate one, where outdoor dining and living are a possibility several months of the year, a kitchen near a terrace or patio is a must to facilitate outdoor food service. If the homemaker wants to join the family activity while she prepares meals, the kitchen may well have to be part and parcel of the family room. If it is to be a kitchen used exclusively by a cook and servants, not all these factors are relevant. In fact, all that may be required is close access to the dining room, breakfast room, and outdoor areas. An architect can help you blend all your requirements and arrive at the best placement, taking into account the location of all the other rooms. He will be able to tell you whether it is possible to follow the recent thinking which locates the kitchen and other service areas toward the less private, streetside elevation of the house, leaving the rear-terrace elevation for living areas which can open onto the outdoors.

Deciding on size and shape

Once location in the over-all house plan is established, your next step is the allotment and shape of space. In bygone days, when it was inexpensive to build, square footage was little thought of and kitchens were often huge. A large kitchen became a status symbol and some of this thinking has carried over to today, when every square foot is costly. Actually, a large kitchen is almost never the answer to present-day needs. It can be quite inconvenient in terms of both dollars and sense. A too-large kitchen can be just as inconvenient as a too-small one, and by this is meant the actual area of food preparation. Of course, efficiency is possible in a large room if the work area is confined to one part of it; a kitchen within a kitchen, as it were, with the remainder of the space used for storage of entertainment equipment, laundry, homemaking desk, dining area, etc. For the actual work area, experts advise that there should be no less than 100 square feet and no more than 170. More space than this means that three basic appliances—sink, range and refrigerator—are too far apart, resulting in wasted steps. Experts recommend that appliances be arranged to form a work triangle with no side of the triangle more than 12 feet and the total of all sides not to exceed 22 feet.

The shape of your kitchen is determined by two factors, the way space is shaped for surrounding rooms and your choice of kitchen arrangement. Certain of the four basic arrangements require a definite shape of room, so it is important to decide on your kitchen arrangement early in the development of the over-all remodeling plan.

The four kitchen arrangements

The U-Shape

At this juncture, therefore, it is important to study the four most popular and convenient types of work centers. The U-shaped kitchen is considered the most efficient and pleasant to work in. (Figure A) A cul-de-sac plan, it permits the sink, range, and refrigerator to be located to form an efficient work triangle, with short distances between these work stations. The base of the U is most often along an outside wall and the sink is located there, under a window. The range then goes on one adjacent leg, the refrigerator on the other. Besides saving steps, its other advantages are that it can sequester the cook who doesn't like people underfoot as she works. It permits her to function in a cul-de-sac with the open end serving as a passageway through which family members can come and go without disturbing her. The wall beyond that passageway can form a storage complex from which the cook can draw special equipment as she needs it. It can also be the location of her homemaking desk, and laundry, provided there is no utility room or other suitable laundry location.

Another great plus with the U kitchen is that it can be arranged as part of a family room, so that the cook can really join in the fun as she works. This is done by making one leg a peninsula which separates the family-dining area, so that the cook can look across and converse openly. In such a plan, a cooktop is usually located in the peninsula which can serve for informal family dining as a buffet from which hot food is taken directly from the pots on the burners. In another arrangement, the sink is located in the peninsula and it serves from the other side as a bar. The peninsula, with stools on the family-room side, can serve as a snack bar.

The only disadvantages of the U-shape are that it requires an extensive amount of countertop area and cabinets, especially corner

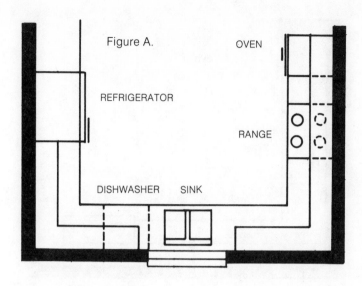

Figure A.

OVEN

REFRIGERATOR

RANGE

DISHWASHER   SINK

cabinets, which are more expensive than others. Also the U must be at least ten feet wide at the base for efficiency, and an even wider span is recommended for freedom at the sink area and enough storage space at the corners. If a peninsula is used for the cooktop, then it becomes necessary to locate wall ovens on the opposite leg of the U or along the wall beyond the open end. Often this open-end passageway leads to the garage or to the service entrance, so that it is important to plan counter space at the extreme end of the leg nearest the door so that other supplies can be set down conveniently. If possible, it adds to convenience to have the refrigerator on this wall near the set-down counter.

The L-shape

Probably the second most popular and convenient arrangement, this one adapts to almost any space, since it requires simply two adjacent walls. (Figure B) A full triangular work pattern is possible only if a corner sink is used at the juncture of the walls; otherwise a modified triangle is created with the sink on one wall (preferably a window wall), with the refrigerator to its right and range or cooktop on the other wall. An auxiliary work island is especially useful, since counter space can be limited in the small kitchen, while the island helps to break up an expanse of space in a large room. With an island,

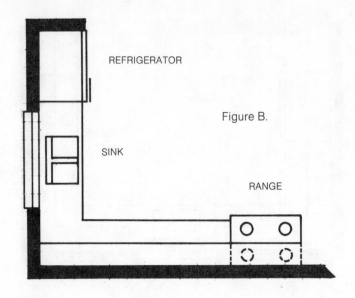

REFRIGERATOR

Figure B.

SINK

RANGE

many variations are possible: the sink can go into the island, making a complete triangle; or an auxiliary bar sink makes the island a convenient place to service a family area beyond; the island can be the top, with auxiliary wall ovens on one wall of the L. The L permits great flexibility in arrangement of appliances, storage cabinets and auxiliary dining space.

For full efficiency, it is important not to break up the two walls of the L with doorways. And in fact, careless planning of doors and windows can destroy the efficiency of any kitchen. Often what seems on paper a more than adequate space for a work center is rendered highly inconvenient in this manner. Compactness of major appliances and cabinets is the general rule for workability. If the two walls of the L are overly long, the arrangement can get so spread out that extra steps result and efficiency is lost.

The Corridor

The corridor or galley kitchen as it is often called can be an efficient arrangement where over-all space planning allots a long, narrow area for the kitchen. (Figure C) Equipment and cabinets are lined up on two long walls, forming a zigzag work pattern as the cook goes back and forth. Advantages are that the cook who so chooses can be completely closed off from surrounding areas. An

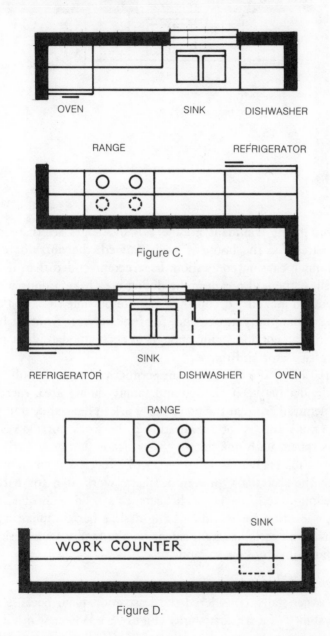

OVEN   SINK   DISHWASHER

RANGE   REFRIGERATOR

Figure C.

SINK

REFRIGERATOR   DISHWASHER   OVEN

RANGE

SINK

WORK COUNTER

Figure D.

efficient triangular work pattern can be created with the sink at the apex, on the outside wall under a window, with the refrigerator and range on the opposite wall on the other corners of the triangle. Fully accessible cabinets can line both walls, with the exception of the win-

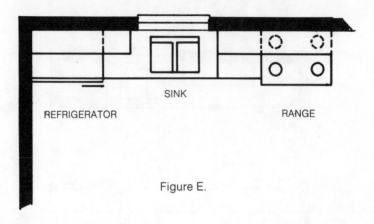

SINK

REFRIGERATOR   RANGE

Figure E.

dow span, giving abundant storage. Disadvantages are that unless the traffic pattern of the house is well planned, the corridor can be a traffic funnel, causing congestion. It is recommended that, if the plan is sleevelike, the end not near the dining area have a door which can be closed and locked. Of course, it is quite possible to have a corridor with an opening only at one end, for food service. Another hazard is not having the corridor wide enough to accommodate door openings of the refrigerator and range.

A variation of the corridor plan permits you to have only a partial height divider between kitchen and family-dining area, thereby creating a peninsula so that the cook can work in her galley and yet partake of family fun. Another variation is the work corridor as part of a large kitchen, with one side of the corridor simply a work counter with base cabinets below. (Figure D) In effect, twin corridors are set up, with the secondary one an auxiliary work area for bartending, salad making, etc. The far wall becomes a solid wall of specialized storage, a location for a homemaking desk, a bar complete with sink, etc. This is an excellent arrangement for the family with husband and wife who enjoy cooking in tandem.

The Line-a-Wall

This is generally considered the least good plan, because it omits any possibility of a work triangle. (Figure E) Where width is a problem, however, it is often the only solution. All equipment is on one wall with the sink, plus flanking work counters in the center, refrigerator on one side, range on the other. It is a popular plan for efficiency kitchens in vacation houses and small apartments, and it can function well in a larger home provided that the equipment is not too strung out, making too many steps between major appliances. It can be a good arrangement for the family who wants the cooking center to be part and parcel of the family room: it simply becomes one wall of this complex. The disadvantage of the line-a-wall kitchen is that there is a minimum of work counters so, where it is part of the family room, an island is useful as an additional work surface and also helps to give the cook a sense of separation. If a second sink is located in it, the island serves successfully as a snack counter and bar.

The three work centers

Within any of the preceding four basic plans, there are three separate work centers which must be carefully detailed. Planning must once again take into account the sequence of steps and the resulting body movements that go into the unloading of food which arrives at the kitchen, its storage, its preparation prior to cooking, the actual cooking, baking and broiling operations, then the serving of the completed meal and finally cleanup. While there is obviously some overlapping of operations in the compactness of the well-planned kitchen, each center should have the requisite capacity and specialization of storage for its function, with each item stored closest to the point of use. This eliminates backtracking from one center to another and saves steps.

Cold Storage Center

This comprises the refrigerator-freezer and perhaps an auxiliary frozen-food locker. As mentioned earlier, this area is best located near the service entrance for convenience of unloading supplies. As close as possible to the entrance, there should be a counter at least fifteen inches wide at the open side of the refrigerator, whose door swing should be taken into account, both for loading operations and for access during food preparation. Usually the set-down counter is at the left of the refrigerator which is hinged on the right. The base cabinet under this counter is a good spot for a mixing center, with electric blender, bowls, beaters, etc. stored therein, in a wall cabinet above, aluminum foil, freezer bags and other items used in the storing of cold foods. If the counter at this location is used as a mixing center, it should be at least three feet long; often it flows into a counter at one side of the sink. The correct door swing of the refrigerator is important and should be ordered carefully: the hinge is described as either left or right as you face the unit. Many refrigerators now permit choice of door swing. Your plumber or carpenter can switch from right to left easily and quickly.

Cleanup Center

This is the busiest of the three centers, and where the cook spends
the most time and for that reason wants it to be bright, and so it is
usually located under a window. However, it is foolish to sacrifice
over-all efficiency just to place the sink there. With today's lighting
techniques, any part of the kitchen can be bright, so don't plan
around one detail at the expense of all the others. The sink should
have a minimum of three feet of counter space to the right and two
and a half feet to the left. The food disposer is a must in this center if
local codes permit it. You will also need a pull-out waste hamper for
cans, etc., in a base cabinet nearby. The dishwasher is another must
for kitchen efficiency and it can be installed immediately to the right
or left of the sink, under the counter. The latter installation is considered somewhat easier for the right-handed person, but the difference
is negligible. The base cabinet under the sink is the place for storage
of soap, dishwasher detergent and kitchen-cleaning supplies.

The Cooking Center

There are four different appliance possibilities and combinations
for this center. First, the freestanding range with cooktop and oven-
broiler in a single unit; second, the freestanding console range with
cooktop and two ovens, one eye-level, the other below the cooktop;
third, the cooktop-oven-broiler unit that drops into a counter for a
built-in look; fourth, the counter cooktop with wall oven and broiler
built into a nearby wall. (As we will see later, an alternate solution
can be to have the oven or ovens on a different wall, since they are
not as extensively used.) In the cooking center, space must be arranged for serving and storage, too. Some counter space is important
on either side of the cooking surface and near a built-in oven, if one is
included, to set down pots when loading or unloading. Base cabinets
at either side should be chosen for storage of cooking utensils, pots of
all sizes, baking pans and small appliances, like toaster, coffee maker,
etc. Some ranges include a drawer at the base in which some utensils
can also be stored. Storing pots in the oven is commonly done, but it
is inefficient, since they have to be removed before the oven is turned
on.

The three centers, of course, share counter and storage space; anything as interrelated as the steps in meal preparation requires a flow
of activity which a cut-and-dried solution precludes. One important
consideration is that the three areas not be broken by doors which
permit cross traffic; again uninterrupted work flow is basic for full
efficiency.

The major appliances

No matter how well planned, a kitchen can function no better than its equipment, especially today's kitchen, which is almost completely mechanized. For that reason it is important to have an intimate knowledge of each of the major appliances, to know the features that are available to you, and to understand the variety in size, shape, and color you can choose from. Then you will be ready to shop for your range, refrigerator, dishwasher, sink, and disposer at your local utility-company showroom, kitchen center, department store or building-supply dealer. Remember, wherever you shop, there are specification sheets available on all appliances which spell out their vital statistics—dimensions, finishes, capacity, and special features. It is a good idea to collect these and study them along with manufacturers' brochures, magazine advertisements and other sources of information before making a choice. As your final selections shape up, they may not all be the same brand; that is, you may want the dishwasher of one manufacturer, the refrigerator of another and the range of a third. This can cause a problem only with color, as not all the manufacturers' tones match exactly. If you choose white or stainless steel fronts, they will blend all right. However, since the advent of the flush, built-in look in appliances about fifteen years ago, they are all designed accordingly, so all will fit together.

The Range

Freestanding ranges vary in size from a 20-inch apartment model to 27, 30, 36, and 40-inch freestanding six-burner units. Depth is standard at about 27½ inches. The most popular model is probably the freestanding 30-inch console range-oven, with a four-burner cooktop, an eye-level oven above the cooktop and a second oven below. The broiler is usually in the upper oven in the electric range. There is also a 30-inch stack-on console with only an upper oven-broiler, the unit resting on a 30-inch base cabinet. Other 30-inch variations include the freestanding unit with four-burner cooktop and oven below it; there is also a one-piece drop-in or slide-in unit which fits into a base cabinet for a built-in look. Almost all the preceding models are available for either gas or electricity as the fuel. Today's gas ranges have automatic ignition, eliminating the old pilot light. In gas console models, the broiler is in a drawer beneath the lower oven. There are now freestanding gas ranges in which a single oven has burners top and bottom for broiling or baking. There is also a console type with cooktop and eye-level oven above, and a dishwasher below.

Oven-cleaning Aids

The big news in ranges is the self-cleaning feature, which is now available in all major electric lines, and many gas lines. There are two types of self-cleaning—pyrolytic and catalytic. The former method literally burns itself clean, with temperatures rising to about 800° F., reducing soilage to powder in an hour-long operation. There is no danger with the high heat which occurs behind a locked door and within a heavily insulated oven. In fact, this insulation provides a bonus, because baking and roasting are better and more economical, since there is less heat loss. The insulation also keeps the kitchen cooler and more odor-free.

The catalytic method of oven cleaning, developed as a partial answer to the pyrolytic method, uses chemical agents which are coated on removable oven liners during the manufacturing process and which cause soilage to dissolve at normal roasting temperatures. Thus the catalytic oven is said to be continually cleaning itself. However,

PLATE 1

Before: Bulky, old cabinets, space-wasting sink on legs in one area, and cluttered pantry in another made for totally inefficient food preparation.

After: The removal of the wall created one large, bright space equipped with new, streamlined cabinets including a large island with chopping-block top. For plumbing economy new double sink was kept in the same location as the old, now illuminated by new Andersen *Perma-Shield* casement windows.

PLATE 2

Before: Dated pine cabinets, worn floor, and bulky, protruding appliances made for both a dreary look and difficult cooking.

After: New cabinets, new appliances are now in an attractive "U" arrangement, flushed for compactness, and forming a work triangle with sink and dishwasher on one point, range and refrigerator on the other two. A brown-and-white color scheme is set by the practical ceramic tile floor by American Olean.

PLATE 3

Before: A narrow corridor kitchen seemed even more confined with dark, strident wallpaper, heavy cabinetry and equipment.

After: A light, new look stems from expanses of white in counter tops, cabinets, and appliances played against the natural tones of wood and·quarry tile floor. Note that tile trims cabinet ends. *Tile is by American Olean.*

PLATE 4

Before: Corner kitchen of a small apartment was crammed between a stair rail and a window. Cabinet and counter space were almost nonexistent.

After: New G.E. appliances in avocado finish, handsome pecan cabinets and avocado laminate counter formed a compact work area. A living look was enhanced by the wallpapered ceiling and an ornate wood-and-iron chandelier by Progress Lighting.

PLATE 1

PLATE 2

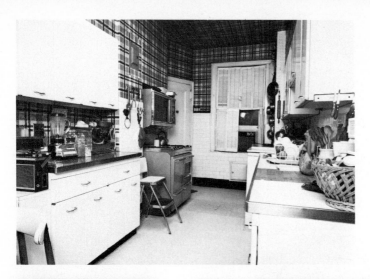

PLATE 3

PLATE 4

PLATE 5

PLATE 6

PLATE 6

PLATE 5
Before: Two small rooms included a dark, cheerless dining room and a poorly planned kitchen that wearied the owner who had to take many steps to bring food over to table.

After: Husband and wife tore down the wall between the two areas, hung the wallpaper, and installed a large wood bay window. Actual cooking and preparation areas are separated from the dining area by a mobile butcher-block-topped island cabinet. Result: one large, bright efficient space.

PLATE 6
Before: A San Francisco kitchen was blocked from a magnificent bay view by an old-fashioned laundry porch. Sink in one area, old stove and refrigerator in another caused needless steps. Cabinets were nonexistent.

After: Taking down the wall and adding a huge scenic window brought the room to life. Laundry equipment was moved to join plumbing lines in a former sink compartment, now a utility room. New sink, cabinets, and electric range line one wall, new cabinets and refrigerator line the opposite wall. Area at the window is a sitting-dining spot which enjoys the great view. *Frigidaire appliances; Armstrong flooring.*

Floor Plan by Thomas L. Bastianon

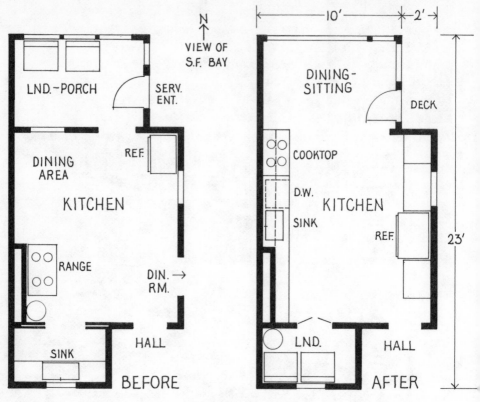

PLATE 6

for full and complete cleaning, the locked-door, pyrolytic type is considered the better method.

There are other cleaning aids in other types of ovens which should be studied. There are lower-priced, removable Teflon oven panels whose special surfaces wipe clean of soilage; disposable aluminum liners are available as an alternate solution. Many ovens can be taken apart and their innards washed at the sink—liners, broiler shields, shelf-glide racks, even oven doors that come off hinges. Cooktop cleaning is facilitated by removable elements, burner bowls and control knobs. There are one-piece porcelain tops (with burner bowls attached) which lift up for cleaning underneath.

Cooktop and Separate Oven Ensemble

Many homemakers prefer to use a counter cooktop and a separate built-in wall oven. This arrangement permits considerable flexibility in cooktop placement and also permits the oven to be located at the exact height most convenient to the cook. There are four-burner and even seven-burner electric units and some six-burner gas ones; there are also combination units with integral grilles for barbecuing and griddles for frying. An interesting advance is the electric cooktop with the elements under a special quartz-glass counter which offers easy cleaning by eliminating the difficulty of cleaning electric and gas elements, burner bowls, etc. There is at least one gas unit under a similar glass counter which has come on the market. The electric unit at this time is available in both a cooktop which fits into a counter and in a 30″ freestanding range; in gas it was first in a double-oven console model. The promise of this feature is great. There is an excellent electric cooktop with a lid which, when closed, can be used as additional counter space, when the burners are not in operation. When the lid is lifted up and the burners are exposed, it becomes a venting system, removing odors and steam right at their source. (You will note that throughout we have referred to electric elements as well as gas components as burners, even though there is, of course, no flame with the former.) Wall ovens come in widths 24, 30, and 36 inches in single oven-broiler units or double ovens (with broiler in one) in a single unit, either one-over-the-other or side-by-side, the latter a 40-inch-wide unit. Two ovens are a convenience for the cook who needs to broil and bake at the same time. With the built-in gas oven, the broiler is in a lower, separate compartment.

Features to look for in cooktops, ovens, broilers

There are many features to study. On the range top: a plug-in for portable appliances; minute-timer which lets you set a time for the appliance plugged in; oven and surface-unit signal lights; infinite-heat controls for burners; electric clock; sensing devices for surface cooking which raise and lower heat as necessary and so prevent spillovers and burned food; cooktop with one high-speed burner for quick heat; cooktops on console ranges which pull out for cooking, close for a narrow, flush look when not in use. Making a comeback is the gallery or shelf to keep foods warm or for warming plates. One model has a two-door compartment that holds food at serving temperatures and can be used to thaw frozen foods. Another model has top-recessed infrared lamps that shine down on foods kept at the rear of a cooktop.

Oven and broiler advances to check include: automatic controls that start the oven at a predetermined time, cook and stop; a cook-

and-hold feature for ovens, which cook foods as per setting, then adjust to hold a roast properly via an electric-thermometer probe until you are ready to serve; electronic ovens in which rays penetrate deeply and quickly into roasts which are given a final browning by conventional broiling for eye appeal; automatic rotisserie attachments for oven use; infrared-gas broiling which uses high-capacity ceramic broiler elements to create an intensely hot flame; variable broiler racks to do steaks to different degrees of doneness without shifting racks; a device which broils both sides of a steak at once.

Another feature, gaining in popularity, is the electric range which includes a microwave oven in addition to a conventional one. The more common use of this appliance is as a separate countertop unit, but more and more manufacturers are offering this electrically powered appliance as a built-in part of the range. One manufacturer has a single oven which can be programmed for either microwave or conventional roasting.

The refrigerator-freezer

Today's refrigerators are so well insulated with urethane that a quite large cubic capacity can be included in floor space that once accommodated a small-capacity unit. Models are flush-sided, with recessed hinges that permit door opening within unit width so that a refrigerator can be set flush even in a corner. Sizes vary from miniature undercounter models 18 and 24 inches wide to upright units 24, 30, 22, 36, 42, and 48-inch widths. Depth varies from 28 to about 31 inches. Capacities vary from six to thirty feet. While the older-type design with a freezer compartment in the inside top of the refrigerator is still found, the more common style is the separate freezer across the top with its own outside door or across the bottom with a door or pull-out bin. The popular "side by side" model with center door opening has a full-height for the freezer section alongside a somewhat wider door, also full-height, for the refrigeration section. This design comes in models as narrow as 32 inches and is a good choice for the small kitchen because of the smaller center-door swings. One disadvantage is that the freezer section is so narrow that large roasts and turkeys may not always fit. The same is true of the cold-storage section, usually on the right, and this is a handicap for the woman who likes to prepare large hors d'oeuvre platters in advance and keep them refrigerated.

For those who prefer cold storage in one unit and a separate frozen-food locker, there are refrigerators with minifreezer compartments for ice cubes only. The complementary freezer can be either an upright or chest model. These have frozen-food capacities from 400 to over 700 pounds, and of course come with lock and key for safe location in a garage or other semipublic area. An alternative to the freestanding unit is the built-in refrigerator and tandem freezer which, installed as separate side-by-side units, present a cabineted appearance in a kitchen wall. There are special cabinets in standard manufactured lines to receive both units which can be easily installed by your carpenter. You can also choose a combination refrigerator-freezer for a similar built-in installation. There are any number of special bar and other small refrigerators, ice makers and combination units which your appliance dealer can show you.

Features to Look for

Here are a few of the conveniences in refrigeration: frost-free operation (now standard with most models of major companies); automatic ice makers which hook up to plumbing lines and fill trays and empty cubes into a bin electrically; wheels which permit easy rolling out for floor cleaning; compartments for fresh meat, butter, vegetables, eggs; adjustable shelves; roll-out elements to facilitate cleaning; an outer dispenser for ice-cold water and cubes at the touch of a glass to the dispenser. There are a few models of different manufacturers that permit you to install an automatic ice maker at a later date. If you don't want automatic ice making, you still have the convenience of an ice-ejector box which lets you remove cubes with the pull of a lever into the storage box.

The sink

Gone is the day of the monster sink on spindly legs, clinically white and with dozens of wasted cubic feet beneath it. Today's sink drops right into a work counter to become part of the built-in-cabinet look. Units are either stainless steel or procelain-enameled cast iron. The former vary in quality. The best stainless-steel sinks are said to be those with nickel in the metal. The gauge marked on a stainless sink refers to the thickness of the metal: the lower the gauge, the thicker the metal, eighteen-gauge being heavier than twenty. The industry minimum of twenty-gauge for residential sinks is set by the Department of Commerce. The best porcelain-enameled cast-iron sinks are those which have three coats of porcelain, which makes them acid-resistant. Regardless of type, sinks come in many sizes and shapes and with single to triple bowls. There are double-bowl corner sinks as well as in-line models. The double-bowl model is a must where there is no dishwasher, permitting washing in one, rinsing in the other. Two separate sinks are a great convenience, one in the cleanup center, another in the preparation area where vegetables are prepared. For kitchens where husband and wife work together, two sinks reduce tie-ups. If the kitchen is open to the family room, a bar-sink and one for flower arranging, children's hobbies, and other pursuits requiring water are useful. Far too often the person remodeling a home regards a second sink as an extravagance and lives to regret not including one when the original plumbing was being done, a time when it would have been economical.

Kitchen sinks are round, square, rectangular, and oval. Sizes range from 25″ for a single-bowl, standard unit to 43″ for a deluxe, triple-bowl design. Side aprons or drainboards can increase this to 66″. The drainboard, which once was standard and then practically disappeared, is making a comeback in stainless steel. It is an ideal place to drain vegetables, place steaming pots that come right from the range, and offers an extra draining area for stacked pans and dishes. The porcelain-enamel sink in an accent color, a decorative feature we'll look into later, is a favorite now. Some stainless-steel sinks are available with a special light, helpful where the sink is in a dark spot. Another useful sink accessory is an electric food center with a blender-mixer-knife sharpener outlet in a side apron.

All manufacturers sell their sinks with or without the fittings, so you buy a faucet set separately. If you do, it must of course, fit the prepunched holes in the sink. There are several kinds of fittings. You can have the now somewhat old-fashioned twin-control knobs to mix the temperature of the water coming out of the faucet, which swings to right or left. This usually includes an aerator built into its tip, which adds tiny air bubbles to the water, making it fresher. A swivel aerator can be added as an accessory to the faucet, giving still more play, directing water in force to all corners of the sink to wash down the drain. An alternative to hot and cold knobs is a single-handle control lever, which the homemaker can swing to right or left with a flick of the wrist to set water temperature, or up and down to change the force of the flow. This is a water-saver, as it can be set at a predetermined, safe temperature and turned off, then on, as water is needed. A variation of this convenient feature is the control-knob faucet, similar to the one more often found in the bath lavatory.

Pulled up, it controls the water flow; pushed all the way down, it shuts off the water; turned left, it increases the hot-water mixture; turned right, it increases the cold. It has the same advantage as the control lever, permitting a temperature setting which remains constant even though the faucet is turned off. There are a number of good brands of faucets, each with special features, so it pays to compare them with the features of the faucet that the sink manufacturer would provide. Faucet accessories include liquid soap and hand-lotion dispensers, spray hose, shampoo spray-hose assembly, dishwasher brush, etc. Not part of the faucet assembly is a water-purifier attachment that hooks up to the faucet, helpful in areas where the water is not up to standard.

The dishwasher

Sometimes homemakers ask: Why a dishwasher? Is it worth the money when it's so quick and easy to do dishes and I don't mind? The answer is that it is worth its weight in convenience. Not only does it eliminate the tedium of washing by hand, it also does away with the unsightly and spacetaking dish rack if you don't take the time to dry by hand. The dishwasher also offers an out-of-the-way storage place for either soiled or clean dishes: you can set the table right from the machine if you care to, and with today's equipment, which requires only the scraping of major food waste, the dishwasher acts as a kind of minidisposer, eliminating soft waste during the cleaning cycle. Some of the new machines have a plate-warming cycle which is another plus, eliminating last-minute oven warming; others include a sanitization feature whereby water is brought up to nearly 180° F. to kill germs in households where there are colds and other contagious ailments.

There are three kinds of dishwashers: undercounter, which are front loading and fit a 24-inch-wide space under a counter next to the sink; the portable model which, freestanding and mobile, usually loads from the top and connects to the sink faucet (one such model is front loading with a counter balance device to prevent tipping forward); and a special variant of the undercounter unit which is expressly designed to fit under a sink in kitchens where space is tight. There are virtues to all three. The regular undercounter is the best for a permanent location, and if your present budget doesn't cover one, it is a good idea to have the plumbing and wiring put in and to leave a 24-inch space so that one can be added later on when you can afford it. Meanwhile, you can include a 24-inch cabinet in this space, to be removed later when the dishwasher is added. The portable is ideal for apartments where a permanent installation isn't wanted. And there are convertible portables, front loading, which can be built in later. Many of these have the same important features as the built-in. However, the portable has an integral advantage in that it can serve, when not in use for dishwashing, as a mobile work island, moving where you need it. Most of them come with chopping-block tops which make excellent work surfaces.

A feature to look for as you shop is the rack arrangement, and here you will want to note whether the upper racks are adjustable and lift up and out of the way for bowls and tall glasses. Split-level racks will hold a double layer of cups; removable racks permit you to wash big platters and pots. More important than the number of place settings which a manufacturer may boast is the provision for random loading, so that you can fit things wherever they will go. It's not a bad idea, if you have special glassware and odd-sized dinnerware, to take a sample with you as you shop and see how it fits. Another factor to be alert to is noise. Manufacturers have done their best to keep it to a low level. However, it is well to listen to a full cycle and notice if the machine fills quietly and if it is insulated against the noise of cascading water when the agitator spins at full tilt.

If you live in the country and have a dug well, it is important to note that a dishwasher uses about fourteen gallons of water in a full cycle. So in certain dry seasons, you will have to watch frequency of use more carefully. In any case, it is best to wait until a full load has accumulated before running the dishwasher; just rinse plates lightly after meals and add them to the load. Most machines use water at 150° F. and take about an hour for the full cycle. All require a special fluid to be added periodically to eliminate spots on knives and forks and glassware. None is guaranteed not to fade antique or hand-painted china with repeated washings. Such pieces cannot stand the high water temperatures and should be washed by hand. However, today's fine china can be washed safely, as manufacturers now make most glazes and patterns resistant to such temperatures. Some machines have a fine-china cycle during which the water is agitated at less than full force. (It has been water force which has caused much of the damage in the past.) Most plastic dinnerware, especially of the melamine variety, is machine washable. If you are in doubt about a plastic item, it is a good idea to test by placing it in an upper rack well away from the heating element, usually a 950-watt radiant tube which dries the dishes.

As far as appearance of the built-in unit is concerned, the fronts come in any of a manufacturer's standard colors and there is also a frame kit which you can order to install your own color in a laminate, a painted or papered plywood or hardboard section or, in fact, any covering you choose.

The disposer

The food-waste disposer is another adjunct of the sink area and is a must where local ordinances permit its use. Installed directly under the drain opening of a sink (you must specify to your plumber which bowl of a twin-bowl model you want it under), it is a special convenience not only prior to washing dishes, but during the preparation of fresh vegetables and many other chores. There are two kinds of disposers. One is the batch-feed variety which you load and then activate by pressing down a partial cover or by turning on the cold water after the cover is put on. The other is continuous feed and is activated by a switch in some convenient location near the sink. With this type, as the cold water runs, you can continue to add food waste to it. In all types the cold water must be running at all times while it is activated, and it is recommended that the water run for thirty seconds thereafter to permit the pulverized waste to travel clear through the drain line. There are models which will take bones and the hardest objects (one model we know will make sand out of glass, although this is not recommended for other than demonstration purposes). A bugaboo used to be jamming on a too-hard object. Now antijamming mechanisms speed difficult items along. A prime advance in recent years has been the reduction of the noise level and this factor is one to look for as you shop and compare. Most manufacturers offer several different models with different horsepower, size, and speed. The size of your family and amount of food waste should be taken into account in your choice. Consult your plumber or the disposer salesman about this.

Cabinets and counters

The compact, built-in look of today's kitchen was only partially the result of new design concepts for major appliances. The advent of modular, manufactured cabinets must be given at least equal credit. And since appliances by their mechanical nature have a contemporary look, it is cabinetry more than any other component that gives the stamp of period style. In other words, if you want an Early American or French Provincial kitchen, cabinets are the first route to it. This leads to an important decision: Should cabinets be custom-made by a local carpenter or kitchen fabricator, or should the home-maker choose from among the many manufactured cabinet collections?

Custom-built or Manufactured?

While the custom cabinet permits considerable individuality in design, interior fittings, and on-the-spot decisions about utilization of space, there are so many more positive factors for a choice of manufactured cabinets that the vote must be overwhelmingly in favor of the latter. Manufactured cabinets of the larger, established firms come in a wide range of sizes and styles, with considerable choice in interior appointments. They are made of solid lumber, plywood with fine wood-veneer facings over an inner core, prefinished hardboard over a wood frame, and steel. The components of each cabinet are cut and joined to exact tolerances under factory-controlled conditions and then given a durable finish, either baked on or chemically treated to make the surfaces wipeable and in some cases, scrubbable. Hardware on the better cabinets is solid.

Manufactured cabinets often offer the homemaker a standard of quality which the local craftsman, no matter how skilled, cannot match, simply because he does not have access to fully kiln-dried lumber and cannot add the kind of finish that assures easy cleaning as well as dimensional stability. The result of the custom cabinet choice is often warped doors, loose moldings, flaking paint, and ill-fitting hardware. On the other hand, manufactured cabinets are usually no more expensive and offer the possibility of many custom options: slide-out garbage hampers, mixing centers complete with electric plug for hookup to house wiring, chopping boards that pull out, tray storage bins, silverware drawers with tarnishproof cloth, liquor lockers—in short, almost every kind of convenience a homemaker might want. And all are part of a modular system that permits you to analyze your requirements and your kitchen dimensions and then choose cabinets as part of an organized kitchen plan.

Two Categories: Base and Wall

There are two categories of cabinets, base cabinets which rest on the floor and form the support for the work counters, and wall cabinets which attach to studs or other wall structures for secure hanging. Base cabinets come in a standard depth of 24 inches and in widths from 9 inches to sweeping sink cabinets of 84 inches. Height is standard at about 35 inches. Manufactured units come open at the top and your carpenter or plastic-laminate fabricator must add a three-quarter-inch plywood top which in turn is given a surface of plastic laminate, ceramic tile, chopping block, marble, slate, or whatever surface you want. The chopping-block top and certain thick stone tops can be installed without the plywood underlayment. As you review a manufacturer's promotional brochure, or specification sheets, you will see the many sizes and special designs that can be arranged, jigsaw-puzzle-like, to form the lower tier of cabinetry that comprises your work counters. Special designs include drop-in range-front units, stack-on range units for upper consoles, peninsula corner bases, sink fronts, desks, drawers, corner sink cabinets, rotating, lazy Susan corner units, etc. Base units can be combined, joined, and topped to form separate islands for counters, buffets, range tops, sinks, etc.

Wall cabinets are standard at 12 inches deep and range in height from 12 to 30 inches and more. Widths range from 12 inches to combination three-door units 48 inches. There are blind-corner designs and lazy Susan units for corners. Wall cabinets can be used in some cases, where necessary because of limited space, as base cabinets, in which instance your carpenter can create a base with a toe setback. The best cabinets come with adjustable shelves for both wall and base units, drawers with smooth-gliding and safety-stop devices, neatly detailed, smooth-finished interiors, shelves, and door backs. Filler strips in consonant finish are available for your carpenter to make final space adjustments. There are also freestanding, tall cabinets for double ovens, utility cabinets, pantry units with swing-out doors and rotating shelves. There are also conversion kits with some lines that permit cabinets to be used as architectural walls in other rooms than the kitchen or in the kitchen as homemaking centers. The variety in the best manufactured lines is really staggering and, with imagination, can satisfy every kitchen-space and decoration need.

Cabinets and Decor

As pointed out earlier, the cabinet more than any other kitchen element helps to establish period style. The most streamlined major appliances fitted around traditionally styled cabinetry seem to take on familiar guise. The largest manufacturers have a line which includes contemporary styling, French Provincial, Mediterranean, Early American, and transitional designs that can be modified in either direction—contemporary or traditional—with other decorative components. They come in many wood finishes, either natural to the type of hardwood actually used—most often birch, oak, pecan, or other hardwood—or a tone to simulate other popular wood finishes like fruitwood, weathered barn siding, distressed pine, etc. This same finish is then applied to the inside core of the door, the frames and interior wood paneling. These areas are often a less expensive hardwood like tupelo (gumwood). Sometimes the backs and sides are hardboard, finished to blend with fronts. The entire style character of the cabinet is actually added by the door fronts and the manufacturer can use standard frames with interchangeable fronts, so you are really choosing door style. In addition to wood finishes, there are standard colors in most lines, and, of course, the better lines will match any color of your choice at a premium. Another contributor to style is hardware, which is designed specially for each style, usually a copy or adaptation of hardware of the period simulated. The best is die-cast and solid brass or other metal. Manufacturers will sell the cabinets with hardware holes undrilled, so that you can place your own pulls, latches, etc., where you wish. This can give a quite individual character to your room. Unless period hardware calls for exposed hinges, the concealed ones are the most attractive choice. There are hinges that close magnetically, too. As you shop for cabinets, look at interior hardware—for adjustable shelves, magnetic catches and friction catches. These will give you a quality-comparison point, too.

Less expensive lines sometimes employ hardboard for fronts as well as backs and sides. If the wood frame is sound, this can be an acceptable construction. Hardboard can, of course, be printed to simulate any wood or other finish and it is dimensionally stable, takes a plastic finish for easy cleaning and holds up well. Filigree hardboard is sometimes used for the doors of wall cabinets for a design effect. Another decorative feature with some cabinets is reversible doors which give the homemaker variety. Usually one side is smooth and can be wall-papered, painted, or fabric-covered to serve as an interesting part of the decorating scheme.

Kitchen Counters

Counters are directly determined by cabinets, since the base cabinets form the platform on which counters rest. The counter is one of the most important elements in the kitchen from the standpoint of a "fit" to the individual homemaker. Young, healthy homemakers often feel tired and yet do not realize it's because they have been trying to fit themselves to work surfaces not designed for their height. Stooping or stretching as you work can be overcome by setting counters at the correct height for you. Research on work heights in the Department of Household Economics and Management shows that elbow height is the measurement which best determines the most comfortable work height. For most activities at kitchen counters, the homemaker needs a work surface three inches below her elbow height. However, for motions requiring the exertion of force or holding a mixer or beater, she needs a work surface six or seven inches below elbow height. So for efficient kitchen work, work surfaces of more than one height may be required.

As for the surface of the counter itself, there are several considerations. The kitchen counter takes a great deal of hard wear, so it is important to choose one that is durable and easily maintained. High-pressure plastic laminate is a good choice. It comes in many colors and patterns, is easily installed and well priced. Edges can be rolled or the installation can be self-edged in the same laminate or a contrasting one, as a color accent. Fabrication can be done by many carpenters, by kitchen specialists, and by companies which do only laminate fabrication. Laminates come in 4×8- and 4×10-foot sheets, 1/16 of an inch thick. There is a 1/32-inch-thick grade which is suitable only for vertical installation, not to be recommended for work counters, even though it is lower-priced. There are special foil-backed laminates said to be heatproof, but these are expensive and better suited to laboratories. The best high-pressure plastic laminate is resistant to cigarette burns, but will not withstand a hot pot set directly onto it. It cannot be used as a cutting surface, as it scars. It is easily washed with soap and water, and stubborn spots can be removed by light scouring with a powder cleanser. Steel wool scouring is not recommended. However, the laminate is practically stainproof so that spots are usually not a problem.

If you want a heatproof surface, consider ceramic tile, stainless steel, or a new glass-ceramic material. Ceramic tile, once disliked because the grout between tiles discolored with various food stains, has now overcome this handicap with new stainproof grouts and makes a wonderful surface. Tile comes in several thicknesses and in many colors, textures, and patterns. The chopping-block top, discussed at length in another section, is a good surface for specific areas where cutting is done. A laminate or tile is the better choice for most counters. The new glass-ceramic counter surface is 3/16 of an inch thick and comes in sizes 16×20, 18×25, and 24×25 inches. It has a nonstick surface good for pastry rolling and dough kneading; it doesn't stain or scratch, so can be used for cutting. Marble has been a favorite in past years for pastry making, but it stains. However, it makes a handsome, elegant surface and if cleaned carefully after each use makes a good counter surface, albeit expensive.

How to draw a floor plan

Now that you have the basic sizes of the main kitchen components, have decided on the arrangement you want from a study of the four possible ones, and know the size and shape your new kitchen will take, you are ready to draw a floor plan. First, be sure of exact dimensions; the wrong ones can necessitate expensive changes later. If your house is in the blueprint stage, note the windows, closets, chimney, heating outlets, and other features of the space you're working with. If you are remodeling a kitchen in an existing home, take a folding measuring stick or yardstick and go around the room, making notations of all the architectural details, length of walls, etc., on a rough plan on a piece of paper. Armed with these statistics, get graph paper (quarter-inch scale is good, with each square equal to one foot) and transfer your dimensions with pencil and ruler. Then, remembering that work counters are two feet deep, draw in the basic form of the L, U, corridor, or line-a-wall arrangement. You may find as you sketch that a variation of the arrangement you had in mind works better, or that you prefer a completely different arrangement.

If you are considering an island or peninsula, cut one from graph paper in various sizes and move it around on the plan to see how it fits. Draw into the counters your range, sink, or refrigerator from known width and depth dimensions, leaving the recommended adjacent work areas. At this juncture you may have to add or subtract counter space to accommodate standard widths of the kinds of base cabinets you want in the different areas. Mark in the necessary electrical outlets with symbols known to electrical contractors. Your electrician can tell you what they are. As you draw, be mindful of the work pattern your plan permits. Is it an efficient triangle? Would it be improved by changing slightly or greatly the location of one or more major appliances and their work centers? What about the traffic problem of the room in relation to that of the rest of the house? Will cross-traffic hamper the cook? Is there a door breaking up the flow of work from one center to another? If the answer is yes to any of these, now is the time to make a change before the structure takes shape. This is the reason for making this test run, as it were, to catch mistakes or poorly planned details in the blueprint stage, because, as in most areas of planning, you get an objective look when something is down on paper, and often, for the first time, glaring errors appear.

Once you have a floor plan you think is right, be sure to draw elevations of each wall. Again, you know the height and width of the

various elements, so draw each wall on graph paper to dimensions
and mark in your cabinets and appliances. This may be the only opportunity to double-check your wall cabinets which don't show up
on a flat floor plan. We know of one kitchen expert who, when planning her own kitchen, failed to draw elevations and failed to order
the cabinet for over the refrigerator as a result. Fortunately, there
was time to order the necessary cabinet at the last minute, but it was
a problem rematching the paint, as it originally had been made up in
one batch by the cabinet manufacturer to the exact shade of the
major appliances.

Mark the manufacturer's number of each cabinet on the face of the
elevation and mark the number of each appliance. This is a good way
for a final check before ordering. The kitchen plan may be compact,
but its very compactness means that each item must have the exact
measurement to take its place properly. Afterthoughts are difficult
and timetaking. It's wise, too, for you to go over your list with a
kitchen planner, architect, or contractor, before ordering. Some utility companies have a kitchen expert who acts as a consultant and
such a person can be of great help at this stage. Too, some department stores offer this service. Take your specifications, graph-
papered floor plans, and elevations there, if you don't have access to
other help.

Decorating the kitchen

We have alluded to decoration from time to time, but held off as you
remember, because we wanted to establish the basic structure of the
kitchen. This room, not unlike others, is largely a matter of surface
coating to strike the decorative note you prefer. To be sure, there are
a few structural considerations and resultant choices you must make
and these should be taken up now. For example, if you want an Early
American kitchen with a fireplace, the chimney must be part of your
architectural plan. Moldings and doors must be specified that blend
with the theme. There are six-panel doors for the Colonial look, flush
doors for the contemporary, arched-panel units for French Provincial, three-panel for Early American, etc., all stock units to be found
at your local lumberyard. The same for cornice moldings and
doorframe moldings. Of course, there's no need to be slavish about a
theme: if you want sliding patio windows leading from an Early
American kitchen to the terrace, have them, but use the kind with
snap-in grilles that will add to the small-paneled look that is authentic

for the period. And the doors can be framed inside and out with the correct moldings.

How to Set the Background

The elements that go to make up the background of the kitchen—which is essentially its decoration—include floor, walls, windows, cabinets, and counters. Let's discuss each in terms of the various themes. We'll build from the floor up. In this room above all others you want practicality, namely a floor that won't show soil, will be long-wearing, and can be easily damp-mopped clean. You also want a floor that's safe, that's not so slick that you have to watch your step as you go through the intricate footwork that food preparation often entails. You also want a resilient surface, or enough resiliency to avoid weary feet, because you are apt to be on them most of the time you're in this room.

So you have these choices: vinyl, vinyl-asbestos and rubber tile, sheet vinyl, asphalt tile, or embossed linoleum; the last two being the least expensive and the least long-wearing. There is wood, provided that it is stained and then given a urethane finish or some plastic finish

PLATE 1

Before: Small bath was located in the part of the house most accessible to a new pool and redeveloped garden. It was also inconvenient and unattractive. Remodeling provided the answer to both problems.

After: Designer Ruth Brooks first extended the window wall five feet and added a door for pool and garden access. A new cabineted lavatory was located on the wall facing the tub-shower, which was retained. New checkerboard floor and leafy wallpaper, which restates the garden theme, completed the decor. *Photographer: Harold Davis.*

PLATE 2

Before: A jumbled lineup of toilet and sink along one wall of a small bath made it seem even more minuscule.

After: A dash of bright color, a new lavatory counter that sweeps across the toilet tank, and new Kohler fixtures changed the whole appearance of the room. The lively blue washbasin is in a cabinet that utilizes formerly wasted space for storage. An overscaled mirror also helps to make this bath seem larger.

PLATE 3

Before: An adequate bath lacked style, but had the virtues of spaciousness and a high ceiling. Also, plumbing and drain lines were located for economical replacement and remodeling.

After: White tile walls and floor set a unified scheme, carried out with white American-Standard plumbing fixtures including a graceful pedestal lavatory. Mirrored ceiling and expanse of mirror over lavatory add to the effect of spaciousness. Plants give a pleasant garden look.

PLATE 1

PLATE 2

PLATE 3

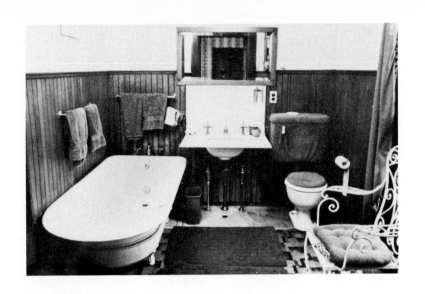

PLATE 4

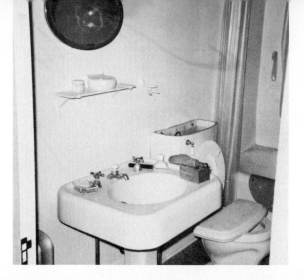

PLATE 5

that makes it more or less impermeable. There is ceramic tile including quarry tile, but if you worry about resiliency you'll want to be sure that it is installed over wood or plywood. The same goes for marble, flagstone, or old brick, all of which are better installed directly over a concrete slab, creating a dense, hard, unyielding surface. The same goes for terrazzo, a most practical material used a lot in Florida, California, and other warm climates because it is cooling. All of these masonry floor materials are totally practical, too, so if you want to use one of them, one solution is to place a rubber section or piece of carpet in the most frequently used section, usually the sink and the path from sink to cooktop. Last and newest in the floor-covering roster is carpet which comes in special, easy-care and soil-resistant fibers and finishes which make it practical and comfortable even when installed over a concrete slab. This kind of so-called indoor-outdoor carpet is relatively inexpensive, good-wearing and comes in attractive colors and patterns.

For a streamlined kitchen the following are good choices because they blend with the contemporary look: choices in masonry include terrazzo, marble and ceramic tile, perferably in light, space-stretching tones. Sheet vinyl, vinyl-asbestos and solid vinyl tile come in colors and patterns that are suitable. Patterns should be small or indistinct, like the vinyls which simulate marble or other masonry, and colors in any floor for a contemporary room are better in light space-stretching tones. For the provincial look, the picture changes, for here dark tones and distinct patterns are required. In masonry, quarry tile, either square or hexagonal, or in a modified fleur-de-lis,

PLATE 4

Before: The owners of this bath liked the old-fashioned look, but disliked the discomfort and inconvenience of this room.

After: Proving that you can have yesteryear charm along with convenience, the remodeling retained the old wainscot, now stripped to the natural wood, and replaced the old tub on legs with a snappy new red tub on legs. Another touch of bright red is the new lav, recessed into a white counter over a wood cabinet. *Fixtures are by Kohler.*

PLATE 5

Before: Here's a bath that looked smaller than it really was, because the fixtures were bunched at one end of the room.

After: Careful measuring permitted a sizable cabineted lavatory, toilet, and even a bidet, without crowding. The disadvantage of the tub-shower along the window wall was overcome with shutter panels of rondel plastic over the window, reducing drafts but permitting ventilation when required. Tub has built-in whirlpool action for hydromassage. *Fixtures are by Briggs.*

trefoil, or quatrefoil pattern is good. The other-than-square design is especially helpful in setting the French Provincial look. Old brick is marvelous for any provincial effect, laid in stacked bond or herringbone pattern; it is especially suitable for the Early American or country kitchen. Any of the sheet vinyls, vinyl tiles, and embossed inlaid linoleums that simulate brick or ceramic-tile patterns are excellent. The kitchens of old usually had rough pine or oak flooring and these can be simulated today with random oak plank, pegged and stained dark, or random pine treated similarly. To get an authentic look with new pine boards, one designer we know has them installed first and gets a distressed look by having all the workmen tramp over them during construction. Then they are swept clean, stained, finished in urethane and lightly waxed. The Spanish or Mediterranean look so popular today is essentially a provincial look with some stylistic motifs added, so any of the preceding would be suitable. The motifs are important and there are a good many designs in vinyl and linoleum taken from authentic Spanish-tile patterns.

Ideas for Wall Treatment

Walls are another main contributor to decor as well as practicality. A washable surface is a must, so semigloss or high gloss paint, plastic-surfaced wallpaper or other covering, plastic-finished hardboard or plywood paneling or ceramic tile are the recommended materials. Contemporary treatment calls for painted plaster or gypsum board, neutral, light-toned, mildly textured wall covering like simulated grass cloth, ceramic tile, again in light tones and usually only to above-counter height with painted plaster above, although a fully tiled wall is good-looking though expensive. For the traditional room, either French Country, Early American, Colonial or Mediterranean, there are documentary wallpapers which come surface-treated or can be treated for easy cleaning. The better wallpaper houses have a wide selection taken from old papers and fabrics; they often have matching fabric, in fact, so that you can blend walls and kitchen curtains. Such a documentary is a sure way to a true look. Wood-paneled walls, either individual tongued-and-grooved boards of pine, or plywood grooved to look random can be used. Plywood comes in many faces, as you likely know, so that you can have pecky cypress, birch, oak, rosewood, and other rare woods besides pine. They come in pastel-toned finishes and most are treated for damp-cleaning. A great look for the country kitchen is with barn siding, and the real thing makes a handsome kitchen, although plywood and laminate panels simulating it give a good effect, too. There are wallpapers that simulate brick and wood, and, of course, hardboard comes in almost any simulated finish you can think of.

Ceiling

The ceiling is part of the background also and for the contemporary room the choice is often a luminous ceiling with light sources behind sheets of translucent plastic, held in place in a metal grid. There are many systems of this kind on the market which are easy to install. The traditional room relies heavily on the counterpoint of white against stained wood. A plaster or gypsum board ceiling with structural or decorative beams makes a good ceiling for the country kitchen. A black wrought-iron chandelier played against it is a dramatic accent. The provincial look can be furthered by an all-papered ceiling or with patterned paper in a documentary design installed between beams.

Windows

The kitchen with a view is one of the most inviting, but even without a view openness is important to prevent the homemaker from getting a feeling of confinement, since so much time is spent there. If the kitchen is one with the family room or breakfast area, it will enjoy an airiness through their windows. For over the sink or any counter, the glider window is recommended over the double-hung, because it is easier to operate. Roll-out casements are easier, too, since they open with one-hand turn of a crank. Whichever kind of window you use, choose a design with open expanses of glass for the contemporary scheme and small-paned units for the traditional. There are even diamond-shaped panes for the Cotswold or cottage look, which can add to the country kitchen. A Dutch door is a good idea for the service entrance, because it adds a rustic touch and also permits light and egress. Here again, you have a choice of oblong or diamond panes. They come in ponderosa pine and in stock panel door sizes.

For control of light, you can use window shades, traverse curtains, cafes, or shutters. Shades can be laminated in fabric to blend with wallpaper and the fabric can be prefinished for wiping clean. Louvered shutters are a good choice for the country kitchen as they can be stained (special walnut is a good stain to use for a provincial look; just apply with a brush and leave without wiping; it looks antique and has a fruitwood appearance on pine). Curtains in the kitchen proper should be the same as in a family room, or any other room, onto which it opens. This gives decorative continuity so important in

making space seem larger. For example, if you have a bank of high
windows over the sink in cafe curtains, use the same fabric as traverse
floor-to-ceiling draperies for sliding glass family-room doors that
open on to a terrace. For the sleek, modern kitchen with sliding glass
doors, vertical window shades are effective, floor-to-ceiling.

Cabinets and Counters as Part of Decor

We have already discussed how cabinet fronts help to set the period style in a kitchen. If you use manufactured cabinets, the brochures in color will give you ideas for decorating your type of
kitchen. They will also help you choose the right cabinet for the
period you want. Suffice it to say here that arched-panel doors are
better suited to the Mediterranean and French Provincial looks;
square-panel doors the Colonial or Early American country look;
grooved-plank doors are effective in the Early American room. The
plainer the better is the word for the contemporary kitchen; flush
doors and simple hardware and as blond a finish as possible are the
order of the day here. As far as painted cabinets are concerned, they
are another sure way of establishing the correct period look. There
are certain colors which denote certain periods (Williamsburg green
for Colonial, for example; antique French blue for provincial; barn
red for Early American, etc.). Using a color closely identified with
the style of your choice will help, also, in your choice of counter
laminate, ceramic tile or other work surfaces. There are many patterns
in both plastic and ceramic that are authentic to traditional periods.
Study these before making a choice. The contemporary kitchen can
use cabinets in bold colors and in several different colors, using them
in large blocks. For example, one bank at the sink, say, in bright blue,
base cabinets of an island in bright yellow; those of the cooktop in
red. Wall cabinets, then, would repeat these colors in blocks, too.
The white look is impressive in the contemporary kitchen—white
counters, white cabinets, white walls, a case of surface treatment following function; clinical white for food preparation. For the natural
wood look in the modern idiom, chopping-block counters are impressive. We have already mentioned the reversible panels for cabinet
doors which permit a decorative touch to tie in with the rest of your
theme. Certain appliances—dishwasher and refrigerator—often permit
decorative fronts to be applied in frames that come with the units or
as frame kits which can be ordered. These provide areas for traditional pattern or contemporary color blocks. If you want the wood

look, you can have it in the same finish to match your cabinets by using the frame kits on dishwasher and refrigerator.

Color and Pattern in the Kitchen

No reference to decoration would be complete without a separate discussion about color. It is one of the most basic and yet least expensive tools you have to work with in the planning of any room. We have already touched on the colors that help to establish the various period themes. The important fact to remember here is that the same color schemes apply to a Colonial kitchen as to a Colonial living room. In other words, study period rooms—in books, magazines, museums—for color ideas which you then apply to the kitchen. Also remember that you have at your disposal an enormous range of color in the components you will use. The only limited color palette is in the major appliances themselves and fortunately the standard line of the major manufacturers includes at least one color suitable for each period style. The colors common to almost all lines include copper, avocado, and a shade of wheat gold plus the noncolor white, which can be worked successfully into almost any scheme. In fact, white is often a good choice, because appliances must be lived with a long time and it is easy to change colors around them in walls, curtains and decorative accessories. In addition, leading manufacturers have more dramatic colors—red, blue and black, another noncolor—but these are usually not part of the full line and, unfortunately, not always in the top of the line, the units with the most prized features. So if you want red or black, you may have to do without an automatic ice maker or a double-oven console range. It is best to inquire what the various colors come in before you get your heart set on a scheme, otherwise you will be disappointed.

Overall, keep in mind that the day of the clinically white kitchen is past; no longer is the slightest hint of red taboo because of the blood association; no longer is the kitchen off-limits to guests and usually to husbands, too. The living kitchen is the rule nowadays and it deserves the same colorful treatment as any other room. If it is part of the family room or some other informal sitting area, it is likely the most lived-in room in the house, and families want to live colorfully. Also, the kitchen is an integral part of the home, in terms of decoration, and it should continue the housewide interior theme; by so doing, it helps to make the whole house seem more spacious. Going from a Georgian living or dining room into a totally crisp, contemporary kitchen makes the whole house seem disjointed and keeps everyone from wanting to gather there. However, if the rest of the house is breathlessly contemporary, it seems perfectly logical and comfortable to find more of the same in the kitchen.

How to Use Pattern

Balance is the watchword here. There is so much going on in the kitchen with the appliances themselves, the many utensils and cabinets, all creating pattern, that this element must be used carefully. As we have seen, certain decorative styles will permit more pattern than others, in fact, some, like Early American, specifically require it. However, it is wise to hold it to certain areas. For example, if you want a busy documentary wallpaper-curtain ensemble, keep countertops and flooring subdued. Or, keep counter laminate in a solid color and the floor in a pattern of about the same scale as the wall covering. If the cabinets permit decorated fronts with reversible panels, then it may be best to keep walls, floor, and counters in a solid color that blends with the dominant color in the print of the cabinet door. Repeat the same pattern in fabric for curtains, table mats, dish towels, and other accessories if possible. If cabinets are in a boldly grained wood, keep to a subdued design in other elements. Don't overlook the ceiling as a source of pattern and color: in the small kitchen, papering exposed walls and ceiling in the same small pattern will help to make the room seem larger. But if you do this, choose pastel appliances in a tone found in the paper and keep counters a plain color and the floor fairly neutral. Or keep walls, cabinets, and appliances—the entire band around the room—subdued, and use patterned ceiling and floor. In the contemporary kitchen, the cabinets and appliances will furnish blocks of pattern, and counters, floor, walls, and ceiling should be in white or a pastel. That way, pattern will result architecturally, a basic role in this style.

The special kitchen

Heretofore, we have been talking about the standard kitchen, a complete and fully equipped room in a year-round house or apartment. However, there are many other so-called special kitchens, less than standard in size and equipment, that are frequently needed. Some of these include the small apartment kitchen, the "efficiency" as it is often referred to, the minikitchen for the large home, as a second kitchen, or for recreation room, second-floor sleeping area, etc. For a minikitchen you have the choice of either grouping an assemblage of small units or buying a unit that combines range, refrigerator and sink. If you choose the former route, you can combine a 20- or 24-inch electric or gas range, a 24- or 28-inch refrigerator and a counter sink 15- to 24-inches wide. So from a total of from 72 to 90 inches you can form a fairly well-equipped work center, a line-a-wall arrangement whose main defect is limited counter space. If you want more wall cabinets, there are undercounter refrigerators 24 to 36 inches.

The alternative is the unitized kitchen, a compact design with the three main appliances in one. Here there are choices too. You can combine a 60-inch unit with gas or electric range-oven and sink with a separate 24-inch refrigerator for a total of 84-inches. There is a system of metal wall cabinets to be used in conjunction. There is also a 66- or a 72-inch unit that includes an 18-inch range-oven, 18- or 21-inch sink and a 30-inch undercounter refrigerator. Again, metal wall cabinets are available for a line above the appliance. Countertop is stainless steel and fronts are white or copper-brown. The refrigerator has a net capacity of 6 cubic feet, a 24-pound freezer with two ice-cube trays and space for nine ice-cube trays. Refrigerator comes with self-contained hinging on right or left, so door swing causes no space problem. Going smaller, you can find a 30-inch unit that combines all three in one with a stainless-steel top which includes two electric or gas burners. A good combination is the 48-inch unit, flanked wth a standard dishwasher on one side next to the sink, and with an 18-inch base cabinet on the other side. These two side elements add 42 inches of counter space. It is easy then to buy a group of wall cabinets to fit the upper area. This creates a highly workable small kitchen.

These units or combinations of units can go into what might otherwise be closet area in a basement or attic recreation room. A 30-inch combination sink, range and refrigerator is a useful addition to a second-floor master bedroom where the owners like to fix themselves a snack. Where possible, it is economical to plan such units so that plumbing can be backed up to that in a bath, and, of course, special heavy-duty wiring is necessary with electric ranges. If it is located in a self-contained niche, folding doors can be installed to hide the minikitchen when it is not in use. Louvered doors are best since the refrigerator must "breathe."

Lighting in the kitchen

Though glamorized to the hilt, the kitchen remains basically a functional room and if it is not illuminated for seeing safely, accurately, and comfortably in a variety of visual tasks, fatigue and irritability often result. Dim, glaring, or poorly distributed light leads to visual fatigue, which sets off an emotional chain reaction that is usually blamed on kitchen drudgery. On the other hand, a well-illuminated, modest kitchen can be far more efficient and pleasant than an elaborate one, poorly lighted. These recommendations will help make your kitchen decor look better, eliminate shadows at work centers along the perimeter of the room, aid in estimating the doneness of foods by seeing true color, and minimize the dangers of working with hot pans and sharp knives.

For general background illumination, a complete luminous ceiling with fluorescent tubes or incandescent bulbs over panels of translucent plastic is an ideal solution. Other than this, an adequate ceiling fixture is a must, one at least 12 inches in diameter and to accommodate either one 150-watt or two 75-watt bulbs. A fluorescent fixture should accommodate either two 30-watt tubes or two circline tubes. These are recommended for a room of about 100 square feet. Specific illumination at work centers is required for supplementary brightness. Recessed fixtures, a pair of high-hats installed in a soffit over the sink, are basic to the well-equipped kitchen. Each fixture would use either a 100 or 150-watt bulb. A 20-watt bulb is adequate for a fluorescent. Both should be warm white. Both require an opaque faceboard of 8-inch minimum depth. At the range, a separate fixture may be required even though the range has its own built-in light panel which is usually sufficient to light the range controls but not enough light for the whole work center. The best answer is a vent hood with a light fixture as an integral part of it. At work counters, there should be fluorescent tubes for every four lineal feet. One 20-watt tube (or a fixture with two 40-watt incandescents) is suitable; the fluorescent is the better solution and it should be fitted with an aluminum, wood, or opaque shield. The fluorescents should be mounted on the wall right under the cabinets. At the cleanup center with cabinets above, you can use a sink which includes a light, if under-cabinet illumination is not sufficient.

Alternatives to the foregoing include luminous panels, cornice lighting around the perimeter of the room and additional recessed ceiling fixtures. Not to be overlooked is the decorative chandelier which adds so much character to the period kitchen, wrought iron or wood for the Country look; brass-ball design for the Colonial room, iron and crystal for the French Provincial. For the kitchen dining area, there are chandeliers which can be raised and lowered according to your needs.

Ventilation

Just as lighting helps keep up kitchen morale, so does the air the cook breathes. Maintaining the air in a home at a constant temperature and humidity keeps the whole family comfortable, happy, and fresh. Since the kitchen drastically upsets the equilibrium of home air with polluted heat, steam, grease, vapor, and odors, as well as by lowering the oxygen content, the cook will suffer more than anyone else. A central air-conditioning system will keep the house warm in the winter and cool in summer while maintaining suitable humidity. However, it is only the first step when it comes to the kitchen. A ventilator is necessary for use when the range is in operation. There are two kinds, those that are ducted to the outdoors and those that are ductless and rely on activated charcoal to absorb grease, odors, and steam which are pulled through by a powerful fan. Obviously the better equipment is the outdoor-vented, because it pulls everything out of the house and into the atmosphere; it is well to check the capacity requirements for the size of your kitchen. Most models have a warranty. The standard rate is 2 CFM per square foot size, and fans made by reputable manufacturers carry a tag certified by the Home Ventilating Institute as to the capacity of the unit. The fan does not disturb the climate balance created by a central air-conditioning system. In fact, it is said that the cost of cooling a home rises considerably when a suitable ducted range ventilator is not installed. However, it is not always possible to vent outdoors because of kitchen location, so a ductless model must be used and its charcoal filter be replaced periodically, since charcoal cannot be reactivated in the home.

Manufactured vent hoods come in most range-width sizes, starting with 27″. They are designed to dovetail neatly between wall cabinets, and under a shorter cabinet directly over the range. So a ventilator becomes part of the built-in, flush look. Ventilators come in all the popular appliance colors—avocado, white, copper-brown—and in stainless steel so that they are part of the decoration. On the face of the unit are push buttons or knobs for controlling the vent fan and the light which is usually part of the unit. One major appliance company which furnishes its own hood includes buttons that operate the electric-cooktop elements as well, a good idea, since it keeps these controls out of the reach of small children. The overscaled hood which is a major part of the decoration in certain traditional kitchen styles is popular and can be found in a few manufactured lines. However, it is most often a custom or semi-custom installation. It can be especially dramatic over an island which includes the cooktop as well as a charcoal broiler or barbecue. Such large hoods are most frequently vented outdoors, but can be fitted with the charcoal filter for ductless installation. Materials can be copper, black metal, or other paint which is chosen as a color accent.

The professional kitchen planner

Here the question is: to use or not to use. Can you get by with your own efforts plus advice from your contractor and/or architect, if you use one? The answers are not easy. Suffice it to say that kitchen planning is a complicated business, with a need for knowledge, not only of new equipment and materials, but also carpentry, wiring, and plumbing. For that reason, and especially if you are doing an elaborate kitchen at great cost, the professional can save you money, aggravation, and arrive at a more efficient room. Remember, that for even the most modest completely equipped new kitchen, you are talking at this writing about a minimum of three thousand dollars, and an elaborate plan can cost ten times that amount. Kitchen planning has become a specialized service in which the trained professional combines the talents of architect, plumbing and electrical engineer, home economist, and interior designer. This combination of talents can be of enormous help to you. However, to get the most out of it, you must help, too.

Before you are ready to pay a professional, you should know the kind of kitchen you want, both in function and decoration. You should have analyzed your family requirements, food-shopping habits, eating preferences, and kitchen-storage needs. You should have decided what other functions you expect the kitchen room to accommodate, and you should know the kind of cook you are, gourmet or three-squares-a-day, a shy cook who needs privacy or a gregarious one who likes company while working. The professional will, in addition, want to know whether or not you intend to have a servant working in the kitchen and whether that servant will live in. The planner will go into detail on how you like to work, how you serve meals, entertain, and your general pattern of living—in short, your image of yourself and your family.

There are several kinds of kitchen-planning services. There is the professional who operates broadly in the kitchen-equipment field and will shop from both custom and standard manufactured lines to satisfy the needs you have outlined. This type of service is most often based on a fixed percentage of the new kitchen. There would be a down payment and then a preset schedule of payments. For supervision, it is much as with an architect: there is an extra fee. Then there is the planner who works much as the interior designer, whose fee comes from the difference between the wholesale and retail prices of equipment and materials. There may also be an hourly consultation fee and, like the designer, he or she may provide renderings or sketches of what the kitchen will look like. A third service is offered by manufacturers, dealers, department stores, retail appliance stores, and utility companies. Here you are limited to the particular equipment they make or sell. Detailed plans can be furnished by specialists, but for a charge, sometimes deducted from the price of what new equipment you buy. In many ways this is the least appealing and successful approach because of the limitations in choice, and because not all manufacturers or dealers carry both major appliances and cabinets, to say nothing of flooring, electrical fixtures, sinks, and all the rest.

Checklist of Do's and Don'ts in Kitchen Planning

1. Don't locate refrigerator next to wall oven, console range, or dishwasher if you can avoid it. Both appliances will last longer and function more efficiently. However, if you must flank them, use at least a 3-inch insulated filler strip between.

2. Don't install a dishwasher in a corner. Its drop-down door may not clear adjacent base-cabinet hardware or the front of another appliance. Use care in planning corners so that you don't set up dead pockets that could be useful storage.

3. Do make sure in a corridor that you have at least 42 inches between counters and preferably 48 inches. Otherwise doors may not swing fully open for access to refrigerator or range.

4. Do plan counter space between a separate cooktop and wall oven. At least 9 inches is recommended.

5. Don't install a built-in oven too high. A good rule is to have the open door 2 inches below the elbow of the person using the oven. Standard placement is the open-oven door at 36-inch counter height. However, tall people often prefer it higher.

6. Don't have doors that swing into the kitchen to cover appliances when they are opened from the other side. If refrigerator door and interior door collide, it can be very annoying.

7. Do locate the dishwasher next to the sink, in-line. Avoid a location around a corner from the sink, because when it is open, the dishwasher door blocks sink access.

8. Do be sure that all door swings of appliances are correct for loading and unloading. Right- or left-handedness of the cook and space-saving should be taken into account, too.

9. Don't locate a range or cooktop at the end of the line in a bank of cabinets. Protrusion of pot and pan handles into the corridor can result in accidents.

10. Do locate all equipment and storage within easy reach of the cook, detailed to his or her height and arm reach.

11. Don't install the sink too close to range or oven; such placement can lead to burns.

12. Do include sufficient electrical outlets at counter height for all small appliances. Electric cords stretched across a corridor can cause accidents. Remember, a great percentage of home accidents occur in the kitchen.

13. Do think flexibly when you plan. Break away from tradition if room size permits. Try curved and angled counters, curved peninsulas, and a round or oval island. The shape will give visual variety and, as long as it doesn't break up your efficiency triangle of work progression, it will be efficient.

14. Don't hang onto aging appliances just because they still operate. They may rob you of time which is expensive.

15. Do use some of the new interior-storage devices in your cabinets—racks and adjustable shelves for china, spices, utensils. Consider those pull-out drawer-type bins which fasten to the underside of cabinets to hold rolls of paper toweling, aluminum foil, and wax paper, and form breadboxes and silverware drawers.

16. Don't buy appliances solely according to price. You are investing in future service and convenience.

17. Do study thoroughly the instruction manuals that come with each new appliance. Don't turn on a switch until you are sure you understand the features of the equipment. Quite often, brand-new units are damaged out of ignorance. You are investing in expensive mechanical equipment. Treat it with respect.

18. Do think ahead when remodeling and plan provision for future appliance and lighting additions.

19. Don't copy someone else's kitchen slavishly just because it looks good. Their work patterns may be the exact opposite of yours. Remember, the kitchen is a personal room. Have one that suits *you*.

20. Don't listen to friends' complaints about particular brands of equipment. They may have gotten one of the few lemons in the whole output. Study the various features of each brand and buy what you think is best for your needs and methods.

21. Do make sure that you know who your service representative is when you buy an appliance, and know your warranties. Be sure to send in your warranty card on each piece of equipment promptly.

22. Do use all the convenience features of an appliance. Experiment with programmed cooking, clock timers, and all the rest. If you are hidebound and stick to the cooking methods you've been using all along, there is no point in investing in new and expensive equipment. Give each appliance a chance to show what it can do.

23. Do make the planning of your new kitchen an adventure in greater understanding of your family's needs. Let it be a broadening experience and as such, don't rush into decisions. Study and learn. That way, you'll appreciate the new beauty and convenience that you have.

The kitchen-remodeling overview

The matter of when to remodel the kitchen in the home you have is a matter of instinct. As homemaker and family cook you "feel" when the facilities you have are outstripped by your family's needs. The kitchen may be too small to prepare meals for the children and their friends; it may be cut off from family fun; you may not have a family-recreation room or have space to include a new one, so it becomes a time to design two needed spaces in tandem. It may simply be a matter of pride: you are tired of comparing your aging but workable kitchen with the new ones of your friends or those you see in magazines. You may need a new lease on life and decide to start where you spend the most time. If you take the plunge, it becomes a matter of degree: what do you save, what do you get rid of at the outset? Kitchen remodeling can start with one new appliance and a plan, so you may begin with a new refrigerator and new wallpaper and go on later as you can afford. If you do this, have an over-all plan, both equipment and decoration wise. If you don't, you'll be buying hit or miss and will be disappointed with the end result.

If you decide to scrap the whole setup you've been using for a long time, remember, this is a good time to take an objective look at yourself and the existing arrangement. Has it responded to your work habits or are you a slave to an inefficient kitchen, wrongly planned in the first place? You may be going out of your mind for more counter space or more cabinets. On the other hand, you may realize that working in the kitchen you have has become second nature to you. In that case, there is no reason to change the arrangement. Just reinterpret it with new cabinets, appliances, and new fresh decor. There may be minor changes in cabinet sizes and appliances, so it is wise to draw a new floor plan and elevations, indicating the existing appliances and cabinets, if any, you plan to keep and the new units you will want to add. You may decide to keep the main work center pretty much as is, but add a laundry, homemaking desk, or a freezer in what was an adjacent closet or pantry, removing the partitions. And, of course, such an addition would also be part of your revised plan.

If you take the former course and scrap everything, gutting the room to the bare walls, so much the better. You'll have a free hand and will benefit from all the previous basic planning pointers. You'll have to draw a floor plan of the existing room, minus equipment, with doors and windows indicated; in the plan incorporate adjacent areas—pantry, closets, closed-in porch, small breakfast room, etc. Then look at the complex as a whole. If the kitchen itself is large, you may not need additional space, but if it is cramped, look into the possibility of tearing down a wall or two and including pantry or porch in a new arrangement. Your architect or contractor can tell you whether walls are load-bearing; if they aren't it's no problem at all. If they are, the existing joists that hold up the second floor may have to be strengthened or replaced with a steel beam. Once you have settled on the area you have to work with, you can start planning as you would for the totally renewed kitchen, the procedure outlined previously. Just decide on which of the four basic arrangements you prefer from the standpoint of your work patterns and then try to relate it to the shape of your room.

You may find, for example, that a corridor plan just doesn't work; in that case, fall back on your second choice. Then as you lay in the work centers, try if possible to locate the sink and range, if it is gas, in the same approximate positions. This will save money provided that the existing lines are still serviceable. If you are adding new house-wide copper plumbing, then it may not be worth the effort. Check this with your contractor who knows the over-all picture and can juggle costs. Don't be slavish, either, about keeping your new cleanup center right under an existing window; the window may not be worth saving anyway, and the cost of adding the new window in the wall where you want the sink may add few extra dollars. Again, your contractor will know. As for saving any usable existing equipment, that is up to you. Often the refrigerator is still operable, even though it may have been designed before the new flush look. Maybe it can be located in an end area or corner, or be part of a built-in wall where it won't be too obtrusive. If so, just be sure there's air for it to "breathe." The door can be spray-painted to blend with your new cabinetry or wall. If you can use a second refrigerator in a recreation room so much the better; that frees you to buy all new appliances. Sometimes cabinets can be saved, repainted, and given new hardware. These are individual decisions that are dictated by budget and other factors. If you can save large sums without compromising your basic aims too drastically, it is usually worth the effort.

When you plan your remodeling, remember that general rules apply. Be sure your structure is sound under and around the kitchen and that the room is well insulated. You are likely to be doing a major replumbing and rewiring job, so go into this with the electrician and plumber to be sure you have electric outlets and water where you want them. This may be the time for an acoustical ceiling; it will certainly be the time for new flooring, new plastering or paneling, perhaps a new bay window, an outdoor deck or more convenient service entrance. This is the time to think about all these factors. You may only go this road once and a few extra dollars spent now will mean worlds of convenience later. Hindsight is terribly expensive in any kind of remodeling.

The Bath: the Home's New Showplace

Of all the rooms in the home, the bath has perhaps come in for the most intensive study and development in the last few years. Gone are the days when it was a tolerated necessity, shut off in clinical white and forced to occupy the smallest possible amount of space. At its best today's bath is also a solarium, a sauna or steam room, a dressing area, a hydromassage headquarters in addition to fulfilling its basic requirements, and the bath serves these new roles in the most attractive guise. What has happened in our thinking to bring about this change? First, in an age of affluence in any civilization, the pampering of the body has always received an extra measure of attention.

—DECK

BATH

SITTING

BEDROOM

CLOSET

CLOSET   CLOSET

BEDROOM

SLEEPING

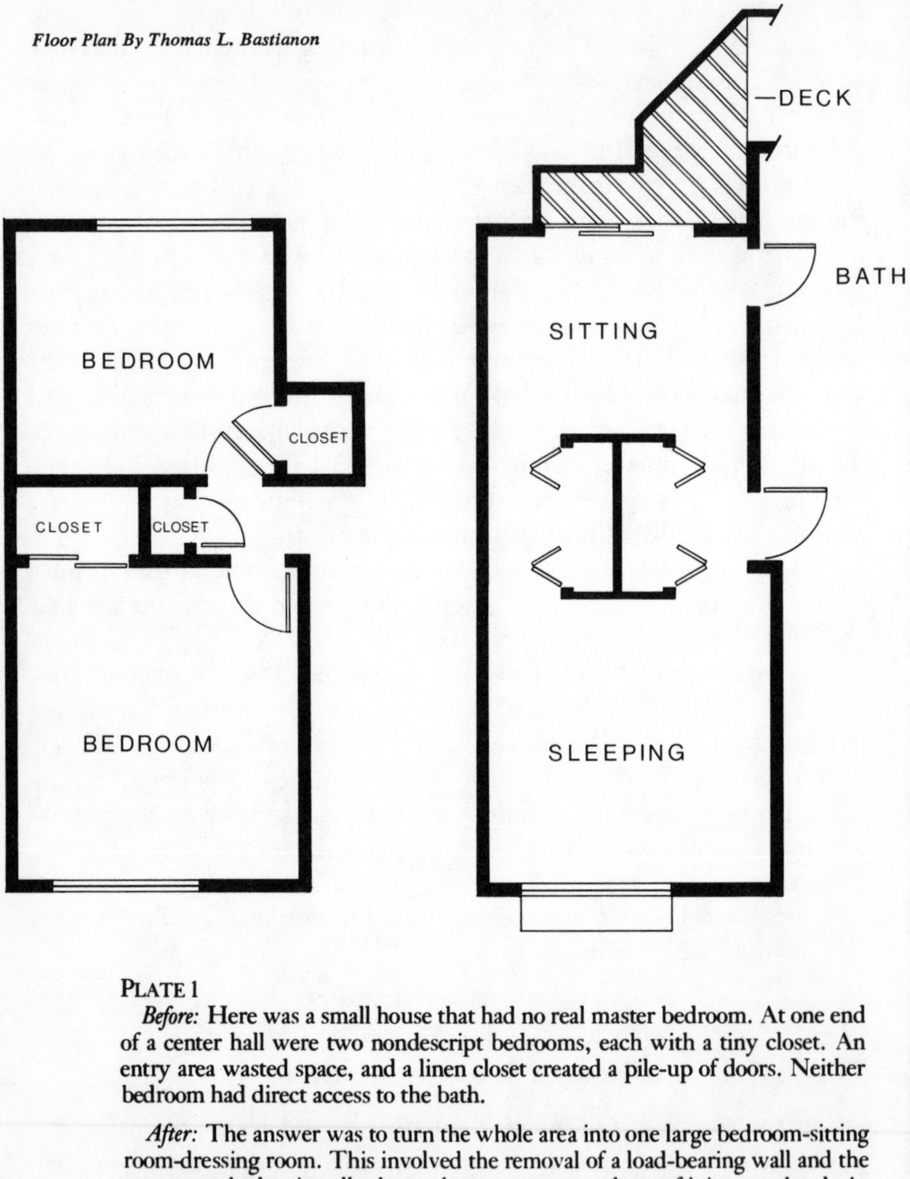

PLATE 1

Before: Here was a small house that had no real master bedroom. At one end of a center hall were two nondescript bedrooms, each with a tiny closet. An entry area wasted space, and a linen closet created a pile-up of doors. Neither bedroom had direct access to the bath.

After: The answer was to turn the whole area into one large bedroom-sitting room-dressing room. This involved the removal of a load-bearing wall and the contractor had to install a heavy beam to support the roof joists overhead. At the bedroom end of the suite, a door now connects to the bath. Plywood was used extensively, to create a closet island with access on both sides, for ceilings and some walls.

PLATE 2

Before: A house with a lovely view of the bay included a guest room on the second floor that took little advantage of its location. A small window and a small-paned French door gave the room a tight, closed-in feeling.

After: The solution was to build a narrow balcony onto the bedroom and add a triple wood patio door. This remodeling provided abundant light, air and easy access to the outdoors. Guests can now enjoy the view from within or without.

PLATE 1

PLATE 2

PLATE 3

PLATE 4

PLATE 5

Today's accent on the youthful image has added to the increased importance of this room. A spot for careful grooming, under good lighting and with efficiently mirrored surfaces, is essential for looking one's best. Other aspects of keeping fit naturally follow: exercise, therapeutic bathing, heat for weight trimming, etc.

Americans demand comfort and beauty wherever it is possible, and now they are aware of the immense possibilities for the bath. So much so, in fact, that the bath has become a new status symbol of the house; husbands and wives show off their baths proudly. We are entering an era when the two-and-a-half- or three-bath house is the rule rather than the exception for the middle-income family. The hope of this chapter is that it will stimulate new thinking on the part of readers to try for the convenience that is within reach in even the most modest bathroom and to open up new vistas of the sybaritic comfort that can be attained as individual fortunes prosper and homes are renovated.

PLATE 3

Before: A spacious but undistinguished bedroom had one pleasant feature: a curved bay window at one end. Owners decided to turn it into a guest room.

After: To take advantage of the windows, designer Betty Castleman treated all of them the same—with movable-louver wood shutters, thus unifying the room at one stroke. A brilliant floral wallpaper, repeated in fabric for pillows, did the rest. A sitting area like this is a thoughtful touch for a guest room, makes company feel right at home. *Photographer: Harold Davis.*

PLATE 4

Before: Children are very sensitive to their surroundings, and the little girl who made this room her realm wanted it changed. She needed more storage space and a freshened look.

After: One structural change did wonders: a storage wall with open shelves above, drawers below, framed the window. Wood-shutter panels dramatized the window. Even a little wall cupboard was given the treatment with a shutter panel. Iron bed, wicker chair, and wallpapered ceiling add greatly to the new look. *Designer: Sylvia Grodins. Photographer: Harold Davis.*

PLATE 5

After: An eighteenth-century Connecticut house, like many others, boasted a ballroom, located in the whole upstairs front of the house. For twentieth-century living, the ballroom gave way to bedrooms, and the vaulted ceiling over the whole space created some problems. The solution was to unify the new rooms by repeating, as closely as possible, the crown molding along the new partition wall. The old pine floors were sanded and refinished, the beautiful, deep windows refitted and painted. *Photographer: Bill Margerin*

Before: An older bath was no longer sufficiently large or well equipped for two daughters. The answer seemed to be twin lavatories to eliminate bath tie-ups.

After: Designer Lillian Chain enlarged the room by removing the window and cabinet and pushing out the wall. This created space for a semiconcealed toilet and one long cabineted lavatory. The other cabineted lavatory is on the opposite wall. *Photographer: Harold Davis.*

Special considerations in bathroom remodeling

First of all, let us define our terms. Remodeling indicates more than surface renovation; we are not talking only of new wallpaper or flooring, but rather of new fixtures, a completely redesigned room with perhaps some structural changes. If you are "doing over" an old house, you may find that it had a quite large bath. Space was inexpensive to build fifty or seventy-five years ago, and ample amounts were often allotted for this room. So if you want to keep the bath in the same area—and this may be an economy if the plumbing lines and vent stack are salvageable—you might ponder the advantages of compartmentation to provide at least two-bath service or an outer dressing-lavatory area off the bedroom hall plus full, three-fixture service at the rear. Once again, take graph paper in hand, measure your space, and draw the area to scale, using one foot for each quarter-inch square. Then move your various sizes of fixture cutouts until you feel you have made the most of space and gotten the service you require.

Your plumber can help you if building codes are in force in your community. The main requirements in most areas are a vent stack for each toilet beyond a radius of five feet; ventilation for an interior bath and in some cities ceramic-tile floor over metal lath and mortar; a marble slab as toilet base; and marble baseboard trim. In some cases the latter are waived on the basis of an "existing" condition. Your architect, structural engineer, or plumber can advise you. But, for example, if you want a carpeted bath you may have to put down a ceramic tile floor first and then carpet over it, rather than using the far less expensive method of laying it right over hardboard or plywood.

As far as the vent stack goes, you can arrange two or three baths in a cluster so that all toilets will be within a radius of five feet, even though they are in separate walled areas. That can save you several hundred dollars especially if an existing vent can be used. In that way you won't have to go through the roof again with the pipe. In some locales, copper plumbing pipe is required and in any event it should be used, because the alternative, galvanized iron pipe, is not nearly as economical in the long run. New plastic pipe, if allowed in your area, should be investigated, especially for vents and drain lines. Its use for water lines, however, is not the best choice, at least at the present time. This has been an area of considerable research and experimentation during the last ten years or more, and great advances have been made. Again, your plumber can advise you. But a word of caution here: the plumbing trade has been an extremely hidebound and conventional one, slow to adopt new ways of doing things, so your plumber may have to be prodded into investigating techniques not familiar to him. Such considerations apply equally to new-home construction.

A most important factor in bath remodeling is to take as much rather than as little space as possible for these rooms. It is often possible to borrow space from adjacent rooms. For example in an old house which has no closets, as you plan new closets for each bedroom, think in terms of carving out an area in the same block of space for a small bath, or for a dressing-lavatory room which can be part of a compartmented complex. Or a small bath can sometimes be tucked into a sloping-roofed area, seemingly useless for other needs, by using the slope section for a tub and the area high enough to stand in for lavatory and toilet. The main thing to remember is that with today's plumbing techniques and fixtures sizes, a bath can be located almost anywhere. You may have to box in pipes that must travel through lower rooms, but this can be done unobtrusively. Often it is possible to plan a closet on a lower floor as you locate an upstairs bath so that pipes can pass through it.

Remodeling is an individual matter with each house and set of conditions and as a result it is difficult to generalize. However, it is helpful to think of a bath renovation project as more than just the substitution of three new fixtures for old, new copper tubing for rusty old pipes, and the more mechanical aspects. Regard it as an opportunity to achieve great new comfort and beauty, to enjoy good lighting, both natural and artificial, and to experience the convenience of many of the new features of improved bath fixtures. However, bath remodeling can be expensive, as is the case with any room where special mechanical equipment is needed. So it is helpful to know there are ways to get the most for your money and still keep costs down. First, if you are revamping an existing room, it is economical to locate fixtures in about the same location as the old. If you are adding a bath, back it to an existing set of water lines in a kitchen or other bath. Second, make every bit of space pay its way: corner showers, toilets, narrow counter lavatories, short and square tubs—all are good bets to consider. Today space is costly, so the more compact your plan, the more economical the room.

Basic bath planning

If you are doing extensive remodeling to an older bath, this section is a must for you to study thoroughly. If you are merely sprucing up an existing bath—giving it a fresh, new look—it is still useful and will give you extra insight into the possibilities that exist. However large or small your impending project may be, you will gain knowledge that will help you work with your plumbing contractor more intelligently. And at the outset it is important to point out that you should work *with* him, rather than turning over the whole matter to him. Remember, the plumber may be a master mechanic and know the mysteries of piping, venting, and installing fixtures; he will know the requirements of local building codes, if any, and he can advise you on the most economical way of locating fixtures, but he is not an expert in the aesthetics of bath planning. In short, he is not usually a person to rely on for the potentials of convenience and beauty. The kind of bath service you require in relation to other rooms in the home and to your individual patterns of living are your special province. If you work with the contractor to exact that service from the floor space you set aside for your bath or baths, you will arrive at a successful conclusion.

Bath planning at its best is no longer a question of simply hooking up three fixtures in the most compact arrangement in the least amount of space that can be spared. A room 5 by 7 feet is considered minimum. Of course, a tiny powder room often has to be shoehorned into a closet or an under-stair area, and there we are talking about two fixtures located as compactly as possible. But when it comes to a major, full bath, a bit of study may prove to you that by allotting a third again as much space as you originally intended, by perhaps borrowing from an adjacent bedroom closet or taking off a bit of the bedroom hall, you may triple or quadruple the amount of service from your bath by being able to include, say, an extra lavatory or a dressing area. These are the pluses that can be understood by a knowledge of the basics.

Location of your baths

Your patterns of living is the determinant here, along with the stern realities of the budget. If you have a sizable home, several children, and occasional overnight guests, you will probably want a powder room adjacent to the more or less formal areas of the home, a bath for the master bedroom suite, and a hall bath to serve the children's rooms and the guest room, or you may prefer a separate bath for guests. In addition, if your children are small, you may want a small, simple lavatory-toilet room somewhere off the informal living area or

family room and near the entrance from the terrace or outdoor play space for the children to wash up before tracking through the rest of the house. On the other hand, if your house is modest, you may be able to locate the master bath (with only a stall shower) so that it can double as a powder room near your more formal entertaining area and place a second, full-with-tub bath near the children's rooms. Think of location in terms of an over-all concept of living, with emphasis on privacy for various family activities, for the scope of your entertaining, and other needs.

As you plan, be mindful of plumbing economies. For example, by backing up two baths you will save on piping and venting. Each toilet must have its own vent stack through the roof, unless a second toi-

Before: Here was a bath that simply needed everything. Two entrances took space, made for a bad arrangement of appliances. There was no shower and decorative appeal was nil.

After: The removal of one door and a partition behind the wash basin permitted a niche for the tub-shower and an open-shelf built-in for towels. A cabineted lav then took the place and the plumbing lines of the old tub. For plumbing economy, a new toilet used the same drain line as the old. For the new decor, a textured, honey-toned tile was used for the wainscot and lav counter, contrasting with splashy floral wallpaper. Textured brown floor tile repeats warm earth tones of the prin.. *Ceramic tile is by American Olean.*

let is within a radius of five feet, in which case both can be on the same stack. Locating kitchen plumbing on one side of a common wall and a bath on the other saves, too, and if you have a two-story house, by locating all plumbing in a core of both floors you can make great economies. Your plumbing contractor can guide you to possibilities here as can your architect or builder. Discuss your needs within the framework of economical location and with an eye to these possibilities. Compartmentation which we will study in the following pages is a helpful concept when it comes to location and it should be explored.

Another aspect of location is exterior versus interior placement. In other words, you can have a windowed bath on the perimeter of the house, or an inside, windowless room. All local codes now permit the latter and it can be just as comfortable and cheerful as a bath with window, through advances in lighting and ventilation. Codes specify that a ventilator go on automatically when the light switch is activated, so study the range of ventilating equipment that is available. Also consider the possibilities of the luminous ceiling, the skylight, and other illuminating devices. The over-all thought is: don't rule out the interior bath. It can ease your space planning and, with clever decoration, be just as bright and attractive as a perimeter bath.

Future needs should be anticipated in planning, too. For example, if you intend to add a swimming pool at a later date, you can run plumbing to an area of the garage which may one day be a pool house, at little extra cost now, cap it, and wait to install fixtures later. The same goes for a basement to be finished off later as a family room, an attic which will provide future bedrooms, etc. A perimeter bath on an outside wall can serve a future pool, too, if it is planned accordingly, with wall space earmarked for later inclusion of an exterior door. The point is, a bit of thought now can save money in the future.

The locations of fixtures

Once the location of the bath, as a unit, is determined, you are faced with choice of location for fixtures. If you are remodeling an existing bath, certain locations may already be chosen for you in the interests of economy. The toilet, for example, is usually best left where it is because of existing drain and vent lines, and there are obvious savings if the tub and lavatory are kept in the same general area. However, if you are starting a new bath from scratch, keep an open mind about

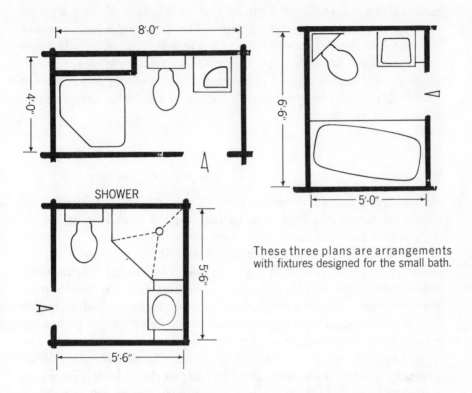

SHOWER

These three plans are arrangements with fixtures designed for the small bath.

placement. Even where space is limited, there are choices and new small-scale fixtures will help you make the most of every square inch. Tub location is the first consideration simply because it takes up the greatest amount of space. There is no need to place the tub across the end of the room under the window just because it seems most logical there. There is nothing worse than a drafty bath or shower and yet in almost every small home the tub is right under a window. Make cut-outs to scale and, on graph paper scaled to the dimensions of your space, move the tub around until an alternate solution emerges.

As you plan, be mindful of the range of fixture sizes and shapes available to you. Instead of the standard five-foot-long tub, you may get a better arrangement with a square thirty-nine- by thirty-eight-inch receptor tub, or you may find you prefer to use a stall shower. The lavatory, the most frequently used fixture, is usually best located near the door, while the toilet should be kept from the view of the door as much as possible. Keep adequate distances between fixtures to facilitate operations; if a lavatory is opposite a tub or toilet, thirty inches is a minimum distance. Side-by-side fixtures, of course, can be located close together. If space permits, create a partition, floor to ceiling, between a toilet and tub located on a long wall. The sense of privacy is worth the extra expense. The lavatory which requires efficient illumination should be near a window if possible; side lighting is excellent for grooming operations. If you are planning to include a bidet, and more and more homes are following this European practice, it should be positioned adjacent to the toilet, in a separate cubicle, if space permits.

The tub

As the largest fixture, the tub deserves first consideration. Tubs come in several shapes and sizes. The rectangular tub is in lengths 4½, 5, 5½, and 6 feet and in widths from about 28 to about 32 inches. Tub opening follows the rectangular shape or is contoured to fit the body by creating an oval in the rectangle. This design creates wider ledges which are helpful for set-down spaces for shampoo bottles, bath salts, etc., or as a sitting-down spot for bathing children or for foot-washing. Rectangular designs are available either for placement into a niche or for a corner arrangement with one open end. The square tub, the receptor, as noted previously, fits a space roughly 40 inches by 40 inches and is designed to offer modified bath service plus a shower base. In both square and rectangular shapes, either right or left hand outlets are available. The receptor tub also comes in a corner model. Sunken tubs are available in manufactured units, rectangular and with a wide overhang which rests on the floor or whatever platform is created. Regular tubs can be made to give the appearance of being sunken, but it is not recommended. Any size or shape of sunken tub can be designed in ceramic tile, marble or concrete; the Japanese even make one of wood, deep enough to use standing up.

Tub materials include porcelain enamel on cast iron and enameled steel, less expensive. Whichever you choose, be sure that the enamel is acid-resistant. Tubs of reinforced fiber glass are new and most promising, being strong yet lightweight. Since they are molded of fiber-glass polyester resin, they can be contoured in flowing designs and can be made as a one-piece unit with shower enclosure, recessed soap dish and set-down ledges all in one. Since most bath accidents occur in the tub and shower, a tub with a textured bottom is a wise choice. Designs include ridges or embossed surfaces which provide a better foot traction than the usual smooth surface.

The lavatory

The washbasin, sink, or lav, as it is variously called, is a wall-hung, pedestal, or counter unit. If the former, it may have chrome legs for partial support at the front which gives it the appearance of being free-standing, with or without side bars for towels. The newer, more popular version is the counter unit which, recessed in the top of a cabinet, appears as a piece of furniture. It can be either self-rimming with an integral lip which overlaps the counter opening to form a water seal or recessed with a surrounding metal rim called a Huddee Rim which provides the seal. Incidentally, the metal rims can be found in finishes to match your hardware, so don't settle for a chrome rim if you have brass or gold-plated fittings. Lavatory materials are stainless steel, porcelain enamel over cast iron, or over steel and vitreous china, which is the most common.

Wall-hung units range from a little over a foot in width to thirty inches or more, and there are corner models when space-saving is a must. Counter basins are square, round, or oval and come in a variety of sizes. Most companies make a long but narrow, twelve-inch counter lavatory for rooms where space is limited. Counter units permit a custom effect; they can be recessed into antique chests or dressers, even into desks for sit-down face washing and grooming. A variety of baked-on designs to fit decorating schemes can be found, ranging from the Greek key design to fleur-de-lis, rose patterns, and many others. Counter units are ideal where two lavatories are needed, since they can be installed in one continuous surface. Generally, counter lavatories are recessed into ¾-inch plywood which has been surfaced in a laminate or ceramic tile. However, they can also be set into marble, slate, or other material. Height is an important consideration with the lavatory. Too often the unit is located so low that grooming becomes a chore. Usual height is thirty-one inches from floor to top of the basin rim. For adults, heights of from thirty-four to forty inches are more comfortable, especially where the users are exceptionally tall. Space between lavatory top and the bottom of mirror or medicine cabinet should be eight to ten inches. Where there are double lavatories in a single counter, allow at least twelve inches between.

The toilet

The toilet, of all the fixtures, has perhaps come under the most intensive study and scrutiny in recent years. The objectives: to make it

Before: A powder room should have an inviting, special air. This one was drab, with its awkward window, small lavatory, and dark wallpaper.

After: Designer Goldie Glassman brightened the room with a long white lavatory counter, striped paper for walls and toilet divider. Twin mirrors cleverly solve the problem of the high window which, covered by a Roman shade in the same stripe, blends into the wall. *Photographer: Harold Davis.*

less obtrusive in appearance, to make it fit the contours of the human body and to make it function better and provide greater convenience. The best toilets are vitreous china and come in two basic types: standing (floor models) and wall-hung (off-the-floor) units. There is also a unit with a power flush mechanism instead of the familiar tank and ball. It has no working parts and eliminates service requirements. However, it is seldom used in residential building because it requires strong water pressure, not always found in certain areas.

Floor units have been the standard toilet for years. They are easy to install and come in many sizes and colors. There are two varieties— the two-piece unit with base and tank and a one-piece model which is quieter in operation. Advances in the toilet include a space-saving corner model; an odor-free unit with a flushing mechanism which has a built-in ventilator to dissipate odors before they reach the room; the nonoverflow toilet which guarantees protection from this unpleasant hazard; and a new water-saving toilet which uses one-third less water than other toilets at each flushing, a good feature for rural and those city areas with chronic water-shortage problems. The wall-hung unit has the advantages of easy cleaning, since it is an off-the-floor design. By its nature, however, it must have a rather circuitous drainage layout and clogs more easily than the standing model.

Spacewise, you must allow 20½ by 27½ inches minimum for the toilet and a maximum of 24 by 30 inches for the larger, more elongated designs. Toilets are much lower than formerly and more attractive as an element of decor. There are also custom models and fittings to be used with standard units which give the appearance of furniture like the *chaise percée* of palace days. Such refinements have helped to create decorative unity in the bath, but for the best visual appearance, a separate cubicle for the toilet is a more satisfactory solution. Other decorative advances with this fixture include toilet seats in designs that blend with decor in a variety of patterns; baked-on designs on tank lids and even lids with integral planters.

The bidet

Almost from the beginning of plumbing in the cities of Europe and before that time in portable, unplumbed units, the bidet has been standard equipment in the best homes abroad. This useful fixture is now, fortunately, coming into acceptance in this country. Where space permits, it is a must for the personal cleanliness of both sexes. A vitreous china receptacle which is available in the usual color lines of

most manufacturers, it is compact and unoffensive in appearance. A
good idea is to pair it with the toilet in a separate compartment. The
fixture permits mixing hot and cold water of a desired temperature in
the bowl, most models have a built-in douche with spray or jet attachments. The user sits astride the bowl, facing the wall and the
valves for temperature and flow control for washing of the pelvic and
anal areas. The unit requires about 13½ by 27 inches of space.

Stall showers

A stall shower is a good solution for the small bath. A space at least
30 inches square and 7 feet high must be allotted. The shower can
be custom built of ceramic tile walls and floor or with a precast
receptor base and tiled walls. Custom designs can be any size you
specify. Today the shower is more commonly a manufactured unit
and these come in a variety of sizes and materials. The least expensive
variety consists of a precast composition base and enameled metal
sides. Better units are one-piece fiber-glass reinforced plastic and
there is also a unit with laminated panels for sides which comes in
36×36- and 48×32-inch sizes. The floor is one-piece composition, and
units come either with the usual shower curtain rod or with doors of
glass or acrylic plastic material.

Tub enclosures

The tub, if it includes a shower, must have special, waterproof walls.
Tubs are made with a lip on the sides which abut walls. The ceramic
tile or other surfacing material is brought out beyond this lip so that
shower water drains into the tub. Ceramic or plastic tile, laminates,
and other plastic-surfaced panels can be used as surfacing. Tile can be
applied with mastic over gypsum board or plaster, or it can be set
into wet mortar, the original Roman way. Laminated hardboard or
melamine-laminated plywood panels designed expressly for this purpose can be attached directly to studs or applied over gypsum board.

Across the front, shower curtains on fixed or spring-tension rods
can be used. An increasingly popular solution is the tub-shower door
with metal-framed glass or plastic panels. The latter are available in
many designs—flowers, butterflies embedded in the plastic; glass is
ridged, grooved, or diffused for decorative effect. Sliding doors are
the most common, but there are accordion-fold doors and hinged
panels, too.

Compartmentation

There are two kinds of compartmented baths, and since both afford extra bath service at little extra cost, they are worth study. The first type is compartmentation within a given bath. For example, by creating a tub-toilet compartment at the rear of the room and an outer lavatory compartment right off the hall, it is possible to have simultaneous multiple use with privacy. This is an especially popular arrangement in a master bedroom suite, permitting the outer, lavatory compartment to serve also as a dressing room with closets and special

Floor Plan by Thomas L. Bastianon

storage for the accouterment of husband and wife. Another variation
is simply a separate compartment for the toilet, which permits a more
decorative effect in the bath. The second type of compartmentation
is more interesting and encompasses total area planning. In a nut shell
the idea is to give two- or three-bath service with the addition of one
or two extra fixtures and a few extra doors. For example, one compartment with toilet and lavatory could be located off the master
bedroom, another with these two fixtures off the bedroom hall. Both
would then have separate access to a tub compartment. Or there
could be lavatory areas off the master bedroom and hall which had
access to a common tub-toilet compartment. It is possible to arrange
fixtures so that a guest room could also adjoin one of the compart-

PLATE 1

Before: The rear yard of this view-endowed house (see chapter on The Turn-
Around House) was an unsightly, overgrown mess. Under the weeds, however, was a geometry of concrete that lent itself to a low-maintenance town-
house garden. Rear door opened onto basement, now a guest suite of bath and
bed-sitting room.

After: New sliding glass wall gives access to a deck which leads to the paved
patio. Existing center circle was surfaced in white marble chips to restate
painted rear wall. Shutters restate pavement tone. Tall window at right, formerly basement door area, now lights a tiled shower of new bath. Planting is
minimal: a few jade trees and other potted plants, Hollywood cypress, and
beds of English ivy. Old, weathered board fence was retained, reinforced, and
accented with tiles and sculpture. Garden overlooks San Francisco Bay and
Oakland hills. *Photographer: Henry Bowles, Jr.*

PLATE 2

After: An old cow barn was the nucleus around which a swimming pool and
deck were designed in the Connecticut countryside. Steel-sided and plastic-
lined 16 by 32-foot pool was surrounded with spruce decking coated in driftwood stain. Tall fence of fir was stained to blend. Part of the weathered boards
of the eighteenth-century structure were taken down from the wall facing the
pool and the decking sweeps inside as a new floor for the old barn. For pattern,
the deck in and near the barn was installed at right angles to poolside deck. The
antique cabana provides changing rooms, cooking and dining facilities, along
with housing for pool filtering and heating equipment.

PLATE 3

Before: Stucco walls, uninteresting rear windows, and narrow, covered
veranda were a challenge to architect Chester Widom, when he and his wife
bought and redesigned this 1948 tract house in Los Angeles.

After: Rear walls were pushed out 17 feet from the existing house, making an
enlarged, new living room out of the former patio. Redwood, used for the new
walls, creates a pattern, horizontal across the fascia, a diagonal design on a side
wall forming one boundary of the new, grid-paved patio. New design makes
the most of the 65 by 125-foot lot. *Photographer: Glen Allison*

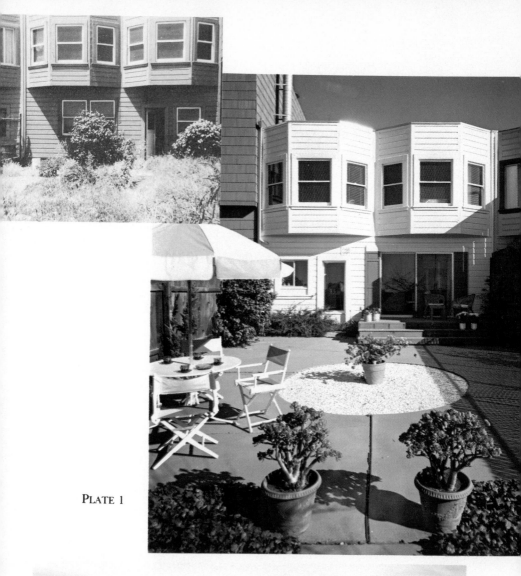

PLATE 1

PLATE 2

PLATE 3

PLATE 4

PLATE 5

ments and so have access to the others, giving the pleasant feeling of a suite. There are accompanying sketches which show a few of the many possibilities.

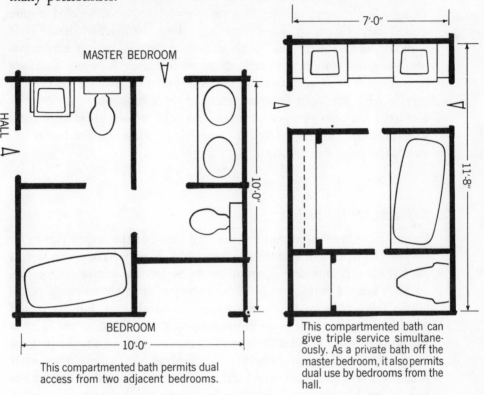

This compartmented bath permits dual access from two adjacent bedrooms.

This compartmented bath can give triple service simultaneously. As a private bath off the master bedroom, it also permits dual use by bedrooms from the hall.

PLATE 4

Before: An awninged, plain-Jane patio of a typical 1948-style house added little to the livability or architectural quality of the structure, located between projecting wings.

After: Owner-designer Elsebet Jegstrup replanned the area which now is the highlight of the home's exterior. Deck, benches, and fencing were built of lower-cost garden grades of redwood, characterized by rustic knots and streaks of cream-colored sapwood. The new deck sets the outdoor living area off from the rest of the garden, makes for easy indoor-outdoor access with interior spaces.

PLATE 5

Before: A contemporary house with a motor entrance close to the road created privacy problems, and the owners wanted to create a carport, gates, and fencing that would blend with the house.

After: Architect Robert Engman found an attractive solution with redwood, used to delineate the carport and to form slatted fencing and entrance gates. A brick-paved entry-courtyard combined with the redwood to give a new look to the interior entry and the outer motor area without costly residing and structural remodeling. Rustic-natural feeling blends beautifully with the house.

The key to success of compartmentation is the type and location of doors. Sliding pocket doors, so-called because they slip into pockets specially created in the walls, eliminate space-taking door swings. Such doors can be designed into new or remodeled homes quite easily. Often an older home has a large bath which lends itself well to compartmentation with sliding doors. Plumbing economies are possible through compartmentation because all water lines are located in a compact area and because you can provide three-bath service with, say, four fixtures instead of the usual nine. A designer or architect can help you get maximum use with compartmentation, and your plumber can also arrive at economical solutions once he understands the principle involved.

Lighting for the bath

Proper illumination, important in every room of the home, is mandatory in the bath. For one thing, most baths, if they have a window at all, have a tiny one which often has to be heavily curtained for privacy. A second consideration is the fact that there are so many possibilities for accidents—taking the wrong medicine, cuts, falls, etc.—and good lighting can be a boon in minimizing them. Illumination follows the same basic principles as in any other room: there should be general background lighting plus specific lighting for certain areas. That is to say that the room should have an over-all glow that can be activated on entering and in addition pinpointed lighting for certain bath activities.

There are several forms of general lighting for the bath. Perhaps the most useful is the luminous ceiling. This generally consists of a system which includes fluorescent tubes attached to the ceiling, a grid of aluminum or wood strips six to twelve inches below, and plastic or glass panels set into the frames. The most common material is plastic, either in flat or corrugated sheets, in squares of two or three feet. This type of system is relatively inexpensive, because it can be put up easily and quickly. It hides ceiling imperfections, helps to lower a too-high ceiling and, most important, casts a diffused, shadow-free glow over every corner of the room. If you do not prefer fluorescents (they can cause a buzz in radios), incandescent bulbs can be used, all switched together for simultaneous illumination.

There are other forms of general lighting: a single luminous panel, circular or rectangular, in the center of the ceiling, which can be attached to a regular ceiling electrical outlet, a chandelier or the conventional fixture with a single bulb and glass globe. None of these is as effective as the luminous grid; however, the chandelier can be used decoratively, to help set period style as we have seen previously. The luminous ceiling or panel is excellent for a streamlined look. Ask your electrical contractor to show you the catalogs of the leading electrical fixture manufacturers and together you can choose the types of units most suitable for your bath.

When it comes to specific lighting, the most important area is the lavatory since it is used the most. Here the best illumination is side lighting, at each side of the mirror. This can be reinforced with a strip of lighting right over the mirror if you have less than adequate general overhead light. For example, if you have an entire luminous grid ceiling, then side lighting is enough at the washbasin. If you have a chandelier which casts a decorative glow only, you may want to have an over-mirror strip, too. You have probably noted the dressing tables of Broadway and Hollywood stars with the open bulbs around three sides of the mirror. This is the best possible kind of light for careful face washing, shaving and make-up. It pours light on every part of the face; nothing is in shadow. On the other hand, if you have used an overmirror light, you have noticed that unflattering and untrue bags appear under the eyes. These are caused by shadows that fall over the face.

There are several different solutions for good mirror lighting. If you have good ceiling light, you can use side fixtures—carriage lamps, crystal sconces or other decorative units and these may be sufficient. Or you can use fluorescent strips running the length of the mirror at each side. Another solution is the dressing-room fixture with a row of bulbs on a bar running vertically at either side of the mirror. Here again, the fixture catalog is an excellent reference. You can have a built-in effect with a luminous soffit over the mirror (good over a long lavatory counter with two washbasins side by side), plus built-in side lighting consisting of frosted glass or plastic panels with fluorescents or incandescents behind. Much of it depends on the decorative effect and the degree of efficiency you want.

Other areas that need special lighting are the toilet and shower. There are moisture- and steam-resistant built-in circular or rectangular fixtures which can be recessed into the ceiling over the shower or tub-shower. There is nothing more pleasant and comforting from the standpoint of physical security than good illumination for bathing. It makes a soothing experience even more beneficial. Such fixtures must be out of reach of children and must not be touched by adults while bathing, of course. If the toilet is in a separate compartment it requires some kind of illumination; if it stands open in the bathroom, and if overhead light is not good, you may need a ceiling fixture or a wall sconce, especially if members of your family read in this area. Other special bath adjuncts discussed elsewhere in these pages—gym equipment, saunas, steam rooms, etc.—all require special illumination and should be discussed carefully with your electrical contractor. Also important is general electrical service which should be discussed at the same time. If the washbasin fixtures you choose do not have a plug-in outlet for hair dryer, shaver, etc. (and, incidentially, many of them do), you'll want an outlet nearby. Heavy-duty outlets for heaters and other equipment which draws considerable current should be foreseen and provided.

Ask your contractor, too, about ceiling fixtures which include not only illumination but also ultra-violet heat and sun-lamp benefits. Several manufacturers make such combination fixtures which permit sunbathing while one shaves or dresses, with timers as auxiliary devices to guard against overexposure. These can be recessed into the ceiling. And, remember in passing, that there are many recessed fixtures for general and specific lighting that are recessed for an unobtrusive look: wall washers, high-hats, pinhole and eyeball fixtures, which you should see in the showroom of a fixture manufacturer or in his catalog before making up your mind.

Fittings

One of the most exciting developments in recent years is the wealth of choice in fittings for the various fixtures. Not only have manufacturers of the fixtures redesigned their standard faucets, handles, shower heads, and other hardware, but special fittings have been developed by companies specializing in this branch of decorative hardware. When you choose your fixtures, be sure to notice what choice you have in fittings. It is especially important to be consistent: for example, if you chose polished chrome faucets, you should have chrome or pewter or some silver-like metal for towel bars, metal rim around lavatory, and even such small items as coat hooks on the back of the bathroom door. On the other hand, if you choose gold-plated fittings, some harmonizing metal should be chosen for all the other metal components.

Polished chrome is the standard metal for fittings. It is applied over solid brass and a few manufacturers offer their fittings in solid brass as it is before being chrome-plated. But polished chrome is the usual

After: A large second-floor bathroom in a Victorian house lent itself to conversion into a bath-laundry combination. Designer G. Allen Scruggs located piggyback washer and dryer in a louvered-door closet and on an outside wall for venting. Tub-shower is on wall at right, toilet and counter lavatory in an L-shaped cabinet on the left. Walls and cabinetry are of Masonite brand paneling.

finish available, and this will run throughout an entire line for all exterior metal parts. A few manufacturers offer brushed chrome, and this soft, dull, pewterlike finish is especially attractive. A few fixture companies are starting to offer gold-plated fittings as an optional extra for the washbasin at least. However, unless they offer it also for toilet handle, tub spout, shower head, and other equipment, it may look odd. There is an incongruity about viewing a powder room with magnificent 14-carat gold-plated faucets and spout at a striking counter lavatory and then turning to see the toilet with a polished chrome handle. Consistency is the route to a really glamorously decorated bath.

Fixture manufacturers are also emphasizing the possibilities in certain plastic materials, notably Lucite, for fittings. This gleaming, translucent, man-made material has a jewel-like quality and can be shaped and faceted to appear quite handsome. It also has a pleasant tactile quality, a softness and warmth that makes it attractive to the touch. Faceting helps to grip the faucets with soapy hands as well as adding the jewel look. Lucite is being offered in amber as well as crystal, and it is equally attractive, especially with certain accent colors for the lavatory. Incidentally, there is nothing incongruous about having Lucite handles for lavatory faucets only, as long as the accompanying metal is the same as for tub and toilet fittings.

Advances in bath fittings have not been limited to the realm of design. Function has been a consideration, too. You'll find it in a single-handle, push-pull faucet for lavatory and tub-shower. The handle is either a lever or a milled knob that is easily grasped. Moving right and left for cold and hot water respectively, it permits the user to set it at a known safe temperature and thus avoid scalding or shock. It is compact in appearance and eliminates the service requirements of washers for leaks, etc. These fittings come in standard polished chrome and certain other finishes; your plumber can tell you which brands are available in which finishes. An excellent fitting for the tub is a five-in-one device that includes a grab bar, soap dish, diverter spout for the shower, tub faucet, and hot- and cold-control knob, all in one fitting. It is easy to install and facilitates tiling in the tub niche by putting so many requirements in one area. There are also special temperature-control mechanisms for showers which automatically prevent scalding. Shower heads are extremely important and deserve study before purchase. There is nothing more exasperating in the bath than a shower which squirts in all directions, which has only a piercing needle spray or a harsh rush of water in one solid stream. There are excellent heads which provide any degree of water stream with a flick of the finger, and which can be rotated to give you the spray where you want it. Some provide a pulsating water spray for hydromassage.

There are a few companies which specialize in opulent bath fittings and they offer some dazzling items. For example, there are gold-plated or silver or pewter faucet sets available with semiprecious stones for embellishment. Malachite, lapis lazuli, onyx, crystal, and rose quartz are a few of the stones offered. Sets can range into the hundreds of dollars and have become a sort of status symbol in expensive houses and apartments. These companies also offer the metal fittings without stones, in many delicate and beautiful patterns to blend with decorative styles ranging from Louis XVI to streamlined contemporary. The chasing and filigree designs on the metal parts are exquisite and do much to create a truly opulent look. And some of these in gold plate are not as expensive as one might at first think. Of course, they never need polishing or special attention, which is a plus.

The patterns of these elaborate faucet sets are often available in co-ordinated tub spouts—in graceful swan, fish, and other motifs—and all decorative metal components. The bath, as a result, can have a similar look throughout, and this part of bath decoration is, in fact, the most thoroughly exploited at the moment. However, it is possible to go overboard, and too much gold plate in too ornate designs can look gaudy and overpowering. Simplicity is the key to the most successful decor in this room as in any other.

Other hardware

As you think of the bath, you will become aware of the many metal items besides fixture fittings that are required—decorative pulls for lavatory cabinet, door knobs, shower-curtain rods, towel bars, and shelf brackets, to name but a few. All of these seemingly small details add up to the over-all effect and should be chosen carefully. There are designs for an Early American scheme in black iron—H-hinges for cabinet doors, fancifully wrought towel bars, simple knobs; and, for a more sophisticated traditional effect, you can find brass hardware with knobs finely detailed with engine turning, milled edges, etc. Again, the tactile quality is an interesting and pleasant bonus.

It may seem too extreme to think about such seemingly trivial matters as the touch of metal to the hand until one remembers that the bath is a highly personal room. It is meant to pamper, to be a source of comfort and solace. Getting up in the middle of the night to use this room and finding the familiar and pleasant touch of a finely milled metal pull or using a cut-glass tumbler for a glass of cooling water can be worth all the time spent in searching out such details.

A dozen ideas for bath comfort

There are many little ways to insure greater comfort and convenience in the bath, little ideas that can pay big dividends in more pleasant utilization of this home necessity. Here are a few in abbreviated form, which your contractor can help you adapt to your own needs.

1. Undertub heating. If you have or contemplate hot-water radiator or baseboard heating, consider extending the hot-water tubing under the bathtub. It will provide a warmer bath by keeping the tub bottom at a temperature comfortable to the touch.

2. Radiant towel bars: Are you tired of towels that take forever to dry out? If you have hot-water heat, it can be piped through towel

bars to speed drying. A less elaborate method is to locate towel holders over baseboards or hot-air registers.

3. Noise control: Bathroom sounds, often embarrassing, can be confined within bath walls in several simple ways. Walls can be constructed with double studding, that is, two rows of two-by-fours arranged in staggered pattern. Then blanket insulation is woven horizontally between the studs and stapled to them. Sounds are trapped within these layers and stifled. Noise also escapes through holes of common bath walls where pipes pass through to a bath in which plumbing is backed up. It is important to stuff insulation material in such openings and pack it firmly, then push a metal collar which goes around the pipe close to the wall on each side. A third area of sound escape is under and around the door. Weather-stripping the door on top and sides will help, and at the bottom a drop closure mechanism can be installed which falls to the floor when the door is closed on the inside. When remodeling the whole house, try to locate bedroom closets along bath walls to block sound.

4. Abundant hot water: The extra cost of a larger water heater and its operation is more than offset by the convenience of hot water for any and all home operations. A sixty-six-gallon tank or larger will provide adequately for clothes washing, dishwashing, tub baths, and the other requirements of the average family and their guests.

5. Shower-head location: There is no such thing as a standard height for a shower, since people are different heights and proportions. Don't let your plumbing contractor locate it for his comfort; determine the height suited to you and your family and have him place it accordingly. The same goes for soap dish, grab bars, and all other shower accouterments.

6. A bench for sitting: If space permits, a small upholstered bench or stool is convenient for tying shoes, sitting at a counter lavatory or just to place a towel before you step into the tub.

7. Tub accessories: There are inflatable plastic pillows and other types of head supports for those who like lengthy, warm tubs. There are also trays which rest on tub sides to hold beauty aids, a book rack for reading, etc.

8. A magnetized shower curtain: After an invigorating shower, it is a bore to have to swab up a lake around the tub. There are shower-curtain liners with magnets sewn into the hem, which grip to the cast iron under the tub's porcelainized surface. They keep the water from spraying out onto the floor.

After: Here's an attractive remodeling idea for use with a self-rimming bathtub. This sleek blue model by Kohler was encased in plastic-coated hardboard paneling, also used for cabinets and walls. Blue moldings on closet doors and tub front repeat tub color accent. *Paneling by Masonite Corporation.*

9. A locked medicine compartment: For emotional comfort and security, if there are small children and even where there are not, it is a good idea to have drugs in a section of the medicine cabinet which is key-locked. All too often we read of people wandering into the bath, half asleep, and taking a wrong drug.

10. Portable heater: For extra heat when you need it on cold mornings or when you plan a long tub soak, a small portable heater is a boon. There are heaters on the market no bigger than cigar boxes which throw out a great deal of warmth.

11. Good storage space: For towels, hair dryers, heaters and all other bath paraphernalia, a sizable closet in the bath is a good idea.

You'll find that it is useful for nonbath storage, too. And don't waste potential space under the washbasin. Use one that's dropped into a cabinet.

12. Luxurious towels: Thick, absorbent towels and large-sized washcloths are a joy for bathing and face washing, well worth the difference in cost and lasting enough to be economical in the long run.

The bath as a health center

With today's new equipment, we are finding that even the small bath can serve as a health center, while the large one presents many opportunities for body care. The hydromassage tub, with a motor which sends pressure-jets of water circulating around the body, is manufactured by at least two companies. The unit includes a separate motor, which operates on electricity but is absolutely safe against shock. Water is drawn into the tub to a height beyond holes which introduce the pressurized air, at whatever temperature the user desires, then the water can be turned off and the switch turned on. The switch must, of course, be located beyond the reach of the bather and in a concealed location to avoid turning on when there is no water in the tub (the motor would burn out otherwise). The therapeutic value is great for those suffering from poor circulation, arthritis, stiff necks, and muscular aches. A hydromassage bath of no more than five minutes is recommended at first, with the user working up to fifteen-minute baths over a period of time.

In addition to the tub with integral hydro unit, there are portable hydromassage appliances which can be lowered into the tub with perfect safety. Such units have long been used by podiatrists and other medical practitioners. They are relatively lightweight, compact, and easy to use. Many manufacturers offer hot tubs, hydromassage family spas, built-in large tubs where several people can enjoy the benefits of swirling water simultaneously.

The sauna is another bath adjunct which is gaining in popularity. Based on the Finnish traditional bath which created intense dry heat in a small hut by heating rocks, today's version is based on the same principle of hot, dry air. Humidity is extremely low—below 6 per cent—enabling the user to withstand temperatures from 175 degrees Fahrenheit and up. One bathes in the hot air in a specially designed redwood-paneled cubicle with a bench or other platform to relax. Perspiration is heavy, and the body is said to be cleansed more thoroughly than with soap and water. After ten or fifteen minutes, a shower brings a feeling of well-being. There are manufactured units as small as 3 feet square and 5×8 feet with a sizable bench. The sauna heater is electric and no plumbing is required. It is thermostatically controlled and contains a fan with sealed motor to circulate fresh air into the room.

For those who prefer the benefits of steam heat, there are devices which permit you to have your own tub or stall shower serve as a steam room. Outside the bathing area, a timer switch activates an electronic steam generator with a steam outlet head placed inside the bathing area. The generator is compact and lightweight, easily installed, and guaranteed not to cause steam damage to bath walls or wall covering. The generator itself can be located in an adjacent closet, overhead in the attic or in a lavatory cabinet next to the tub or shower area. A bather can set the timer and, when the steam cuts off, can proceed with an invigorating shower. This kind of wet heat is said to beneficial in cases of arthritis and inflammatory joint ailments. It is safe and easy to use.

Where space permits, the bath is an ideal location for a massage table, exercycle, and compact weight-lifting, gym, and other equipment. After completion of a prescribed set of exercises, a warm shower is conveniently at hand. There is a variety of equipment manufactured in sizes that permit use in the bath without difficulty.

THE MASTER SUITE: CONVENIENCE FOR HUSBAND AND WIFE

The master bedroom

The bedroom is the most personal room in the home, especially the master bedroom, which should be a comfortable retreat for husband and wife, a place to be alone together. If one of your reasons for remodeling is to create such a refuge, then you'll want to think in terms of a suite which includes a sitting area, a separate dressing area, a bath or baths, and perhaps even two bedrooms connected by a bath-dressing area. There are many possibilities limited only by the amount of space you can allot and what you can afford to pay. The first consideration in planning a master bedroom suite is privacy. So as you think about possibilities for location, keep this factor uppermost in mind. An attic or upper floor, a rear basement area that opens to the garden, a new wing positioned away from other sleeping rooms—all these are possibilities.

Whichever location you choose, there are basic pointers to keep in

mind. First make a room plan, again turning to graph paper, quarter-inch scale. Inches are important, so measure and draw carefully. If you're thinking in terms of a single-story addition, position your windows for privacy from neighbors and from any outdoor area where other members of the family might congregate. If it is to be a basement room overlooking the garden, be sure that you create not only separate access to the yard from the rest of the house but that you screen off a deck or terrace that can be the private preserve of the master suite. If possible do not locate windows on the east wall, since that elevation will admit harsh morning light not conducive to sleep. As you plan, make sure that you have an unbroken wall that is large enough to accommodate the bed or beds you intend to use. Remember that a double bed flanked by two night tables takes about eight and a half feet of wall space; twin beds with one table between about the same amount; a queen-size bed with two tables takes nine feet and a king-size about ten and a half feet with two tables. By all means avoid locating bed or beds under a window because of drafts and light.

Before: A 1917 home was using a former sunporch as a makeshift summer bedroom until they needed a year-round room for a teen-age daughter.

After: Rotted wood was torn out around windows; shingles were removed from one wall; two windows were eliminated; insulation was added where walls were opened. Then paneling, a prefinished hardboard, was applied to walls. The rest was frothy decor, suitable for a young girl. *Paneling by Masonite Corporation. Designer: Penny Hallock Lehman.*

Size the room, too, for inclusion of dresser, bureau, and whatever furniture you need for your dressing and grooming requirements. If you intend to have a separate dressing area, built-in cabinetry with drawers may eliminate the need for storage pieces in the sleeping area proper. Bedroom furniture, however, is bulky and takes considerable wall space, so plan accordingly. Try to include a comfortable sitting area with sofa, love seat, chaise longue or comfortable upholstered armchairs. There will not be room for all of these, but choose to fit your needs. It is pleasant to have a dining-height table and chairs near a window for snacking, games, writing, or sewing. Or you may want to have desks, one for husband and another for wife. Think carefully about what conveniences you and your spouse really want.

Choice of materials

Wall-to-wall carpet is good for the master bedroom, as it provides warmth, softness underfoot, and absorbs sound. Visually it enlarges the room and unites various furniture sizes and shapes. If full-size car-pet is not possible, have at least a room-size rug. Windows are espe-cially important in the bedroom, where control of light and air is critical. You'll want light for daytime activities but will want to ex-clude it for afternoon naps, night slumber, and lazy mornings. Casement windows are a good choice, because they can admit air while deflecting unwanted drafts; large sliding glass panels are not the best solution either for air control or security (especially if you are on the ground floor). Better to think in terms of a glass door that can be closed and locked, combined with, say, fixed glass panels above and operating casements below—all to form an expanse of glass over-looking a garden or patio off the room.

For window treatment, there are window shades available in a room-darkening material that looks translucent but blocks out sun-light. There are venetian blinds, in regular width or the newer nar-row style, that control both light and air. There are some designed especially for the bedroom that close with a tight overlap to prevent light streaks; for greater darkness, some even have channels at the sides and bottom to mask light leaks at these spots. Louvered shutters are a good choice, too, as they can be manipulated for light and air. If you live in an area where air conditioning is required part or all of the year, you'll have to consider its placement, which will affect your window planning.

For artificial lighting, valance illumination over your window ex-panse is efficient and attractive, casting a pleasant glow over shutters, window shades, traverse drapery, or whatever window treatment you choose. This is a good source of general background lighting and has to be built in, so arrange this in your over-all electrical wiring system. For specific lighting, you'll want bedside reading lights which can be mounted on the wall, focusing directly on the oc-cupant of the bed, individually adjustable. Other possibilities are standing lamps on bedside tables, a built-in strip over the headboard, or a wall bracket that sheds light both upward and downward. For the latter, two separate fluorescent tubes and two switches are desira-ble. Other necessary illumination might be a table lamp at a window grouping, a suitable lamp for a desk, and perhaps built-in strip light-ing at either side of a mirror over a make-up table.

When it comes to choice of walls for the master bedroom, it is wise to avoid paneling and other heavy, textured wood surfaces as they tend to make the room look dark and heavy. Such materials are better left for the study or informal living room. If you surface the walls in gypsum board, it can be painted or wallpapered after it is taped and seamed. You can avoid the taping and cut costs with fabric—an eminently suitable wall covering. Fabric creates an amazing aural effect that is conducive to sleep and repose. The absorbent fabric sound-deadens the room, making the acoustics somewhat like those in a recording studio. A wall of heavy drapery can give somewhat the same effect. And for a more complete sense of enclosure, you can fabric-cover the ceiling or create a tentlike effect. Just as important as what presents itself on the inside wall is what is behind it. Be sure to insulate the new walls of an addition and the old walls of an attic or basement.

The master bath

For the master bath, consider the possibilities outlined in the previous section on bathrooms. A compartmented bath works well, giving both husband and wife privacy with minimal fixtures. This is the spot for a hydromassage tub, hot tub, sauna, steam enclosure, and all the other health and body-pampering niceties. So earmark space for what you want and can afford. As for the dressing area, first take inventory of your and your spouse's clothes and allot closet space accordingly, for hanging garments and drawer-stored items. Include a full-length, well-illuminated mirror somewhere and, if you don't care to have it in the bedroom proper, add a dressing table in this area. Be sure to arrange for plenty of dead storage—over-the-closets is a good spot—for luggage, extra bedding, and the inevitable miscellany. Think carefully of storage needs before starting construction. Remember, you can never have enough storage space anywhere.

The guest suite: home away from home

If you enjoy regular visits from in-laws, other family, or close friends, you may have reached a point where you just can't cope without separate and full-service quarters for them. Places to find the space are the same aforementioned areas of the existing house—attic, basement, garage, etc.—plus another possibility: combining two smallish bedrooms to form a bedroom-bath complex. The same planning principles apply as with the master suite, except that you can be a lot less luxury-minded in your approach. What guests need is privacy, adequate hang-up storage, comfortable beds (twin are a better choice, as not all guests care to share a bed), and a good bath with tub and shower. If you have room in the bath for a tiled or laminate-topped counter for a toaster and coffee maker, with an undercounter apartment-sized refrigerator, these appliances will eliminate kitchen tie-ups and keep guests happy in their own little world until meal or entertainment times, when all of you want to assemble together. Guest bath aids might also include hooks for the back of the bathroom door (indispensable), extra towel storage, a commodious medicine chest, wide towel bars, wastebasket, and, by all means, a small drying rack for the inevitable minilaundry guests must do as soiled linen accumulates.

PLATE 1

Before: While attractive enough, this sprawling house didn't have a period style definite enough to suit its owners. Also, they required additional bedrooms and the existing attic was not usable.

After: By raising the pitch of the existing roof and adding dormer windows, designer Walter Simmonds was able to increase living space. At the same time, the new dormer windows, half-timbered siding, and small-paned windows gave the French country look the owners wanted. *Photographer: Harold Davis.*

PLATE 2

Before: 1930s beach bungalow had little going for it other than compact space and a water view. Owner-photographer Bruce Harlow and his architect, William Kirsch, worked together to give it added comfort and architectural distinction.

After: New windows on the old porch opened the house to the view, and redwood, used in several forms and ways, gave new life to the exterior. Resawn redwood plywood siding covered the old, dilapidated clapboard, and was accented with redwood battens, trim, fascia, and window framing. Brick chimney was encased and given a design with redwood trim and, along with vertical battens, gives the illusion of greater height.

PLATE 3

Before: Large house had simple lines, an unimaginative mix of stucco, clapboard, shutters.

After: Street-side elevation is now imposing, with wrought-iron gate and high wall. Setback entry space was used for a new foyer and impressive entrance door. Railing above added Italianate style, carried out in pictureframing for windows. All exterior walls were stuccoed and painted terra cotta to heighten Italian look. *Photographer: John Hartley.*

PLATE 4

Before: Spanish-style 1930s bungalow looked dated, but its new owner saw possibilities for a contemporary appearance.

After: Here is an excellent example of what can be done with encasement. By building a new redwood wall right in front of the old stucco, designers Aris Kotzamanis and Christian Dante gave an up-to-date look with one stroke. Redwood trellis and boards in herringbone design, plus new double-door entrance gate are highlights of the redesigned façade. *Photographer: Harold Davis.*

PLATE 1

PLATE 2

PLATE 3

PLATE 4

PLATE 5

PLATE 6

PLATE 7

The living room: make it more livable

The living room is one of the most remodeled rooms in the home, probably because in many ways it is the home's most important area. Not only does it get the most family use, it is the room most often on exhibit to friends and business associates. It is where major entertaining is done and as such it becomes a status symbol. For these reasons, it holds the most important furniture, woodwork, flooring, and all the surface materials that go to make it look impressive. Most often, this room is revamped to make it larger, and space is borrowed from other, less used areas, or new space is added to it, taken from the land.

In older homes, the living and dining rooms used to open onto each other, either through an archway or through doors that could be closed to give privacy to either when desired. Many families feel that

PLATE 5

Before: A 1950s rambler-style house was typical of thousands throughout the country, with shingle siding, stone accents, and uninteresting entrance detailing.

After: New design incorporates bold detailing with American Plywood Trademarked Texture 1-11 plywood applied horizontally and accented with lumber battens. The dramatic boxing of the windows protects them from the weather, reducing heat loss, while a dramatic wood entrance deck lends privacy along with heightened visual appeal. New siding was applied directly over the old with nails after stone wainscot was stripped away.

PLATE 6

Before: Another bungalow, like thousands seen everywhere, had good living space inside, a dull appearance from the street.

After: An imaginative design combining trellis painted dazzling white and red brick turned it into a little gem of a pavilion. Trellis sweeps across entire length, defining windows and carport. Brick, full-width steps, and white roof add new distinction. *Designer: Anton Vogt. Photographer: Harold Davis.*

PLATE 7

Before: Designer Jamie Ballard saw this 1920s bungalow as the answer to his needs for home and office, largely because of its proximity to the decorating centers of Los Angeles and because it had a two-car garage he could convert to an office, separate from his residence.

After: To gain privacy and design continuity, Ballard chose used brick and lattice to soften an otherwise unbalanced design and create a shaded terrace for greenery. A new window design masked narrow glass panels with louvered shutters, topped with a louvered fan over the whole. Garage door gave way to a board-and-batten façade for the office, brightened with tall, small-paned windows. A hedge separates the brick-and-grass paved office courtyard from the lawn of the main house. *Photographer: Harold Davis.*

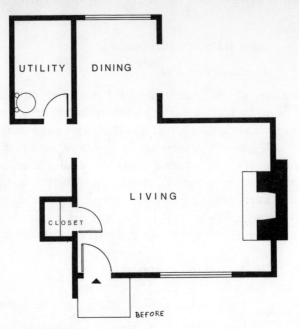

Before: Dreary living room of a tract house had several bad features. One was that, since the house had no foyer, access was directly into the living room. A dining ell was cramped and lacked storage space.

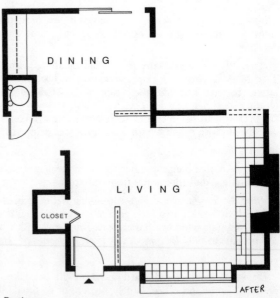

Floor Plan By Thomas L. Bastianon

After: For entry privacy, a short partition wall was built delineating a small foyer. Protruding fireplace was integrated into over-all room design by creation of a raised tile hearth, at a level repeated under the front window as a plant ledge. To make the dining ell more functional, space was borrowed from two directions: a utility room took unneeded space for one water heater, so the wall was taken down, the water heater given a tiny, doored compartment, and the remaining space made for dining storage and extra space. On the other side, the wall was moved a few feet, permitting a larger dining window. *Photo courtesy of American Plywood Association.*

space was wasted on a formal dining area and have created workable dining space in an informal family room off the kitchen or, if the kitchen was large, in one part of that room. In most cases, since the ceiling joists are transverse—from one side of the house to the other— it is a simple matter to remove the stud walls which are not load-bearing to form one large living space. If there is a fireplace on a side wall of the old living room and it now seems off-balance, use a large piece of furniture—a bookcase or wood cabinet—on the same wall of what was the dining room. That will improve symmetry. If you are lucky enough to have had a fireplace in the dining room on that same wall, so much the better. You can create two conversation groups. If there was a chandelier in the former dining room, it should be removed. In fact, in most cases it is better to remove chandeliers in remodeled areas and have a wall switch activate a base plug that can be used for a lamp. (Building codes in most places now require that there be such a switch in all rooms.)

Include a fireplace

If you are adding space to an existing living room or revamping one that doesn't have a fireplace, it is a good idea to include one. It creates an excellent focal point for furniture arrangement and also adds an emotional warmth and cheeriness to the room above and beyond its thermal contribution. If you can afford an elaborate brick or stone construction, that is one solution. A simpler, more economical solution is to use a prefabricated firebox that combines the burning area and facing in a metal unit that can be built into a stud wall faced with gypsum board, wood paneling, brick veneer, or whatever surfacing material you choose. Your carpenter can create necessary depth, and the inner workings—firebox, flue pipe, collar, etc.—will be concealed. You'll have to add a hearth in some masonry material—slate is a good choice—to the depth required by code, usually at least eighteen inches. This can be framed on the three jutting sides by quarter round or some decorative molding and stained to blend with the surrounding floor. It is important to remember that the flue pipe must rise higher than a neighboring roof by whatever local building codes require (three and a half feet in many areas).

Another good solution to a fireplace, where codes permit, is a freestanding Franklin stove type of unit. These now come in a variety of styles, from the traditional design (which old Ben Franklin made to fit into a brick or stone fireplace opening) to very stream-

Before: The living room of a 1915 apartment was dominated by an overscaled mantel and spoiled by an underscaled chandelier. Other features—parquet flooring, bay window, cove ceiling—were attractive.

After: An antique Venetian trumeau was adapted to form a mantel, with verde antique marble plinths and ledge. The plinths were required to raise the trumeau to give correct proportion to fireplace facing. A ten-branch Williamsburg-style brass chandelier added to the new style.

lined units perfect for a contemporary decoration scheme. Most of these units come with a top or rear opening for the flue pipe, so that you can vent it through-wall with the flue bracketed to the outside wall of the house or, if it is a one-story structure, leave the pipe exposed for decorative pattern. It is well to have the unit rest on some nonflammable masonry and have a sheet of asbestos cement attached to the wall directly behind the unit, if it is plaster, gypsum board, or some other burnable material.

Living-room lighting

The living room is likely to provide more lighting problems than any other room in the house, for two simple reasons. It usually is the largest space to be lighted, and as the focal point of the house it sets the mood for other areas.

Here are a few questions you might ask yourself as you consider remodeling your living room with light. Is this an all-purpose room or is there a separate family room or den? How much entertaining do you do? How many groupings of furniture do you have? Will certain areas involve conversation, reading, or playing the piano? Is a dining area included? What decorating styles blend best with the architecture of your home—Early American, contemporary, period? What decorative accessories do you wish to accent? Remember that to avoid the bland, unimaginative look of many living rooms you will need to highlight interesting textures, areas, or objects. Lighting is one of the tools you can use to stamp your individuality on your home.

Let's consider lighting rooms of three different sizes.

The small room needs to avoid clutter. That means eliminating as many small lamps as possible. A flexible pull-down fixture can do double duty in a corner which may be devoted to conversation or reading or occasional sewing. A valance will dramatize a window, at the same time providing some general illumination. A collection of plants in a window can be accented with two or three swivel spotlights set in the ceiling, or a wall of bookshelves can be lighted with strip lights under the shelves, or incandescent spots to bring out the color of the book jackets, or a cornice between the ceiling and the top shelf.

·When a room has several built-in units, as is apt to be the case in a small living room, the elimination of portable lamps is particularly desirable. However, if you do use lamps, perhaps on either side of a sofa, be sure they are scaled to the size of the room, and that their height from the floor to the center of the shade is the same throughout the room. This helps to create a unified effect. Dimmer switches are recommended for living rooms of any size.

The average room offers you a little more flexibility, since you will probably be dealing with 125 to 225 square feet of space—for example, a room 12×18 feet. A combination of fixtures and wall lighting is desirable here, and if you're using a valance, cornice, or wall bracket, it should be at least 12 feet long.

One of the effective ways to light paintings, bookshelves, a collection of porcelain, or a stereo corner is to mount an electrified track on the ceiling about two feet from the wall you wish to illuminate. Since the track carries power along its full length, just clip on shielded spotlights evenly spaced at intervals (every three feet perhaps) and focus them on your treasures. If the spots are dimmer-controlled, they will lend a greater enchantment.

Perhaps you feel that chandeliers belong only in the largest, most formal, or most elegant rooms. This is no longer true. An airy, graceful chandelier can be used in a low-ceilinged room. Two precautions must be taken—it must be placed so that no one will inadvertently hit his head, and if it is used over a cocktail table, the bulbs, even though small and flame-shaped, should not shine in the eyes of anyone. If possible, put it on a dimmer switch to give the soft glow of candlelight where desired. If you're using portable lamps to supplement your lighting, aim for balance in their positioning, and be sure they are in proportion to the tables they rest on. Many decorators prefer that all shades in a room be white and that the same material (linen, silk, parchment) be used for each shade. If there is a great deal of reflected light in the room, a dark shade lends contrast.

The large room, measuring over 225 square feet in area (that is, a room 12×20 feet), should definitely have built-in lighting. This should include at least 20 feet in cornices, valances, or wall brackets, plus whatever spotlights are needed. In a large room you will need to achieve some feeling of intimacy by grouping furniture and defining each area with light, either from table lamps or shafts of light directed downward from the ceiling. A large room also gives you the opportunity to do interesting things with wall washing from recessed fixtures. On a 24-foot-long wall you could use eight fixtures 3 feet apart. Wall washing helps to give depth, warmth, and character to a room. Ceiling recessed downlights add still another dimension.

Frequently you can live with a room for a long time before realizing how poorly it is lighted. This happened to a New York family whose large living room was lighted by a blazing torchlike fixture on the fireplace wall at the far end of the room, and two table lamps, one beside a wing chair and the other beside a sofa. A handsome portrait of their daughter over the mantel was unlighted. In fact, the glaring fixture on the same wall actually prevented a clear view of the portrait.

The solution? Removal of the disfiguring wall fixture and installation of a dimmer-controlled valance to dramatize the attractive bay window. A ceiling track with three spotlights attached was installed near the fireplace wall. One spot was focused on the girl's portrait, another on built-in bookshelves, and the third on the wing chair near the fireplace, thus eliminating an awkward little table and its lamp. A pair of big matching table lamps was placed on either side of the sofa. As the owners themselves readily admitted, the results were spectacularly successful.

Flooring

Oak-strip, parquet, or wood-block flooring are most commonly found in the existing living rooms of houses twenty to fifty years old. Homes older than that often had pine, fir, or some softer wood (in Louisiana, for example, floors in very old homes were often cypress). Wood is a good choice for a living room which gets a lot of traffic, so if your house has this kind of floor, it is well to retain it if it can be sanded and refinished to look and function well. (You'll find tips on sanding in a later chapter.) If you are adding space to a room that has a fine wood or other floor, it is a good idea to surface the addition in the same material. If the existing floor isn't all that good, use plywood for the new floor, then carpet or use tile or whatever over the combined expanse. Wall-to-wall carpet gives a lush, snug look to a living room (tips on carpet choice are also in a later chapter), and if a suitable fiber is chosen, it can wear long and look well. In warm climates—Southern California or Florida—ceramic tile is marvelous. It wears forever and can easily be damp-mopped. Quarry tile in the classic terra cotta or other neutral color is both practical and attractive; patterned tiles must be chosen carefully as part of an over-all decoration plan. The same must be said of patterned carpet. In fact, plain carpet is the best choice in the long run—neither patterned nor sculptured.

Other tips on living room renovation

New windows, if for an addition, should blend with the existing fenestration. For example, if you have double-hung, small-paned windows in the original room, windows in the addition should blend to keep the traditional look. If the addition includes a glass wall opening onto a garden, use small-paned french-type doors, which are stock items at the lumber yard. If the existing windows are in too poor a condition to repair, they should be replaced, and if you want to create a more contemporary look, aluminum-framed units are a good and relatively inexpensive solution. A study of the yellow pages of your phone book should lead you to a glazer who can have these units custom-sized to your existing window openings. Frames can be either the natural, silver-toned aluminum or anodized aluminum to give a more sophisticated bronzy, dark appearance. Casements that open out are usually the best choice both from the standpoints of function and appearance, but double-hung aluminum units are available, too. This type of window can be combined with large sliding glass panels, also aluminum-framed, if you want full-height, glass expanse opening onto a deck or terrace.

If existing walls and ceiling are plaster in poor condition, cracks and holes can be repaired. However, if large sections of plaster are not securely locked into the lath underneath, it is well to nail gypsum board right over the entire expanse. If sections of the ceiling look suspicious, take a broom and gently tap. If they seem to be secure, you can leave them. A plasterer will be able to tell you what can be saved. Don't worry about one wall being gypsum board and the others plaster; you'll never know the difference once everything is painted. If existing walls are a textured plaster, a sand finish or other, as in many houses built in the nineteen twenties and thirties, a good plasterer can surface new gypsum board to blend. So don't worry about closing up an unwanted door or window. The carpenter can remove the casing and the unit, add studs in the opening, insulate and patch the hole with gypsum board. Then the plasterer will blend it with the surrounding wall area so that you will never be able to tell where it was.

Perhaps you'll want to replace a dated fireplace treatment. No problem. The mantel can be easily removed and you can plaster for a mantel-less, modern look, or add a new mantel. Your lumberyard can show you brochures with various styles of ponderosa pine mantels that are stock items you can order, or you can look in antique shops for an old mantel. If you see a picture of a period mantel you want, a good carpenter can copy it. The old fireplace facing—around the opening—can be changed by adding slate, marble, or other masonry material. The hearth can likewise be resurfaced. An updated look for an old fireplace wall can make a world of difference in a room. And while you're improving the appearance of a fireplace, why not improve its function? If there is no damper, by all means have one installed. It may be high time the chimney was swept, and if the fire brick or plaster at the rear of the burning area appears damaged, have that repaired too.

Before: What can be done with a room with dated 1920s Spanish features, including a bulky fireplace and poorly proportioned windows?

After: Designer Lawrence Limotti found a solution by encasing the fireplace and trimming a new fireplace area with magnificent fluted pilasters. Shutter panels disguise the windows and add appropriate scale while permitting passage of light and air. French door to porch was closed off and made part of a sofa wall delineated into panels with decorative molding. The result: a distinguished period room. *Photographer: Harold Davis.*

The dining room: a new look

As living has become more informal, there has been a lot of new thinking about the dining room. In homes thirty years and older this room was apt to be as large or larger than the living room. As the cost of space has increased and family dining has become less of a ritual, many homemakers choose to enlarge living areas—the living room and family room—and assign dining to a multipurpose area. This is often a part of the kitchen, but arranged so that there is some separation from the cooking section. Another popular solution has been to combine dining and recreation in a family room or to use convertible dining furniture in one end of the living room. A drop-leaf table or a console that opens to a dining table with leaves that can be stored at other times along with folding chairs—there are many ways to have a fairly formal dining grouping and at other times make the room appear solely as a living area.

So if you are rethinking a house with a too-large kitchen or one where you plan to remove a partition between living and dining areas to make one large living room, you may want to think in these terms. If you have an old house with a back porch off the kitchen, that may be the logical solution for dining, with easy service access and a pleasant garden view. In your renovation plans you may be able to arrange access from the living room so that it wasn't necessary to pass through the kitchen to get to the dining area, which can be somewhat disconcerting at formal parties. If the porch is a step lower, it may be a good idea to raise it up to the house level, as a step down or up can cause spills for someone serving from the kitchen. Also the porch probably had a sloping floor for drainage and a new floor can make it level. New windows, heating and electrical lines would about complete the transformation. If there is a window opening into the kitchen, it can be closed or perhaps turned into a pass-through to facilitate food service.

However, if your family has and wants to keep or has not and wants to create a separate, formal dining room, here are some tips. If your house has an archway, double glass-paned doors, or some other quasi-barrier into the living room, close it off and make the dining room truly separate. (Of course, the swinging door into the kitchen and any other egress should be kept.) That will give privacy to the living room and an extra wall for furniture placement in the dining room, which requires considerable bulky furniture. If there is no alternate access to the dining room from the living areas of the home, you'll have to provide one, to avoid having to pass through the kitchen. In that case it is better to reduce the size of the opening between the two rooms and simply install a door which can be closed. If the dining room relied on the old archway for daylight, it may be necessary to open up a side or rear wall with new fenestration. Or you might want to construct a terrace opening off the dining room for summer meals alfresco. There seems to be something instinctive in human beings to want to eat their food near a window, or a view or out in the open to one degree or another.

There is no need to be hidebound about the arrangement of furniture. Instead of the conventional table in the center of the room with a chandelier overhead surrounded by chairs, you might consider a drop-leaf table near a window or a mix of two or more smaller tables.

Flooring

As in the past, you're not necessarily stuck with the floor that comes with your dining room. If you have a wood floor, you can alter its appearance enormously by staining, bleaching, painting, or stenciling. Or you can add any number of completely new floors and change the surface completely. Since you are remodeling your house, and are in the planning stages, you can decide upon random-plank flooring, parquet, flagstone, terrazzo, travertine, marble, ceramic tile, brick, slate, or mosaic tile. Or you can put down a solid-color flooring or a gaily patterned one in the form of an easy-to-maintain durable vinyl tile. And don't overlook the vast array of plastics that emulate the natural wood and stone materials described above. Often these vinyls so closely simulate the natural material that they can be distinguished from them only by touch.

Whether you leave your floor bare or punctuate it with a solid-textured or delightfully patterned area rug will be determined by the style of the room as well as budget considerations. Today there are so many different kinds of area or accent rugs from which to choose in every style, price, and size. Your choice of rug also offers you a chance to introduce an exciting eclectic note into an otherwise conventional room. One example of this would be putting down an oriental rug in a sleek modern setting. Another would be to blend a contemporary carpet texture with formal French furniture. While many prefer wall-to-wall carpet in the dining room, from the standpoint of even wear and cleanability, the area or accent rug idea is a more prac-

Before: Entrance hall of a Colonial-style home was spacious and impressive but lacked a sense of drama. The area around the entry door also had a cramped look, with narrow coat closets flanking it. Flooring which continued into rooms on either side kept the area from appearing to be a separate entity.

After: In remodeling, the coat closets were removed, and leaded glass windows were installed on either side of the door. Then the flooring was removed and plywood put down over which ceramic tile could be installed. White woodwork now contrasts dramatically with dark-painted wainscot and brocade-patterned paper on walls above. Highlight of the foyer is the new floor, American Olean's Birch Hexagon Primitive ceramic tile.

tical one. From an aesthetic standpoint, too, the area rug used on an attractive smooth flooring offers more interest than a blanket of carpeting. In considering cost, unless the rug is a quality product, it is not going to last or look very well for a healthy period of time. A good rug is a good investment.

Lighting

There is never much question about what activity occurs in the dining room. It centers, of course, on eating, and this immediately raises two concerns. First, the lighting must make the food look appetizing, bringing out its varying colors and textures, and second, the mood of the room must be relaxed.

Have you ever really studied the lighting in restaurants? Possibly not, because in better restaurants the lighting is so subdued you're not conscious of it. Yet it is an important factor in creating the atmosphere the management desires. It can range from the bright, cheerful lighting of the quick lunch places to unobtrusive lights in a restaurant that encourages leisurely and gracious dining. Here the lighting will frequently combine mellow contrasts, subtle downlights, and diffuse illumination from coves, valances, and soffits. Downlighting is particularly effective in catching the sparkle of silver, crystal, and china. Ideally a table should be lighted from several directions for a natural, flattering look to both people and food. Dimmer controls are strongly recommended.

Perhaps you have no clearly defined dining area, but must eat and entertain in a corner or ell of your living room. You might borrow the idea of a New York lighting designer. Although he claims to dislike theatrical effects in residential lighting, you may think the way he lights his dining room—consisting of a big wooden buffet table against a wall of his living room—rather dramatic. Above the table are a series of recessed downlights which, at small dinner parties, are dimmed during the cocktail hour. When dinner is served, the lighting level is turned up to cast a rosy glow on the food, guests, and a brilliant tapestry hanging on the wall behind the table. Later, when the last morsel is gone, the table will again recede into dimness. Living-room lights are adjusted for the guests' mood, and sometimes lazy dancing patterns of color float across the ceiling. One way to achieve this is to conceal a rotating projector with colored plastic discs behind a cove near the ceiling.

If the dining area opens directly from the living room, the lighting in both must be blended and co-ordinated. In any room where the family or guests sit around a table, the light on the table itself is of prime importance. This can be accomplished by downlighting from recessed spotlights or by a fixture hung directly over the table.

While dining-room chandeliers provide some light, they are essentially decorative and should be supplemented by other sources of light—possibly from a valance, a soffit, or a wall bracket. The type of chandelier you select will, of course, depend on your furnishings. Among those appropriate for a dining room are brass fixtures with globular lamps, wrought-iron candelabra, crystal chandeliers, and pewter reproductions. Whatever your mood—Mediterranean, English country, formal French, Early American—you can easily complement it.

If your furnishings are contemporary and your dining area is small, you might prefer a group of pendant lights, adjusted at varying heights, or a pulley fixture that can be lifted or lowered and is mounted on a traverse track to slide across the ceiling. This type of fixture is particularly desirable if the dining table must double as a study or work table.

To achieve dramatic effects in a formal dining room, remember the technique of wall washing (especially if you have a mural or a collection of art) and use recessed spots or concealed strips to highlight a collection of heirloom china or a niche filled with crystal. And don't forget that while many people love the romantic glow created by candlelight (real or electrified), others like to see the food they are eating. You may be able to appease both by bathing the tabletop in soft light from two adjustable shutter pinpoint spots.

Actually there's no limit to the effects you can create. In one home tiny pinpoints of light embedded in the ceiling were controlled to suggest twinkling stars. For an alfresco atmosphere, plants and feathery trees (real or artificial) can be silhouetted against a luminous panel. In one house a luminous wall was made of cutout plywood with shirred white sheer fabric stretched on the back and backlighted by yellow, blue and pink fluorescent tubes. These combine to give a white light of depth and distance.

PART THREE

Special Areas

CHAPTER SIX

REMODELING THE OUTDOORS

MORE AND MORE today, outdoor areas are thought of as rooms, planned, designed and used as alfresco counterparts of interior areas. To be sure these rooms are freer, but thought of in this new light, they can be areas with floor (paving), walls (fences and screens), and even ceilings (canopies, awnings, trellis, and other forms of shelter). Seen in this perspective, outdoor rooms stimulate the imagination to the fullest. House walls open up for easy access to and from exterior space; design crosses the threshold—colors, patterns, decorative accessories, and furniture bring as much man-made beauty to the landscape as they do to the enclosed structure, or as much ugliness if they are not planned in tandem with the beauty of nature. For one of the first rules in exterior remodeling is to let nature set the pace; planting and natural elements should call the tune in terms of color and design; what we bring outdoors should be held in subservience. And this applies not only to areas open to the sky or partially so, but any separate garden structure such as a gazebo, teahouse, pool house, pavilion, or whatever.

How do we classify these various outdoor rooms, what are the names for them and what do they mean? What are the differences between a deck, a terrace and a patio? Suffice it to say that deck, terrace, and patio are used by millions of people interchangeably. Millions of others have regional terminology: for example, on the West Coast, the Southwest, Florida and other formerly Spanish colonial areas, the word *patio* means outdoor living area. Although the term actually originated as a courtyard, walled in the Mediterranean manner, today it refers to almost any outdoor space adjacent to the house. In the East, where the heritage is English, *terrace* is most frequently used, which means any flat, raised level of earth, supported on one or more faces by a wall, according to Webster. *Deck,* to most, signifies the use of a wood platform, raised above the earth either slightly for the free passage of air and drainage of rain water, or fully, as over a hillside at the rear of a house.

THE CITY HOUSE TERRACE

For the city or suburban house where structures front on the street and side yards between neighbors are narrow or nonexistent, the terrace must almost always be located at the rear of the house for privacy. As a result, there is little choice of orientation for prevailing breezes, sunlight, etc. If the rear yard happens to face south, so much the better, but you may have to temper the afternoon sun with some form of overhead "ceiling" in at least one portion of the terrace. If it faces west, you will almost certainly need shading devices against the late afternoon sun, while a northern or eastern exposure will require no special consideration.

If you are remodeling a city house rather extensively, you have an opportunity to relate the functions of interior rooms and terrace quite closely. For example, most older city houses used to have the kitchen and dining room at the rear, the living room at the front facing the street. Today, architects are reversing this order and putting the kitchen and service areas at the front for ease of delivery and because these rooms require no special privacy, and relocating the living areas to the rear, where there can be a view of terrace and garden beyond plus easy, private access for outdoor living. In some cases, the solution is a combination dining-sitting area at the rear so that the adjacent terrace can be used in similar fashion. It is important to arrange convenient passage to the kitchen for easy service of refreshments outdoors.

Earlier, referring to the city or suburban house we said that the terrace was "almost always" located at the rear. It is important to point out that, today, both in the remodeling of older houses and the building of new ones, there is another interesting solution which places the terrace at the front, but completely protected by enclosing walls which make it a sort of entrance courtyard. In one way at least, it makes a lot of sense, because often with older homes there was a sizable front yard, completely useless unless it was enclosed. The courtyard is a way of making the most of idle space. To create such an entrance terrace, it is important to check into local zoning to determine setback requirements. If they permit, it may be a good idea when you are planning the remodeling to consider both a front and rear terrace.

With houses close at the sides, privacy will be an important factor. You will want to check city ordinances about the maximum height of fencing and other types of screens and baffles. Go as high as is permissible and construct a kind of fence that offers seclusion along with breezes. There are designs of fences which give closure from view but with openness for air passage—for example, a fence which has wide boards nailed to both sides of horizontal stringers, alternating open and closed on each side. Woven cedar and other types of close pickets permit air and privacy. Many families, of course, continue some such screening around the entire rear property, but where possible it is pleasant to have a visual sweep of space, with rear yards open to each other and privacy fencing used only at the outdoor living area.

While the terrace can be at the same level as the rest of the yard, it is well to have it somewhat raised for drainage. And be sure to provide for this in your plans, for while you may not be able to use the garden shortly after a heavy rain, if you have good drainage and suitable paving, you can use the terrace. It is important that the terrace slope away from the house so that rainwater will not collect near walls. For paving there are many choices in masonry units or natural material, and this kind of paving sets the terrace apart from the wood deck, which we will discuss later. Brick laid in sand or in mortar is excellent, and for a rustic, country look, old brick can't be beat. It does tend to crack, however, with freezing and thawing, and it is rather expensive, both for labor of installation and for the bricks themselves. Your landscape architect or contractor will know of various kinds of precast masonry units—concrete squares or rectangles, some of them integrally colored. You will find these at wayside garden shops, and they can be laid in gravel or sand, or embedded in mortar. It is best to choose the natural masonry color, however, because it makes for easier decorating. Green, terra cotta, and other tones can be used, but you may tire of them and the color scheme which they dictate. You can find flagstones at such centers, and there are excellent copies, also precast masonry, colored and finished to resemble flagstone. These make a handsome terrace. For special, more elegant effects, you can also use marble and other luxury stone.

Another excellent terrace can be made by pouring concrete into a grid of wood. For example, redwood or some other type of 2×2s or 2×4s impervious to rot are arranged in a geometric pattern over gravel and the slurry of concrete is poured into the openings. At the building-materials or hardware dealer you can buy bagged mixes to which you add only water in prescribed amounts. This makes a distinctive terrace that permits you to arrange a pattern of your own design. A rough pebble aggregate on top adds interesting texture.

Before: Town house backyard measured about 50 by 25 feet and was an over-grown wasteland with a cement walk up the middle.

After: For low maintenance, most of the area was resurfaced in brick, with four parterres, each a different pattern. White marble-chip paths were dividers. Major new planting included five trees against tall trellis panels of redwood and a hedge along a side fence. The rest was established planting and pots. *Photographer: Henry Bowles, Jr.*

These materials, you have noticed, are all hard, durable, water-shedding, easy to sweep clean or hose down. This is important for an outdoor expanse near the main house, because of tracking in leaves, grass, and mud. It also explains why a grass terrace is really no terrace at all, or rather no suitable outdoor living area. As you plan, don't overlook an outdoor water connection (be sure your plumber uses the new kind, which doesn't require draining in winter). It is useful not only for hosing down and watering plants but also as a water source for drinks and outdoor cooking and entertaining.

With your "floor" and "walls" decided on, you can consider materials for "ceiling," provided one is necessary. If space permits, it is always wise to have some part of the terrace sheltered at least, so that you can move under cover in a mild shower or find respite from the sun. An awning can be an attractive part of your remodeling scheme as well as a water-shedding, hardy material. Canvas and plasticized or plastic materials can be found in abundance in all colors and in stripes and other patterns. The material can be hung on hinged pipe attached to the terrace wall and raised when you choose or can be stretched over more or less permanent pipe, creating a kind of pavilion. In the latter case, be sure there are openings for drainage, otherwise the material will collect water and ultimately bend the pipe framing.

There are many varieties of plastic sheets, flat and corrugated, tinted or plain, all in 4×8-foot and other modular sizes which can be used as part of a ceiling structure. These sheets can be drilled and then nailed to wood members, one attached to the back wall of the house and others creating a sloping framework supported by posts resting on the terrace floor. It is important to calculate your loads carefully, taking snow into account where necessary, so that you use sufficiently strong supporting members. Water will drain off the smooth sheets nicely with even the slightest slope. Wood frame can be painted or stained to blend with an over-all plan. These tinted plastic panels create a most pleasant effect with the sun glinting through and make an excellent contribution to the contemporary home. While not totally discordant with traditional architecture, they must be handled more carefully, designwise.

Another interesting outdoor "ceiling" can be created with trellis in the manner of a pergola. Although such a structure gives only token shelter overhead, it is an attractive way to temper the sun, if not the rain. Lattice strips found at any lumber yard can be nailed crisscross to 2×4s to create panels which in turn are supported by 4×4-inch posts. Similar panels can be used as side privacy panels if desired.

SIZING OF THE TERRACE

The city terrace will have size limitations dictated to you. However, it is important to create an area at least eight feet wide. Anything narrower than that will make it awkward to use a chaise or a table for four people, and a 10- or 12-foot depth is preferable. As to width, for the row-type city house with the neighbor's yard immediately contiguous, it is good visually to run the terrace the full width of your house, to go fence to fence, as it were. This will give pleasant scale and make the rear of the property much more impressive-looking. In the case of the suburban house, which may be wider than the 25 or 30 feet of the standard city house, full width isn't necessary. A rule in this case might be to make the terrace as wide as the interior room it adjoins. Or where the ranch house has both dining and living rooms across the rear, you may want one long sweep with some kind of divider to demarcate living and dining terraces. Where sliding glass or other doors open only from the living room, there is no problem: you simply size to that room. As far as depth is concerned, that will depend on your outdoor needs and the depth of your lot. There should be a good visual proportion between garden or grass area and the paved terrace. Anything over twenty feet in depth makes furniture and other outdoor appointments look lost and isn't necessary for convenient use.

THE SUBURBAN HOUSE TERRACE

What has been said about materials is equally applicable to the suburban terrace. What differs is the attention to orientation. Where you have more land and openness, there is greater flexibility in location, so you can take into account views, prevailing breezes, the path of the sun and other factors. As you remodel to make a new home, it is important to plan outdoor and indoor living areas in tandem: you will have your architect take orientation of terraces into account. This is no problem, as it is axiomatic to plan indoor rooms for views, sun, and breezes, so that the outdoor counterpart of each will automatically make the most of these natural elements.

During temperate months—in most parts of the country a full five —the terrace is apt to be the center of much daytime and even night-time activity. So you will want expansive, convenient, colorful, and attractive outdoor rooms. In addition to the usual living and dining terraces, you may want to include one off the master bedroom for a

Before: Ranch-house patio was essentially a narrow porch with access from the living area and from the kitchen.

morning cup of coffee or a last cigarette under the stars before bed. Remember, the successful house is one which offers enormous variety in living appointments, and the more intimate, inviting areas, you have inside and out, the more interesting the home, both for guests and family members. There is nothing duller than a large, expensive house that reveals all its charm at once. A small place tucked away where a cocktail or a cup of tea can be enjoyed along with a special view at the end of the day can be far more appealing than the most expansive and expensive terrace at the rear of a million-dollar mansion.

The country property offers opportunities for small terraces away from the house. There may be a secluded spot under an apple tree, overlooking a lake or pond or in a special part of the garden that cries for a paved area where you can enjoy the view, take a bit of picnic lunch, do a bit of sewing, painting or other hobby, or sling a hammock and laze away the day under the trees. A little imagination will help you make the most of the living potential of your property.

After: Window on a side wall was removed, sliding glass doors added for better kitchen access. Raised bed and tree were taken out and a stepped-up brick expanse provided a sizable new lounging-dining area in the ell of the house, plus a larger brick patio for sunning. *Designer: Virginia Heap. Photographer: Harold Davis.*

Special Terraces

There are a few of what might be called special terraces and these demand special attention to detail. The swimming-pool terrace is really a continuation of the pool border and looks best when it is the same material. Requisites are that it be a material free of grass, gravel, or anything which might be tracked into the pool and play hob with the filtering system. It must also be hosed down and be relatively unaffected by the inevitable splashing around a pool. Concrete, ceramic tile, and almost any kind of masonry are good. Wood is excellent, too, and one workable solution, easy to install, is a system of duckboards—1×4 inches nailed to 2×4-inch runners, with about a quarter inch between boards for drainage. Spruce, fir, or redwood are all excellent for this purpose, the latter being especially resistant to the effects of water. So that grass doesn't grow between the boards, use a chemical soil sterilant on the ground, or a good idea is to lay plastic sheets over the gravel bed which you lay on top of the earth. Puncture a few holes here and there for the water to pass through. Plastic drop cloths found at the hardware store are good for this purpose and can be cut into strips. Size of the terrace will vary with the amount of land and the size of the pool. Generally it is sufficient to have a sizable terrace only along one side or an end of the pool, the other sides merely flanked with decking or masonry three feet or so in width, just enough for use as a walkway. If concrete or other masonry is used, be sure it slopes slightly away from the pool for drainage. The main sitting terrace should be sized to accommodate several chaises, a dining table and chairs with an umbrella, and should be adjacent to the pool house or some shelter where outdoor furniture and pool gear can be stored and simple change of clothing can be made. You will need shelter for location of filtering and heating equipment anyway. A common pool size is 16×32 feet, and a good solution is to have the terrace at the diving-board end, say 24 feet wide and 16 feet deep. This creates a sizable space for lounging and its relation to pool scale keeps either from seeming dwarfed.

The Deck

A deck is usually wood, sometimes concrete, and always a raised platform which permits drainage and an easy flow of air below. It is especially prevalent with the beach house, ski cabin, and other vacation cottages. While useful and attractive as an outdoor living area on flat property, the deck really fulfills its potential on sharply sloping property. Singlehanded, it makes what is often thought of as an impossible building site highly desirable, simply by hanging out over the slope and offering a whole new world of versatile outdoor space. So if your house is on a lot that slopes sharply off at the rear, remember that a deck can make it as functional as flat land. And remember, the deck is by no means limited to the vacation house, or a California or Florida kind of climate. It is suitable and useful in year-round homes anywhere and in summer months will provide a marvelous escape into the sun and air.

Since a deck does not rest on the ground and must rely on its underpinnings to support human weight, there are almost always strict local building codes to which it must conform. So it is important to check with your planning or building commission for approval before going ahead. Besides foundation requirements and load limits, building regulations may specify height and projection limits and railing detailing. Therefore it is important to be conversant with local codes in order to plan your deck precisely, to prevent construction delays and assure ultimate approval by the planning commission. If a deck is high and the terrain difficult, it is mandatory to hire a professional architect, landscape architect or contractor who will design and build in accordance with the strength requirements of local codes. As to how a deck is supported, suffice it to say here that the deck structure must be designed to gather the weight load of the platform and transmit it down to the earth. The platform is the decking itself and rests on joists which in turn rest on beams. These transmit the accumulated load to posts which rest usually on concrete footings which rest on or in the ground. Since the footings anchor the entire structure to the ground, building codes are usually quite explicit on the subject. Generally, they must extend to undisturbed soil or rock and in cold climates, below the frost line. On quite low decks, the beams may rest directly on footings. In this case concrete blocks or precast footings may be used, seated firmly in the soil. At the beach where sands constantly shift, concrete footings are often bypassed in favor of pile-driven posts or telephone-pole-type columns. For a streamlined, contemporary look, a deck may also be cantilevered out from the house in which case especially heavy joists continue out from the understructure of the house foundation structure to support the decking. The weight of the house itself then holds the deck weight in balance. Steel beams are often used for especially long spans and where the platform is reinforced concrete.

If you're remodeling on hilly land, chances are your motor entrance will be off the higher, street side of the property and your slope will

Before: An unattractive and dangerously steep stairway was the sole means of access to the yard of a wood-shingled New York house, making food and drink service from the kitchen almost impossible.

After: A new deck for al fresco dining and relaxation solved the problem and conveniently masked the air-conditioning condenser. Cabinet under the kitchen window permits easy passage of plates and glasses outdoors, holds seat pads and other accessories below. Foundation posts and finish trim are clear heart redwood, resistant to insects and decay. Remainder of the structure is garden grade redwood. *Architect: Thomas J. Mannino.*

be at the rear. In that case you have little choice about location of the deck. However, if you're remodeling a house at the beach or mountain you may have a great deal of flexibility, so once again, you must plan for the best orientation to views, prevailing winds, the sun, etc. View-siting is most important, for one of the main advantages of the deck is the exhilarating feeling one has of hanging out over space to view the distance beyond and below.

To plan a deck, first decide on the placement according to the above criteria and in relation to the room or rooms the deck will serve. Then decide on the height relative to the doorway of these rooms. The deck should be nearly level with the floor of the house, or one easy step down, although this is better avoided if possible. (There are so many home accidents caused by failure to notice a step.) One inch below the doorway is the best level. For decking lumber, you have a wide choice—clear all-heart redwood is excellent because it is resistant to decay and termites and requires no preservative chemicals, even when in contact with the ground. Redwood treated with water repellent retains a buckskin beige hue; untreated, its original color will gradually change from beige to dark brown, then to a soft gray when exposed to the weather. It also takes stains so almost any color can be attained. Spruce is a good choice, also Douglas fir, western red cedar, larch and southern pine, properly pressure-treated. All of these weather beautifully without finishing, although if you want a driftwood look at the outset, you can easily get it with an oil stain. One application, and then you can leave the deck to weather naturally. Be sure that any lumber you choose has been certified "Kiln Dried."

Wood supports that go into the earth or sand must be treated. Pressure treatment with pentachlorophenol or creosote will guard against rot and termites. If the supports or posts rest on concrete footings, treatment is advised but not absolutely necessary, as water will drain off the concrete. The posts, incidentally, are attached to the concrete footing via a special metal fitting which is inserted into the wet concrete and hardens integrally with it. As far as the decking is concerned, the spaces between boards will permit quick drainage of rainwater and subsequent drying.

Depending on the size of the deck, you have a choice of lumber weight for the decking. It is best to use 2×3s, 2×4s or 2×6s. Space supports should be about four feet apart if 2×6s are used, or 2×3s or 2×4s laid on edge. Space supports about three feet apart if 2×4s are laid on the face. When face-laying 2×4s or 2×6s, be sure to lay boards with their bark side up (this can be determined by the arch of the ring marks being at the top of the board). Spacing should not be

more than a quarter inch; this is sufficient for drainage and is not apt
to trap spike heels, but it will trap small objects and keep them from
falling through. A most important pointer, especially at the beach or
other corrosive climates: be sure that you or your carpenter uses hot-
dipped galvanized- or stainless-steel nails and other fastenings. Otherwise, you will have unattractive rust stains and eventually a weaken-
ing of the structure due to corroded nails.

DECK DESIGNS, SIZES, AND DETAILS

The platform needn't be rectangular or square, nor does it have to be
modestly sized. A deck which follows the free-form contours of the
site and which fits around existing trees or has openings to let trees
through makes for a most interesting and attractive outdoor room. Be
imaginative, too, when it comes to the pattern of the deck lumber: it
can be laid on the diagonal, in a herringbone pattern, in parquet
squares, in blocks which are themselves at right angles to each other.
Your carpenter can tell you which of the designs that interest you are
feasible and most economical. Photographs in this book will give you
ideas about possible patterns.

When it comes to size, be expansive. You will regret a too-small
deck almost immediately, but never a too-large one. Many a quite
small house has a deck larger than its interior space. In a salubrious climate, everyone will be outdoors most of the time—for sunning, reading, napping and for meals from breakfast through barbecue-
prepared dinner. The deck, in fact, becomes an outdoor house. This
is the main deck; other decks off bedrooms and other less frequently
used rooms can be smaller, but anything less than an eight-foot depth
is fairly useless. You'll want enough space to use a chaise or at least
two folding chairs and a small table.

As your carpenter builds, ask that, as far as possible, his men protect the planting below the deck. Natural growth underneath is the
best landscaping in the world. Not only does it help to protect the
land, hillside, or whatever against erosion, but it takes away any stark
look and helps to relate deck to site. As trees and shrubs begin to
push against the underside of the deck, they can be thinned out, or in
some cases it may be possible to cut a hole in the decking to let them
grow through. A landscape architect can advise you at the beginning
on how to foresee such planting problems.

When it comes to design, the deck as a straightforward architectural element should have a streamlined contemporary look. In
most cases it is an appendage of the contemporary house. The simpler

the detailing of railings, stairs, and other elements the better, plus the important factor of sturdiness. The railing is especially important when it comes to strength, as people are apt to sit and lean on it, no matter how often you may forbid it. Railing supports should be securely fastened to the deck framing to provide adequate resistance to outward forces. Simple toe-nailing to the surface of the deck isn't enough; railing supports must be bolted to joists or beams or may be an extension of the supporting deck posts. Posts and railings can be decorative and many designs are possible.

When children use a deck, it is well to use some kind of grille or screening to protect them from falling through. Screening of this kind will allow breezes and view to be enjoyed and protect the tots. Again, if expanded or other forms of metal grille are used, be sure they are aluminum or galvanized iron. If the house is close to neighbors, the open railing space can be infilled with many kinds of decorative paneling for privacy. Frames with translucent plastic can be attached to the deck and railing; louvers which let air pass but prevent views are another solution. For greater protection, you can design and build a system of detachable 6- or 8-foot-high panels which can be held in place with hooks in screw eyes attached to rail and decking. It is a good idea to have grommeted holes in canvas panels or drilled holes in plastic sheeting to let air blow through, otherwise strong gusts may dislodge even the stoutest connection. That is, unless you have a specific wind problem and want panels as windbreakers, in which case you make them as tight as possible.

For the house of traditional architecture, you can use turned spindles for the railing or splat patterns and other motifs associated with Swiss Alpine ski lodges and rustic cottages. Wind and privacy screens, outdoor furniture and planting can also help to establish design style. Plantings are a basic part of deck living. If the deck is above ground, a planter can be installed at deck level or raised above it to give a visual break in the expanse of wood. Remember as you consider planters that they will increase the weight load on the deck greatly, as the earth is heavy, so you must detail your structural framing in advance to accommodate these loads.

As you plan your design, make sure that your deck and its adjacent indoor rooms work well together. Here is the place for sliding glass walls and full indoor-outdoor access, so that it becomes difficult to tell where one type of living begins and the other ends. As far as function is concerned, the same rule applies to decks as to terraces: keep them convenient to the kitchen for easy service of food and drinks. Don't rely on portable barbecues and other equipment to solve all your problems. There is still a lot of running back and forth for outdoor meals and it is wise to foresee it and minimize tie-ups with good positioning.

THE TOTAL SCHEME

As you plan your outdoor living world, remember to take all elements into consideration, just as you would with an interior room. Your floor may be a wood deck, weathered or new, flagstone paving, stone, brick, or concrete, and each one of these will help to dictate a color and pattern scheme. If it is wood, you have a natural expanse to play against, so you can be bold with bright colors and large patterns. If it is brick, which has so much pattern and a dominant color of its own, you are more limited: big expanses of solid colors may be better for chaises and sofas. If it is stone or flagstone, you'll need fresh, light colors to play against the grayness, while if it is marble, your choices will have to be carefully formal in pattern and color.

Similarly, the walls of the house will play a part. White clapboard will allow a free choice; brick or stone a more limited one. The materials themselves and the design of the house, its windows and other architectural features are important to consider. If your terrace has a wall with a bank of french windows leading into the living or dining room, they may dictate the beginning of a country, even rustic look in chintzy patterns and fresh colors. Very contemporary furniture in solids of primary colors wouldn't look nearly as good, but it would be perfect against an expanse of glass doors in a contemporary house. If part of your terrace is covered or you are decorating a porch, the ceiling must be taken into account. One way to jazz up an old porch is to paint its ceiling with bold stripes or a colorful stencil design or to cover it with gay fabric, draped like a tent or stretched and tacked flat. This will probably be the dominant note for the area, so you can play subtle color and pattern against it on the floor and wall, also in furniture and accessories. A trellis over the terrace dictates its pattern similarly, canvas awnings the same.

As you can see, the point is to play one element against another for visual contrast. Decorating the outdoor room is the same as doing an indoor one: it is a subtle tapestry, an intricate weaving of pattern, color, scale, and, above all, the emotional associations that we all have with these elements. If this all sounds too pretentious and elaborate for doing a simple porch or patio, keep in mind that the aim is not to be stuffy, but to spend your money wisely, no matter how much or little, and to arrive at the most comfortable, pleasant, and good-looking scheme you can. Many people with nothing but money can make an otherwise lovely terrace quite ordinary just by failing to understand these principles.

TERRACE STRUCTURES

The architecture of the garden is especially interesting, first perhaps because it is miniature and all of us are intrigued with the dollhouse concept, and second, because it has been associated with luxury, with the expensive estate and the large, important garden. Today it is no longer an extravagance but a practical and useful addition to outdoor living, rather than something to view in the distant landscape, as of old. The large terrace will most certainly need some form of protected living space whether it be an awninged pavilion, a trellised gazebo, a teahouse in the Japanese manner or a pool house, if the terrace in question borders a swimming area.

Again, the first rule in design is that the structure have some architectural relationship with the main house. It is an extension of the house, part and parcel of the property, so you can't give way to too much whimsy and have a pleasant effect. You can't, for example, have an aggressively oriental teahouse behind a pure French Provincial house complete with mansard and long shutters. They just won't mix. You can mix the Japanese house with a contemporary main house and a trellised or louvered gazebo with the French manor style. If you're in the slightest doubt, it is well to get professional architectural help; it will be worth the cost, because these little houses rely greatly for their charm on authenticity of detail and the trained designer knows such matters.

The structure needn't be large, but you'd want at least 100 square feet to make any use of it at all and 225 would be better. The latter would give you an area 15×15 feet, the former one, 10×10. The latter is enough to have a table and chairs for games or light refreshment. The former would provide enough area even for a mini-kitchen with a refrigerator, sink, and small electric cooktop in one 48-inch-long undercounter unit. This is a marvelously convenient adjunct for outdoor drinks and parties. Such a structure gives the terrace a lot more use: it is an evening party headquarters, with the bar and some seating under cover, dancing on the adjacent terrace.

The pool house needs to be somewhat larger. It must provide space for the filtering and heating equipment, if you have a warmed pool (and more and more families are stretching the swimming season this way) and also for changing and showering room or rooms. For the average pool and family, one changing area used by the sexes in turn is probably adequate. You'll also want the pool house to provide storage space for all the paraphernalia of poolside living—skimmer, cleaning, and vacuuming equipment, chaises and lounge chairs, towels and all the rest, plus some kind of wet bar and refrigerator setup. Because, you might as well face it, almost all summer outdoor living will be poolside, and unless you want to be lugging refreshments from the main kitchen incessantly, you may as well provide a minikitchen outdoors. Of course, the ideal pool location is as close to the house as possible, but this is not always feasible from the engineering standpoint and you may not want it from the visual standpoint. Some families like to view the pool as a reflecting pond at night and when it is not being used. However, it is well to remember that in areas where winters are long, the pool area can look quite dismal.

As far as materials for the garden structure are concerned, wood is the economical answer. A masonry structure would be prohibitive for most families. Plywood panels can be trimmed with shutters and stock ponderosa-pine moldings and then painted to provide any architectural style. A red cedar shingle roof will weather beautifully and, for a small expanse, is well within reach economically. And it will weather naturally, so there will be no maintenance. If the architecture of your main house is contemporary or in a provincial style, it is a good idea to use some of the new rough-sawed lumber or plywood that will weather without the need of any exterior finish. There are redwood, cedar, fir, and other panels that come in 4×8 feet and other modular sizes that can be easily and quickly installed over a light stud framework. Stock french-window panels or sliding glass doors can be added for access or you can have the openings completely accessible. The gazebo usually is open on two or more sides. And if you plan to use any type of garden house in the evening, you'll want it screened.

How to Create Privacy for Outdoor Rooms

This is one of the most desirable finishing touches of the terrace. Without it, if you have neighbors in close proximity, you have no outdoor living at all, and since this is the place for total relaxation in bathing suit or the most informal attire, you want to be as free as possible. There are several different ways to attain a measure of privacy outdoors; we say a measure, because unless you have vast acreage, total privacy in the open air is practically impossible. However, there are things you can do. First, case your terrace area in relation to neighbors' views. It is an easy matter to screen the side boundaries, but notice what they may see from their upper-story windows, if any. Then if you can afford one area of the patio to be covered, earmark space that would otherwise be on view from their upper rooms.

For the sides, you can use either fencing or planting. If you decide on the latter, choose pine, fir or cedar trees that will keep their foliage year round. Ask your garden center which of the nondeciduous trees are the fastest-growing and use these. Don't plant them too close together; follow your landscape dealer's instructions; remember, they will grow, and you don't want them to be cramped. If you decide on fencing, there are many designs and materials. Plastic panels that are translucent and let light through but not views can be framed in wood to make excellent screening devices. Be sure to check local ordinances to determine the allowable height in your area. It is usually 6 to 8 feet. Go as high as you can; 8-foot panels are recommended not only because they are higher, but also because most materials come in 4×8-foot modules and there is no waste.

Plywood in its many faces is excellent—and be sure you get the sheets that are manufactured expressly for use outdoors—specify exterior grade. It comes in 4×8 and 4×10-foot panels and can be painted or stained any finish you wish. There are forms other than the smooth sheets to consider—grooved, which gives an old-fashioned board-and-batten kind of look, rough-sawed, sand-blasted, etc. You can also nail batten strips at regular intervals for the colonial look. Check all of these before deciding. Plywood must be framed, that is, nailed to 2×4s or other heavy lumber. You are wise to use at least half-inch-thick plywood; anything less than that is apt to bend, no matter how carefully fastened to the frame.

Hardboard is an excellent screening material. Properly framed, it holds its shape outdoors if painted. It is good, however, to nail it to studs within the frame, 16 inches on center just like a real wall; that will help the material maintain its dimensional stability. Asbestos cement (now called mineral fiber) panels make good fences, too, and will weather durably and in fact get stronger over the years when exposed in their natural gray color. They can also be painted. These panels are heavy and, nailed to a frame of 2×4s, a 4×8-foot panel may need some diagonal bracing to make it wind-resistant. And while we're on this subject, it is good to take the vertical supports for these panels well into the ground, using lumber treated with pentachlorophenol or some other rot- and termite-proofing.

Remember, too, that any of the 4×8-foot panels can be cut in half lengthwise, if you feel that the full width is awkward. Then the breeze can bounce off the side of your wood screen and come in at the open top. You can also help with noise by making sure that your outdoor mechanical equipment, if any, is in tight enclosures. Water pumps, pool filters, window air conditioners, etc., all create sound which can be stopped from entering the surrounding area only by the sound waves hitting a solid material and stopping dead.

STORAGE

Few things help frayed nerves more than abundant storage, both inside the house and outdoors. Dragging pillows, folding furniture, and all soakable items, indoors at the first drop of rain is a bore which can be minimized by making provision for a good bin or locker right near the outdoor living and dining areas. It can be concealed behind a fence or some baffle or even be the lower part of a permanent cabinet along the rear wall of the house. The latter can have a handsome top which will serve as a buffet or console table. When the top is raised, you have a convenient and commodious bin for many items. Properly designed and built, it can serve as a location for winter-stored things.

THE LANDSCAPE ARCHITECT

Should you or shouldn't you use one? If you can afford a professional, it is always better to seek the advice of a sound, reputable one. And this goes for any home-centered need—interior decoration, architecture, kitchen-planning, etc. If you are spending a lot of money, they can guide you to better ways to get the most for it. They can also bypass a lot of pitfalls. Check the local chapter of ASLA (American Society of Landscape Architects) and contact a recommended one.* You can inquire as to his rates and decide whether you can afford him. For a flat fee, many will come and give you ideas, not only for terrace design, paving and materials but also recommend plants for various locations. If you want elaborate sketches and plans, of course, the fee will be higher. Some are willing to go further and contract the labor and supervise the project to completion for a percentage of the total expenditure.

However, if your ideas are fairly simple ones, you can plot the terrace or patio yourself. Here are a few helpful pointers. First, buy graph paper—quarter-inch scale is best—and make a drawing of the area you have to work with. Indicate the windows, doors, and other

* If there is no local chapter, write to American Society of Landscape Architects, 2013 Eye Street, Washington, D.C. 20006.

architectural features of the rear wall or walls of the house, the lot boundaries at the side, walls, fences, etc. that are close to the house and must be taken into account. Then make several versions of proposed terrace size and shape, keeping in mind your budget, space requirements, the size of the pieces of outdoor furniture and equipment you want to include, etc. If your landscape contractor or builder who will do the paving and other work can give you a rough idea of cost per square foot, so much the better. You can keep close touch with cost as you plan, since each square of the graph paper will represent a square foot of space.

Mark in any trees, shrubs, and other established planting you want to include. Once these elements are on paper, you will get a better idea of how they will work together. You will be able to juggle the various living, dining, and planting areas until you get the best solution, in terms of sun, prevailing breezes, convenience to the interior of the house for serving. Be sure to indicate a place for an outdoor storage locker or some space where you can keep equipment out of sight and out of the rain when necessary. Also indicate a drying yard, service area, or whatever your mode of living demands, locating and designing it for maximum convenience and unobtrusiveness. Make a list of all the elements you must include and then check them off as they are included in your drawing. Once you have completed it, review the whole design with your contractor. He will be able to suggest changes to make it more economical from his standpoint. Once these revisions are made, you are ready to go ahead with confidence.

CHAPTER SEVEN

POINTERS ON CREATING A RENTAL UNIT

MUCH that has been already written applies to a rental apartment you might care to make in your home as part of a remodeling plan.

There are economic advantages with a rental unit. The homeowner can live in the building, rent the unit, declare the income on his or her tax, but also deduct a portion of the home mortgage, any expenses for repairs and maintenance and a part of water, sewer, and whatever other charges the tenant does not pay. The house can be set up as income-producing property and depreciation can be taken on income tax—perhaps even a bit of the cost of maintaining the owner's unit, on the basis that he or she is conducting a business and uses telephone, automobile, in-home space, etc., in the course of gaining the rental income. A tax accountant can tell a homeowner what is legally possible in all this.

There are intangible advantages, too. If a family that owns and lives in the same structure as the apartment it rents is out of town, on vacation or whatever there is someone living on the premises to maintain security, keep an eye on things, water the garden, etc. If the tenant-owner relationship is a pleasant one, it is comforting to have someone else in the house who could help out in case of illness or accident. This is especially important to older, retired people who may be fearful about being alone in a big, old house.

The disadvantages include loss of privacy, the uncertainty of tenancy (although most cities have a shortage of apartments in good areas), and the problems of noise and mutual disturbance that sharing quarters under the same roof inevitably produces.

MAKE SURE YOU ARE ZONED FOR RENTAL

The first step is to be certain that your property is zoned for multiple dwellings. Go to your city planning department or building department and find out if you are so zoned and whether the zoning permits one, two, three, or whatever number of units. Some cities have ordinances which permit multiple dwellings provided that the building has off-street parking on a one-unit, one-car basis. This may affect how you remodel existing space. There will also be the matters of dual egress in case of fire, the necessity of smoke alarms, sprinkler systems, and metal fire escapes depending on the number of units you wish to include. In most cases, a two-family use of a building has far fewer restrictions than does a three- or four-unit building. There will also be height limitation ordinances that may affect your plans, if you were thinking of adding an additional story. Creating an apartment building takes you into a whole different world of city and state supervision and control, because of the need to protect tenants against fire, theft, and other possible dangers, so it is important to explore all the angles before entering this kind of home ownership.

In certain residential areas where rental units are illegal, there are, however, many so-called "in-law units" created without benefit of building permit. The risk with such is that, if they are discovered by the building department, the owner must rip them out, or pay a fine and get a variance which can be difficult. A guest suite is usually legal as long as it does not include a kitchen sink. This appliance seems to be the sticking point. In other words, there can be a makeshift kitchen for guests with a small refrigerator and an assemblage of small appliances—a toaster, hot plate, etc., but when a kitchen sink is installed the unit becomes rentable and as such illegal.

How a rental unit can be fitted into a single-family residence is an individual matter and it is usually wise to have an architect work with you. He or she is equipped to explore possibilities based on street access, the existing arrangement of rooms, possibilities for dual access, etc. We show here one example of how a large basement which had been a family room with cooking equipment first became a separate apartment for a relative and was later turned into a rental unit. The plans for each step are presented to show how the problem of separate dual access from the garage and into the garden were handled when the unit became income-producing. As long as the

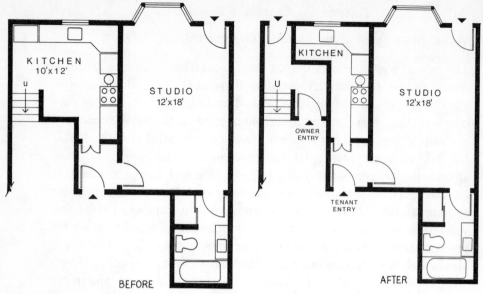

KITCHEN
10'x 12'

STUDIO
12'x18'

KITCHEN

OWNER
ENTRY

STUDIO
12'x18'

TENANT
ENTRY

BEFORE

AFTER

Floor Plan By Thomas L. Bastianon

For photographs of apartment see the top of page 48.

apartment was inhabited by a family member, the owner who lived upstairs was able to walk through the unit either to go from garage to quarters upstairs or to pass through the unit en route to the garden. Obviously this was no longer acceptable when the apartment was occupied. The plans show how this problem was solved. See also the first color section for photograph.

How to Make a Rental Unit Rentable

Here are a few pointers of items to include to make an apartment attractive to tenants. A good kitchen is especially important and, if possible, with a dishwasher. Most tenants are busy working people who look for time-saving devices; they don't mind a compact kitchen as long as it has as much automatic equipment as possible. A laundry with washer and dryer for use by the whole building is important, too, installed in some common area such as the furnace room or garage. If possible, vent the dryer outdoors, as it tends to expel humid air. Doorbells and automatic entrance door opening with a buzzer system and a vocal annunciator are important, too, in areas where security is a problem. Be sure to include plenty of storage space in your plans for a rental unit; nobody ever has enough closets and it is a good idea to provide a locked storage area in the garage or some common area.

A dressing room or an area of the bath with good lighting, a make-up or grooming counter, and big closets is a tenant-getting feature. Be sure to include a tub-shower combination. A stall shower as the only bathing convenience will turn off a lot of prospects; these days a lot of women, and men too, like to soak away tensions in a tub. Provide a big medicine cabinet, behind a hinged mirror and/or in a cabinet under the lavatory counter. A standing or wall-hung washbasin, as noted earlier, wastes valuable storage space. A far better solution is a basin embedded into a laminate counter which rests on a storage cabinet. Be sure to have good lighting at this area; strips of incandescent bulbs at each side of the lavatory mirror are the best illumination for make-up, shaving, and general grooming. If carpet is permitted by code it is a good solution for underfoot comfort, provided that it is loose and can be taken up and cleaned. An extra strip around the base of the toilet is advised.

Make the living and sleeping areas, no matter how small, as light as possible. Add as many windows as tenant privacy permits. A bay window with window seat is attractive because it gives tenants a sit-down area in addition to the furniture they may have. Painted walls are preferable to wallpapered, because while one pattern may please a certain tenant, another may dislike it. Paint walls white, off-white or a light neutral color like beige or gray. Everyone's furniture looks better against a light background. Draperies or whatever window treatment you provide should also be light-toned, preferably blending with the wall color to make the space seem larger. Carpet is a good choice for both living and sleeping areas, especially if your remodeling calls for plywood subfloor or you want to cover a poor existing wood floor. It then becomes more economical than hard-surface flooring. Buy a good grade of carpet with a fiber content recommended for easy cleaning. Again, a light neutral color is best, as most people feel comfortable with it. However, if you have good wood floors in the areas made into the apartment, sand and refinish them, adding a urethane or some other protective top surface. A medium walnut stain is a good finish, as a too-light tone looks old-fashioned and a too-dark one will show the dirt and wear. If you decide on vinyl tile or linoleum over the plywood subfloor or over bad existing wood, again select a neutral color and a quiet, subtle pattern. You will, of course, have to put down hardboard over the old floor first for a smooth surface.

If possible by all means arrange some kind of outdoor living, even if it may only be a balcony or a tiny part of a garden. Most people like to have a few plants or some living growth around them. If direct outdoor access isn't possible, you might consider a greenhouse window and certainly a window looking out on greenery. Lightwells can be turned into window gardens and, like a prefab greenhouse window, can be the location of potted plants that give a room an attractive focal point. A wood-burning fireplace is another distinct plus in an apartment. Almost everyone has an atavistic yearning for the glow of a friendly fire. If there is a fireplace or even a chimney in a room of the apartment, by all means open up the flue or rebuild it to make a workable fireplace. A Franklin stove or some other prefab unit can also be hooked up to an existing chimney or you can vent the flue pipe through a wall or leave it exposed atop the unit and vent it through the roof, using a prefab chimney on the rooftop.

Be sure that separate meters are arranged for gas and electric service. In cases where these utilities are included in the rent, it can lead to misunderstandings where a landlord feels the tenant is using too much energy fuel. In this light, it is also wise where possible to have a separate heating system for the apartment, so that these charges go directly to the tenant. Radiant electric baseboard heating is relatively economical to install and is effective, but it can be costly to operate depending on the care a tenant takes. The baseboard units are on individual room control, so if the tenant turns thermostats down or off in rooms not used during the day, money can be saved. Where tenants work during the day and turn down the thermostat, this kind of heating is economical. Of course, in cold climates rooms that have water pipes must be kept at least at 55° F.

Perhaps the most important element to include in a rental apartment is privacy—for both tenant and landlord. Inevitably, there are times—like when the rent is a few days overdue—when the tenant doesn't want to encounter his landlord and times—like when the landlord has not made a repair he promises—that he doesn't want to bump into the tenant. Also there are always points of contention when any two households are under the same roof. For all these reasons, it is important to create access to both their units separately. If possible, have each outside entrance on a different wall of the building. If both must use the same garage, have separate spaces clearly marked where each belongs. Have responsibility for payment of trash collection, water, and any other services spelled out in a lease. Above all, make certain that sound conditioning is built into your remodeling plans. Insulate between floors if the rental unit is above or below your own quarters, taking up the floor to add this, if necessary. Common walls should be double-studded with blanket insulation wrapped between the studs to reduce sound transmission to a minimum. Nothing raises tempers more than too-loud hi-fi music coming through the walls, either direction. Carpeted floors, acoustical tile ceilings, heavy drapery—all these will help absorb sounds within rooms. Another good way to cut down sound transmission is to build clothes closets along common walls. In fact, any kind of bulk storage in a closet with a solid door will help cut the passage of sound. The sum of all or even part of these details will add up to considerable cost, but all are niceties which will pay off in terms of good tenants and less turnover, plus higher rents.

CHAPTER EIGHT

APARTMENT REMODELING

How and When Is It Feasible?

If you own a condominium or cooperative apartment, it makes sense to remodel it on the same conditions and for the same reasons as you would remodel a house you owned. So all the previous discussion of evaluation holds for this kind of dwelling. However, in the case of the rented apartment, you are faced with an entirely different set of factors. Generally speaking, it is foolish to invest a lot of money changing living quarters that somebody else owns, unless the landlord agrees to underwrite part or all of the remodeling expenses or is willing to deduct them from the rent you pay. There is another pitfall in renovating a rental unit: the lease indicates that any attached improvements become the property of the landlord. So as you plan improvements, be sure they are ones you can take with you when you move. There are ways to include built-ins so that they slide out and can be dismantled and go along with your furniture. If you wallpaper, the landlord can be nasty and insist that it be removed or that he have it removed and bill you for it. If you substitute light fixtures, keep the ones that go with the place and put them back before you leave. As mentioned before, it is usually not economically feasible to make a lot of permanent improvements in an apartment, unless you have a long lease at low rent. In that case, you can amortize the improvements to make them sound. For example, if you have a five-year lease and put two thousand dollars into a new kitchen sink and bath fixtures, the pleasure you derive from these improvements may be well worth the dollars a month extra you will be paying.

Before you move in, be sure to buy a quart or so of the paint mix from the painter who redecorates the apartment. It will be helpful for touch-ups, matching the built-ins you may add, etc. Usually the painting contractor is on the premises when you are looking at apartments and you can, for a small tip, buy a quantity of your particular mix. And speaking of paint, you usually have a choice of four or five fairly muted and neutral shades. By all means, select off-white or white, light beige or gray; avoid the greens and pinks. The most neutral shade is the easiest to live with in small space and is easiest to decorate around.

Replanning Your Space

The ultimate aim in the small apartment is to get as much visual and living variety as possible. Each area should be planned so that you have a feeling of being in a separate space, and yet all must be planned together for over-all visual harmony. It is difficult, but it can be done.

First of all, if the entrance door opens right into the main room, you may want to create the sense of a foyer for privacy, which can be done with a folding screen or some kind of baffle. Most buildings are a standard 8 feet high, so one or two panels of 4×8-foot plywood can be used. One interesting approach is to have two panels cut to provide four 2×8-foot sections which can be joined with butterfly or two-way hinges and either painted to blend or contrast with walls or wallpapered. For an investment under ninety dollars, you can have something good-looking which can move with you and always be used somewhere in a future home.

Next, you can concentrate on your largest room. Just because it includes four walls, it doesn't have to be a single space. There are ways to partition areas according to function and to give privacy and variety. If the kitchen is off the part of the space closest to the entrance, as is usually the case, you can take, say, eight feet and form a dining foyer by installing plywood panels coming out from each side wall, with a space in the middle leading to a sleeping-living area or extending only from one wall, creating a passage to the rest of the space at one side. By positioning the panels cleverly, you can also create privacy from the entrance door. If light is a problem and you don't want to create a dark foyer, you can use translucent plastic panels, framed in wood like Japanese shojis (they can even slide to go all the way across the space); or another idea is to use old paneled doors, which can often be bought from demolition contractors for as little as a few dollars apiece. By hinging them or adding plywood to top of bottom to get floor-to-ceiling height, you can create a handsome partition for little money. It can be painted, or, if you are very ambitious, the doors can be stripped of paint to the natural wood and stained, to accent the rest of your decorative scheme. If you do the project yourself, here is the way. To attach the doors, fillers, ceiling track, or whatever, you'll need metal plugs, angle irons, and screws. Side walls of plaster present no problems, but if the ceiling is concrete, you'll need a heavy-duty electric drill. Use a bit the size of the lead plug, insert it in the hole, and use screws to attach the panel (which already has one part of the angle iron attached) to the lead plug and hole. The lead will expand as you drive in, making a tight bond.

Depending on the location of windows, it may be possible to partition to form two completely separate rooms. This is often feasible in a corner apartment with windows on two walls. If the apartment is a two-and-a-half with an ell which has a window, it is an easy matter to close this off as a separate sleeping room, or if you prefer to use dual-purpose bedding in the living room, the ell can be a private study. Here you will have to include one hinged panel for access. You can even frame in a regular door or merely hinge one 4×8-foot plywood panel to open. A ceiling track for drapery or narrow, hinged panels can also be used clear across the opening, with panels accordion-folding to one side as you need access.

Speaking of plywood, remember that there are many grades and several sizes. The least expensive is the common fir plywood, which has a heavy, rather ordinary grain. This is quite satisfactory if you are planning to paint or paper it. Be sure to pick out your panels at the lumber yard, if possible. Be sure to get at least one good side free of knots and indentations and two good ones, if the screen or paneling is to be exposed on both sides. For better appearance, choose one of the many other wood finishes—oak, birch, even teak and rosewood, if you prefer. And again, if the panels are to be seen on both sides, specify two-faced panels. While you are at the lumber yard, study the variety of stock ponderosa-pine moldings that are available. They can be used across the top of a partition to hide disparities, fillers, etc., and can be stained or painted to blend. Molding can also be used at the base and can be chosen to blend with the usual clamshell molding used in most new buildings as baseboard. If you don't do the project yourself, specify to the carpenter what you want or go with him to the lumber yard and choose the items together. He'll be amazed and pleased that you know something about it, and it will help to arrive at a meeting of the minds. Nothing is more discouraging than being "surprised" by what a carpenter does.

APARTMENT IDEAS TO STUDY

Floor treatment

When it comes to floors, the usual fare in apartments is oak strip or oak block for the main area, ceramic tile in the bath, and asphalt or vinyl tile in the kitchen. If the building is new and you rent before the wood floors are finished, you may have a choice of light or dark. Most building managements will finish the oak the standard blond way, in the mistaken belief that most people prefer it and that it is "safe." Actually, dark floors are considered by discriminating apartment dwellers not only more attractive as a background for furniture and other decor, but also more space-extending and more practical. So if you can control the initial finish, specify a medium-dark walnut with a liquid urethane coating, topped with urethane and a coat or two of paste wax, machine-buffed. That will give you a floor that will hold up attractively with routine care.

Carpet for the main room is another matter. It can be costly, and although you can take the carpet with you when you move, it seldom if ever fits another space. However, a piece 12 or 15 by 22 feet or so is a general size that can be trimmed and bound relatively inexpensively to serve as an area carpet in another home. It can be cut to give two 9×12-foot pieces which are always useful, so you may decide it is a good investment. It is certainly easier than having floors scraped and refinished. If you decide on carpet, keep it a light, neutral shade that will blend with your color scheme. In fact, if your walls are light gray or beige, carpet in the same tone will make the place seem quite large. Such neutral color will prove to be more useful in a later home, also.

If you want the streamlined look of vinyl tile and one of the many decorative effects it makes possible, there are ways to install it so that it can come up when you leave. Vinyl tile is expensive, and this is usually a consideration, plus the fact that there may be the danger of having to pay for its removal if it is semipermanently installed. And remember that with today's mastic, it has to be literally dug up off the floor for removal, which is costly. An alternative is to put down heavy kraft paper over the wood floor with double-faced mastic tape, using the tape along the borders and joints only. Then the tile can be installed over the paper with regular cement. When it comes time to move, the tile will come up fairly easily and chances are it can be used again. In small areas—foyers, kitchens, baths, entranceways—vinyl tiles can be put down individually with double-faced mastic tape. Foot pressure and gravity will assure a tight bond. A large space like the main living area may not respond to this type of installation, and, in addition, it is a time-consuming and tedious chore which you probably would have to do yourself, since a professional tile installer would not want to take the time to put each tile down on tape. If you decide on this method, be sure to buy 12-inch-square tiles rather than 9 inch, since there will be less taping involved.

Various patterns of vinyl can create the illusion of extended space. Alternating light and dark tiles laid on the diagonal like a checkerboard can lead the eye beyond room dimensions. Other pattern possibilities are limitless. If you create a highly patterned design, however, keep other elements in the room plain—drapery, upholstery, etc., to avoid a too-busy look that will seem confining. Usually the best solution with tile is the same as with carpet, a light, neutral, or white (if you don't mind the maintenance problem white always brings).

If you retain the existing wood floor or put down tile, you will also want area rugs. Choose them as an integral part of your color and pattern scheme, whether they be orientals, plain broadloom, the new textured Moroccan, Spanish, or other accent rugs. Area rugs can be most helpful in the one-room apartment to define various areas. For example, you can demarcate a sitting area of sofa, a pair of chairs, and a coffee table with one rug, a dining area with another, a TV corner with a third. A foyer that opens directly into a living room can be made to seem like an entity with a rug. If your floors are slick wood, be sure to put down rubber underlayment to guard against slipping. If several area rugs are used, they should relate to one another color- and pattern-wise, or you will create a hodgepodge that looks cluttered. Also, do not change styles of rugs: if you want orientals, use all orientals and preferably the same kind—Hamadan, Herez, or whatever. You can't mix Moroccan, American Indian, and oriental. It can be interesting to use rugs of the same style and pattern, but in different colorations that are part of your color plan. That way you get variety and demarcation but also design harmony.

Lighting tips

Standard apartment illumination is meager and uninspiring—inexpensive and unattractive ceiling fixtures in foyer, kitchen, and bath, plus the legally required minimum of base plugs and wall outlets. To gain drama in the foyer or living area if it has a ceiling fixture, invest in a handsome chandelier, take down the existing fixtures and put them away for replacement when you leave, and install your own. An electrician can do this for you at nominal cost. An elegant crystal and iron or brass ceiling fixture will go a long way toward creating an interesting entrance into the apartment and one in the living area will make it gain importance as a substantial home rather than a temporary shelter. Proper scale is vital with a chandelier: a too-small one looks puny and a too-large one overpowering. A 12- or 15-foot-wide room can take a fixture three feet in diameter nicely and perhaps even 40 inches. It is better to overscale slightly than the opposite. Be sure to select one, however, that doesn't drop too far into the room; you'll want at least 80 inches of clearance from the floor. So if you have the standard 8-foot ceiling height, you'll need a broad, shallow fixture. There are some handsome ones in Colonial Williamsburg style with shallow, sweeping branches for candlelike bulbs. Study the catalogs in the electrical shop in your neighborhood and look for one with a depth of 20 inches or so.

There isn't too much that can be done in the bath unless you want to replace the chandelier there too. There is most always a fluorescent fixture of some kind for mirror illumination. Unfortunately it is usually over the mirror, which is the worst kind for grooming, since it is so unflattering. You can buy fluorescent strips to flank each side of the mirror, which is the preferable kind of light. If you are in an older building with a too-high bath ceiling, a simple and relatively inexpensive way to gain intimacy and good light at the same time is with a dropped luminous ceiling. A fluorescent fixture with two or three tubes can be installed in the existing outlet; then a metal strip is fastened around the room at the height you desire. Into this a metal grid fits which holds panels of translucent plastic, either flat or corrugated. This goes a long way toward modernizing a bath and is worth the money, if you have a long lease. The same treatment is excellent in the older kitchen, providing shadow-free illumination that is so restful while meals are being prepared.

In the kitchen, undercabinet fluorescent strips are a must. If they are not already there, you can buy fluorescent units—the same kind used vertically to flank the bath mirror can be installed horizontally under cabinets to give marvelous work light where you need it. In a new building where ceilings are not high, the insignificant ceiling fixture can be replaced or given new interest with whimsical paper covers such as the Japanese ones which simulate Tiffany stained-glass globes. The regular oriental paper lantern can be fastened around the fixture, too, to give a pleasant and strong white light. Incidentally, use a bulb of good wattage, at least 150, to keep the kitchen from being a dungeon.

Storage

When one thinks that even millionaires in mansions bemoan the lack of storage space, the plight of the apartment dweller seems especially acute. Apartments vary greatly in number and size of closets. Standard fare consists usually of a closet near the entrance and another, larger one, either adjacent if there is a longish hall off the foyer, or off the main room. If the unit has a sleeping ell, there is apt to be a clothes closet between it and the bath and often a small linen closet on the opposite wall. A medicine cabinet and wall clothes hamper in the bath and base and wall cabinets in the kitchen complete the storage inventory. If it is a large apartment, each bedroom is apt to have a sizable sliding door closet. If the bedrooms are large and there are other windowless walls, it may be a good idea to create some additional closet space. If you do, be sure it looks architectural—that is, like part of the original structure with fronts that go to the ceiling and closet doors that blend with the original.

Bath

Here you will probably find a five-foot tub with a shower and ceramic tile enclosure, toilet, and lavatory, either wall-hung, or, in the better new buildings, recessed into a cabinet with a hinged door giving access to shelves for medicines and bath supplies and also to plumbing controls for emergencies. There will also be a wall medicine cabinet, with hinged, mirrored door. By law in most areas the floor must be ceramic tile and the baseboard marble.

The bath will probably be an interior room with a wall or ceiling opening to a central vent. Sometimes there is a vent-fan that goes on when the electric light switch is activated. This is usually not enough air in summer, and a portable fan is helpful. There will not be auxiliary heat, so a small heater will be a comfort, too. There will be a wall plug near the lavatory for electric hair dryer, shaver, etc., and it can be the source of power for a combination sun-lamp-heater which can be positioned for sunning while you groom yourself at the mirror.

If your lavatory is wall-hung or on legs with exposed pipes below, it may be useful to have the carpenter create a closed cabinet to make use of this wasted space. With shelves and a hinged door, towels and bath supplies can be stored there. Once again, look up—see if there is wasted space up high. If so, shelves for towels and special equipment or for out-of-season clothes in attractive boxes can be installed. You may have to supplement the meager offering of one or two towel racks. A clothesline in the tub area is usually a must for an apartment dweller; there are new devices which pull the line out of a concealed holder which attaches unobtrusively to one end wall.

A piece of carpet is a nice touch in the bath, and its color can be coordinated with adjoining rooms for continuity, or, if you prefer, a sharply contrasting tone. Sometimes it is interesting to decorate the bath as a powder room in dramatic contrast to other areas of the small apartment. In which case, treat yourself to an elaborate wall-covering (make sure it's vinyl-surfaced); since little is required, you can afford to splurge on this and on the carpet. Beautiful towels, bath mat, etc., are investments that move with you.

Kitchen

Most new apartments are fairly standard when it comes to size and equipment in the kitchen. It is usually a smallish corridor or U-shaped arrangement with fewer cabinets than one would like, with a dishwasher, most often a gas range-oven, and a refrigerator with a freezer compartment. To this you may want to add a trash compactor and/or a waste disposer. Counter space may be limited, so you may want to provide laminate-topped, drop-down counters hinged to the wall or the door for extra work area. The rest is a matter of decoration to your taste. When storage space is limited one good idea is to make pots and pans part of wall decor or buy a black iron or metal pot rack which can be hung from the ceiling with hooks for your cookware. Condiment shelves and see-through storage bins for staples —flour, sugar, etc.—can also go on the wall, providing extra cabinet space for china and glassware. If space permits, another useful adjunct is a mobile work island, with either a chopping block or laminated top, which can be rolled wherever you need it, perhaps even to the dining table like a tea cart.

In the older co-op or condominium apartment, it is likely that the kitchen will be antiquated or not up to present-day work requirements. In that case, you can proceed with remodeling the same as with a house kitchen, described in an earlier chapter. If one or more major appliances can be retained, so much the better. If they are copper-toned, white, avocado, keep to the same color with whatever new appliances you buy. These older apartments sometimes have fairly large kitchens so that you will have good space to work with and can plan plenty of storage space in your new cabinets. Or you may be able to salvage the existing ones, having a carpenter refit them for easy opening, equip them with magnetic catches and new, good-looking hardware. It's also possible to keep the cabinet structure and replace the doors in any style you want. Don't make do with obsolete lighting. You're in the kitchen a lot and it is hard on the eyes and the temper. Think of a luminous ceiling with diffused plastic panels in a grid system for excellent shadow-free illumination. Be sure to have undercabinet fluorescents installed for point-of-use lighting where you work. If space permits, include a home office—desk, chair, and telephone. The apartment kitchen is the place to consider compact, new multi-use appliances. For example, there is a console unit which combines a cooktop, high oven, and a dishwasher below the cooking surface. There is also a compact, 24-inch-wide washer-dryer if you like to have the laundry in the kitchen. This can be a good solution for an apartment, because plumbing lines are already established in this room.

CHAPTER NINE

THE TURN-AROUND HOUSE: A CASE STUDY

A COMMON PRACTICE with houses built over thirty years ago was to locate the living room at the street side. Sometimes there was a big front porch with windows looking into the living room, the idea being that it was important to be aware of what was going on in the neighborhood. This was commonplace not only in city homes but also with those in the country or suburbs. Whatever part of the property was at the rear was considered utilitarian, to be used for drying clothes, keeping a watchdog, or perhaps for a small vegetable garden. In the last twenty years the concept has changed, in part because of the emphasis on outdoor living. Families began thinking in terms of private relaxation in the garden, and so the back yard, as we have seen earlier, began to be thought of as an outdoor room, a terrace or patio.

The obvious corollary, of course, was that the basic plan of the house had to be changed to fall in line with this idea: the plan had to be reversed. Instead of having the kitchen or bedrooms or any nonliving areas at the rear of the house, the thought was to move the living room to the rear with access to the garden or at least to a view of the garden. At the same time it made a lot more sense to locate the kitchen and service areas at the street side for easy delivery of food and other supplies. Not every older home could be adapted in this fashion from the standpoint of either structure or economy, but where it was possible the livability of the house was greatly improved.

HOW A 1932 HOUSE LENT ITSELF TO A NEW PLAN

Here is a case study of a modest house built in 1932, a type of plan and design style found in many cities across the country. Of doubtful architectural lineage, it was, when built, classified as Spanish stucco

Floor Plan by Thomas L. Bastianon

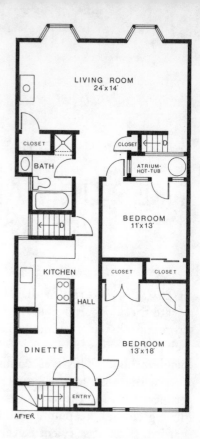

LIVING ROOM
24' x 14'

CLOSET

BATH

CLOSET   D

ATRIUM-
HOT-TUB

D

BEDROOM
11' x 13'

KITCHEN

CLOSET   CLOSET

HALL

DINETTE

BEDROOM
13' x 18'

U   ENTRY

AFTER

BEDROOM

BEDROOM

CLOSET

CLOSET   CLOSET

BATH

ATRIUM

D

DINING ROOM

KITCHEN

DINETTE   LIVING ROOM

U   ENTRY

BEFORE

DECK

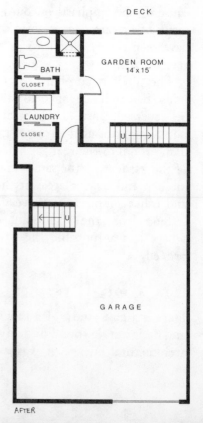

BATH

CLOSET

GARDEN ROOM
14' x 15'

LAUNDRY

CLOSET

U

U

GARAGE

AFTER

style. The structure 50×24 feet, comprised 1,200 square feet of living space on the upper floor which included two bedrooms, living room with fireplace, dining room, kitchen, bath, and small entrance foyer. Below this was a ground floor of the same dimensions with space for two cars, the furnace and water heater, with two windows and a door opening to the rear garden. The living room, which faced the street, was relatively small, 18×13 feet, and was entered from the foyer through an archway. At the rear next to an inglenook wood-burning fireplace were two paneled doors which could be open or closed to the dining room. Across the foyer in the other direction was a paneled door to a dinette which opened directly to the kitchen. The two bedrooms, each 12×14 feet, were at the rear and had a panoramic water view plus a view of the garden.

Since the dinette-kitchen area was at the front of the house with established water and gas lines, it made sense to turn the plan around and make the bedrooms into one large 14×24 feet living room. The existing living room then became a pleasantly sized master bedroom with the nicety of a fireplace. In turn, the dining room became a second bedroom. The addition of closets for both bedrooms claimed space from the erstwhile dining room. New dining was arranged at a bay window in the living room and the dinette was kept for informal meals.

A new central hall had to be created

The main architectural problem was the lack of a central hall. As the plan existed, the only access from the foyer to the rear of the house was either through the kitchen to the left or through the living and dining rooms to the right. Both routes lead to a rear hall with doors to both bedrooms and to the bath. (See before plan.) The answer was to demolish the coat closet in the foyer, borrow kitchen space (where the range had been located), and make a new central hall, patching with new oak-strip flooring to blend with the existing floor and with gypsum board to blend with adjacent plaster walls.

Another ambitious part of the new plan was the creation of a suite of sitting room and bath-laundry in the rear of the lower-floor garage space. The concept was of a garden room with access to a deck and the garden beyond, a kind of informal sitting room which could double for guests with a sofa bed (or, with a regular bed, it could serve as a master bedroom with its own bath). Big sliding-door closets in the bath could then serve both husband and wife. A washer and dryer were included for convenience, and the bath would have a shower for use after sunbathing.

Before and After: Exterior of Spanish-style town house was left unchanged except for painting. Typical of the 1930s, it has counterparts everywhere. Façade belies space within: three bedrooms, two baths, big living room.

Before: Former living room at the front of the house had corner inglenook fireplace, double-paneled doors to dining room.

After: Former living room became a large, new bedroom with a fireplace. Doors to dining room were removed and wall closed except for door to closet. Casing and door of old hall closet were moved to new location here.

Before: Entry door opened onto a tiny foyer and directly ahead, a small coat closet. This was removed to create the central hall.

After: New central hall leads directly to rear living room. Space was borrowed from the old kitchen and hall closet; oak strip flooring was patched for continuity.

Since demolition and reconstruction were extensive, the house was stripped of furnishings, leaving only the carpet in the former living room, which was wanted for the new master bedroom. In mid-May, a building permit was applied for at the city's Bureau of Building Inspection along with before and after plans for both levels drawn to scale on graph paper. At that time a team of carpenters, a plumbing company, and an electrical contractor were lined up to begin work within the month. Work began mid-June with the permission of the building inspector to do everything except take down the bearing wall between the two rear bedrooms, since the Bureau felt that calculations were required from a structural engineer for that step of the remodeling. A licensed structural engineer was engaged who submitted drawings and calculations to the Bureau of Inspection early in July, which were promptly approved.

Reconstruction retained original detailing

To keep architectural continuity, all existing paneled doors, original hardware, door frames, etc., were kept and moved to new locations. For example, the archway from the foyer to the old living room was rebuilt into a stud-wall opening into which a door previously used between living and dining rooms was installed. Another door, formerly of the foyer coat closet, became the entrance to the new master bedroom closet. A second door that had been part of the pair between the living and dining rooms was combined with a swinging door from the kitchen to form sliding closet doors for the second bedroom in what was dining space. All casings and door frames were carefully removed and put aside during demolition, because the moldings were of a kind no longer available. As it turned out, there were just enough moldings to frame the new openings. The original Art Deco door hardware was brass and, buffed with fine steel wool, gleamed as of old. All of this proves, perhaps, that even older homes of modest architectural significance have interesting details that are well worth keeping, even treasuring. And unless the new remodeling concept calls for a complete change of architectural style, it is important to save what exists and use it for decorative continuity.

The kitchen lost about twenty square feet of space to the new center hall. However, the new area, $7\frac{1}{2}'\times8\frac{1}{2}'$, was adequate for an L-shaped work center with a compact arrangement of refrigerator with ice maker, sink and new gas range in an efficient triangle. A dishwasher was installed under an existing counter, borrowing a bit of depth space from a stairwell to the garage. The old sink and its tiled counter and splash were retained, while a double-hung window nearby was replaced with a new aluminum-framed casement opening over the sink counter. A roof projection in this lightwell permitted a kitchen window garden to be made with redwood decking and trellis. Illuminated by a floodlight at night, it creates a colorful picture and offers extra work light at the sink area. The existing cabinets were retained, the doors being refitted and equipped with new hardware. New cabinets to blend with the old had to be made for the wall built to define the new hall. A wall cabinet was fitted with an exhaust to the roof for a vent hood over the range; a new bank of base cabinet with laminate counter stands to the right of the range.

One of the most pleasant features of the old house was a small atrium opening from the former dining room via a french door. This became a plant-filled adjunct to the second bedroom. The clapboard wall opposite the atrium door was opened up and a 4×5-foot fixed glass panel was installed, permitting a view from the bedroom through the living room and to the water beyond. On the other side this panel lights the stairwell to the garden room downstairs. To hide pipes and other eyesores in the lightwell of the neighboring house, a diffused-glass panel was installed at one end of the atrium. An outdoor electrical outlet makes possible night lighting up through the plants, which gives exotic illumination viewed from both the living room and the bedroom. The atrium also became the location for a recessed hot tub.

The living room was an ambitious project

The most complicated part of the project from the structural standpoint was the creation of the 14×24-foot living room, made possible by taking down the common wall of the two former bedrooms. New supports had to be devised to hold the roof structure in place when the stud wall came down. Main support is a 10×12-inch joist which rests on a post embedded in the outside wall at one end and, at the other, rests on a new lintel supported by posts which carry the thrust down through supports in the lower floor. This formed the new opening from the center hall into the living room. A heating duct from the forced-warm-air furnace which had run to bedroom outlets in the wall now removed, had to be rerouted to a new location in the floor of the living room.

Where the partition wall had been, new oak-strip flooring had to be laid just as oak strips filled the areas of the center hall which had formerly been closet and kitchen. Then the living room and hall floors were sanded and refinished in medium walnut tone. At the end of the living room toward the best part of the view, a wood-burning fireplace was built with a stud wall enclosing a prefabricated metal firebox and flue. Surfaced in gypsum board, it was painted the soft beige color of the new room. A black slate hearth was added, trimmed with molding stained to blend with the oak floor. At the other end of the room, a delicate railing of wood spindles and banister delineates the stairway to the garden room below. The big new living room seems spacious beyond its dimensions because of two large bay windows, originally bedroom windows. At the end of the room near the fireplace a former bedroom closet has been kept for general storage.

Before: At the rear of the house, two doors led to bedrooms. Since these had the big water view, partition wall was taken down to form the new 24 by 14-foot living room.

After: New living room comprises space of two former bedrooms. A fireplace was installed at one end. Oak floor was patched where partition had rested. Heavy new joist was added to support roof structure. Room commands view of garden and San Francisco Bay.

Part of the garage is now a garden room

On the lower level a platform was built over the concrete garage floor to form the new combination guest-sitting-garden room, 14×15 feet. Small rear garage windows were replaced with an 8-foot expanse of sliding glass panels which lead to a deck of 2×6-inch hemlock stained driftwood. The deck, 8×12 feet, has two steps down to the garden pavement which is stained a terra cotta color. A new bath with shower and dressing area opens off the garden room in a space that once housed old laundry tubs, so that existing water lines could be tapped. A rear door from the garage to the garden was replaced with a panel of tempered glass which became the rear wall of a stall shower-with-a-view, possible because the garden has total privacy from neighbors. All the new electrical lines and furnace ducts were concealed above a luminous ceiling of translucent plastic panels in an aluminum grid, with three four-foot fluorescent strips located for maximum light over grooming and dressing areas. New plumbing included a drain connected to the main garage drainage system and new copper piping to counter lavatory, shower, toilet, and washer.

Before: At the rear of the basement-garage of the Turn-Around House the semblance of a room had been constructed. Its only virtue was that it could be opened onto the garden. As raw space, it could be remodeled to any use.

After: The need in this case was for a combination room that could serve as informal living room, garden room, and, when guests were in residence, guest quarters. Access is two ways: independently through the garage from the street or via a stairway that was built from the living room above. Understair space was filled in with bookshelves and a unit with hi-fi and TV.

After: Biggest change was replacement of the small, dreary windows with an eight-foot expanse of sliding glass doors. A deck was added beyond for indoor-outdoor access. A sofa bed does double duty. Other furniture includes light chairs that can be easily moved when the bed is opened. A table provides guests with a place to dine, play games, write letters. At other times it is a family game table. Guest bath is again multipurpose: it has twin louvered sliding-door closets for guests' gear and so serves as a dressing room (see page 193). It is also the home's laundry. Interesting feature is a shower which overlooks the completely private terrace and backyard.

Floor joists were installed to the same level as the garden room and the plywood subfloor was covered in linoleum which simulates quarry tile, chosen to keep the same feeling as the hand-painted Mexican tile used for the shower and the lavatory counter. The garden room plywood subfloor was covered with underlayment and carpet.

The work covered a period from mid-June to mid-August, a short time considering the scope of the project, and made possible because the owner subcontracted the work and dovetailed the various plumbing, electrical, and carpentry elements, supervising the work closely. The owner also did some painting, although the big expanses of new living room, kitchen, and hall were painted professionally.

PART FOUR

Project Specifics

CHAPTER TEN

REMODELING VERSUS RESTORATION

IF YOU HAVE a house of some vintage, the thought may have crossed your mind that, while you are improving the structure, perhaps it is time you made the most of its architectural heritage. In short, you may wonder if you should "restore" it. That brings up the question, what is the difference between remodeling and restoration? It is a provocative question and one that is not the easiest to answer, because while restoration inevitably requires remodeling, the opposite is not true.

Not long ago friends took me to a home in the East that they said had been "fabulously redone." The owner kindly gave me the five-dollar tour, at the end of which she mentioned what a marvelous experience it had been "restoring" her two-hundred-year-old house. At this remark she saw I looked puzzled. "Oh," she said, "you're like everyone else. You can't believe it's an old house, because we've restored it so thoroughly." Puzzled I was, because the woman had not restored the structure but rather remodeled it. In her zeal to create a home that looked up-to-the-minute, she had covered up or destroyed almost every vestige of the old.

The experience got me to thinking again about what the two words mean, the differences between them and the perils of confusing one with the other. *Restoration* implies a period house—Victorian, Thirties Art Deco, Spanish, French Country, or Tudor English, to name a few styles that were endlessly copied in the nineteen twenties, thirties, and forties. Every change that is made should extend the basic, existing style.

For the traditionalist, nothing can beat the charm of an older home, provided it has all the comforts of a new one. Even a person who gets dewy-eyed over a run-down Victorian soon loses enthusiasm when it comes to coping with a dilapidated kitchen, an outworn heating system or a smelly bathroom. So obviously, there has to be some remodeling in the restoration process. The functional parts of the house have to perform.

However, that doesn't mean that the kitchen of a Victorian has to look streamlined contemporary. There are newly made cabinets that are in a period style compatible with Victorian, French, Spanish, or what have you. Ceramic tile walls and counter tops can underscore a traditional theme; certain paint colors evoke certain styles, to say nothing of wall-covering patterns. If a new window is needed, there are unitized models that slip into the wall in one piece and look for all the world like old ones. And snap-out grilles will give the small-paned look so attractive in some period styles.

The same approach can be applied to the bath: tile, fixture colors, cabinet style, period hardware—all can be chosen to blend with a house-wide restoration theme. And while you're at it, there's no reason why you can't include a whirlpool bath or sauna for health and comfort.

The main thing to remember in restoration is to keep what you can of the old and give it new beauty and life. Sand and refinish old wood floors; repair old walls and paint or paper in colors and patterns that are part of the period in question. But above all, retain any period detailing—moldings, doors, stairways, cornices, façade trim. That's what gives the flavor!

REMODELING MEANS NEW

As noted before, while there is some remodeling in restoration, the reverse is not true. *Remodeling* means to change the model, to make all new, to transform it into something else. Tradition is less important in the scheme than streamlined comfort for a lifestyle that is up-to-the-minute. With remodeling, of course, the homemaker is much freer. There need not be any clinging to the old, no attempt to save flavor.

Remodeling can do wonders, as we all know, for the nondescript house, and there are many such structures of indeterminate architectural origin everywhere. Built fifteen, twenty, or thirty years ago, these sturdy structures are often excellent candidates for remodeling, because they offer good space at reasonable cost.

When embarking on your remodeling project, keep your mind open to the wealth of new ideas, materials, and equipment that are available today. As you visit home shows and dealer showrooms, evaluate each item you see in terms of what additional use, value and comfort it can give you. Try not to lock yourself into a set scheme until you have studied every possibility for that new kitchen or bath.

Restoration means old, with convenience

If you're restoring a house, the places to look for ideas are museums, old house tours, books on architecture, and magazines that present traditional houses—all this in addition to home shows and the market place for new convenience in kitchen and bath equipment. Restoration requires study; you have to become a specialist in Early American, Victorian, Federal, or whatever, if you don't want to botch the project. Fortunately, manufacturers are helping with authentic reproductions of almost every facet of restoration. There are period lighting fixtures and bulbs that flicker like the gas jets of old. There are box locks and other hardware in gleaming brass much like eighteenth-century handmade prototypes; special millwork—paneled doors, moldings, and windows—is available in many architectural styles. Plaster ceiling medallions—anaglyphs—are offered by Victoriana manufacturers. Pegged-oak or pine flooring can be found in manufacturers' catalogs, and a good carpenter or flooring contractor can copy, in oak or whatever wood you choose, many of the intricate parquet patterns of the past. Again, the point is to preserve what you can of the authentic parts of the house and replace what is missing with authentic copies.

CHAPTER ELEVEN

FLOORING

CHOICES

If you remember, in the various chapters dealing with room remodeling, there are many types of flooring to choose from, some especially suitable for the functions of various rooms. They are resilient flooring, natural hard-surface flooring, and carpet.

RESILIENT FLOORING

Because of its durability and easy care, resilient flooring has grown immeasurably popular, and you will find almost anything you wish from an expensive product to a do-it-yourself installation.

All the fabulous textures, fresh colors, and exciting patterns are enough to make you plunge right into a spending spree. The purpose of the following is to give you some beforehand knowledge of how each type of resilient flooring performs. This information can serve as a money-and-mistake-saving guide for you and make your shopping days easier, too.

Floorings based on man-made vinyl are truly resilient, strong, easy to maintain, and resistant to soil. They come in two basic forms: tiles, which are cemented in place to serve as a permanent floor, and sheet goods, which are also cemented in place for a permanent installation. However, some types of sheet goods may be cut from the roll to fit a room's size and can be put down without being cemented to the floor.

In general, resilient tiles come in nine- and twelve-inch squares. Most major companies can give you special custom-cut designs in special dimensions, but, of course, these cost more.

With few exceptions, sheet floor coverings come in rolls six or twelve feet wide and in continuous lengths, usually up to ninety feet.

Before spending any money, consider the condition of the floor you wish to cover. Your subfloor (which is what the floor under your new flooring is called) has a great deal to do with the eventual look of the new resilient floor. While the new one will bring color, beauty, and function to any room or area, it cannot cure defects that already exist, such as roughness, springiness, unevenness, and dampness. Resilient floors have a tendency to take on any bulges or bad grooming of the floor beneath them. Make certain your subfloor is clean, even, smooth, and dry.

Discuss any special symptoms showing up in your floor with your flooring dealer. Let him advise you if you need a new underlayment (such as plywood or hardboard). Also, be certain to tell him just where the new floor is going, that is, on which grade level in your home.

GRADE LEVELS

While shopping you will hear floors described as below grade, on grade, and above grade. This is what is meant:

Below grade. Below the level of the ground, such as a basement which is in direct contact with the ground.

On grade. This is at grade level; for example, a house built on a slab without a basement beneath it.

Above grade. Any floor that is over another area such as a basement, or is a second story that is never in contact with the ground.

Any solid vinyl may be installed on any grade level provided you use the proper adhesive. Conditions vary in different sections of the country; therefore it is always best to consult your dealer before making an installation.

ABOUT MOISTURE

If you live in an area where excessive ground moisture penetrates the slab and collects under certain parts of the resilient floor, a special type primer (or whichever product is recommended by the manufacturer) should be applied to the concrete before installation.

FOOT TRAFFIC

You are the only one who knows how much soil your new flooring will get from the daily tramping in and out by adults, teen-agers, energetic toddlers, and pets. Color, patterns, and durability in a specific type of flooring should be determined by the use a room gets. Mixed colors in floorings will show less soil and dirt than a solid color, and textured surfaces will help to hide heel and scuff marks.

Tips on types

What you pay for your new resilient flooring will depend upon design, amount of vinyl, whether or not you install it yourself, and the condition of your subfloor. Here are some of the popular types of resilient flooring that make up most of today's market.

Vinyl-asbestos tile. One of the most popular for do-it-yourselfers. High stain resistance. Good durability. Easy to maintain. May be installed on all grade levels.

Solid vinyl tile. Excellent wearability and easy to maintain. Wide color selection. Available in special sizes. Can be installed on all grade levels. Check your dealer for special adhesive for on and below grade.

Asphalt tile. An all-purpose flooring. Can be installed on all grade levels. While it has excellent resistance to alkali, it is low in resisting grease. Considered very serviceable as a flooring when the budget is an important item.

Cork tile. Wears well. Extremely resilient and is great for cutting down on noise. Has a fair resistance to grease but a poor resistance to average soil. For easy maintenance, some cork tile is coated with a clear-plastic finish.

Rubber tile. Excellent resiliency, hushes footsteps and is easy to maintain. Has a fair resistance to grease. Comes in a fine range of colors.

Linoleum tile. Good selection of colors. Long wearing, economical, and easy to maintain. Comparatively resilient. Must be installed above grade.

Sheet vinyl (inlaid). Inlaid means the pattern goes all the way through the thickness of the wear layer. Makes for the greatest durability. Comes in a variety of backings and is resistant to stains and indentations. Known for keeping its good looks for years.

Sheet vinyl (printed) felt-backed. Pattern is printed on the surface. Not all felt backs are for permanent installation; some are put down without being cemented to the floor.

Cushion-back sheet vinyl. Has a thick backing of vinyl foam that gives when you step on it. Comfortable underfoot and muffles noises. Some cushion backs are available in sheet goods for permanent installation; some can be simply cut from the roll to fit the approximate dimensions of the room and installed without being cemented to the floor.

Rotovinyls. Rotogravure-printed surface design topped with a coating of clear vinyl for protection. Felt or moisture-proof asbestos backing. Usually less expensive than inlaid vinyl.

Linoleum. An old reliable that is durable, greaseproof, economical, and long-wearing. Easy to maintain. One drawback is that it must be installed above grade.

BROWSE BEFORE BUYING

Browse around, make a tour of the stores, take note of color, pattern, and texture in resilient flooring before you make your own selection. Take time to visit the flooring showrooms where you can view the new designs at your leisure and very often get ideas from special settings of flooring and other home furnishings. Also, you can get any information you need for your own special rooms, then go on to your favorite flooring dealer to make the actual purchase.

So much has been added in new designs and new ways to use these easy-care, hard-surface floors. In addition to the good decorating effects gained from simulated flagstone, slate, terrazzo, mosaics, beach pebbles, and marble, dealer showcases now include:

Bold geometrics, some of which are adaptations of the weathered tile of a Moroccan courtyard. Colors are flamboyant reds and clear tropical blues.

Wood patterns that range from the elegance of parquet, displaying simulated squares of bleached oak and light maple colors, to the random planks that depicted an early America.

Adhesive-backed tiles with the three-dimensional translucence and richness of marble; or in a stone-chip design that can widen optically with the use of accent strips.

The unified floor. An exciting new decorating idea presenting two types of flooring, vinyl and carpet, as a new floor team. For example, an area rug in a lovely hexagonal pattern can be used to top its vinyl teammate in the same hexagonal pattern and in the same color tones.

These are just a few of the hundreds of designs you will meet on your marketing trip.

Resilient floor tiles are a spur to your imagination. You can work out designs of your own with the regular nine-inch tiles by including among them, at selected locations in a room, some of the very unusual tiles on the market. There are border effects, centerpieces, and many other tile types to bring out your own creative ideas.

Ask your flooring dealer to show you how to create further flooring interest by combining plain or patterned flooring with feature strips. These come in various widths, some narrow, some wide, in a broad range of neutral colors or in deeper tones of green, turquoise, blue, red, and orange.

To evaluate all the many new materials in floorings is a big undertaking. When shopping, your best guide (as said before) is the good name and reputation for quality of an established brand-name manufacturer and the reputable name of your flooring dealer.

How to Measure for Resilient Flooring

To give your flooring dealer some idea of the size of any room you wish to cover, measure it before you go shopping. For sheet goods: multiply the length of the room by the width to get the square footage. From the square footage, your dealer can give you an estimate of the cost, including the price of installation. Most manufacturers recommend that you have an expert put down sheet flooring for you. However, as mentioned under types of floorings, there are some types of sheet goods which can be cut from the roll to fit the room size and put down without being cemented to the floor. This is found, for example, in the cushion-back sheet vinyls or felt-backed printed vinyls. (Ideal for renters in apartments when the landlord does not permit cementing down a new flooring.)

If you are handy, it will save you money if you install your own tiles.

The size of a room, or other area, and the number of tiles needed determine the cost. For example, to get an approximate idea of the number of nine-inch-square tiles required, multiply the length of the room by the width to get the square footage, then multiply the square footage by two.

To get the cost, multiply the total number of tiles required by the cost of each tile. Ask your dealer to recheck your estimate to make certain you have enough. It is a good thing to have a few extra tiles, and it is also advisable to buy all that you need at one time.

Read about what you intend to use

In speaking with many of the tile manufacturers, whose products are known around the world, this sentence kept repeating itself: "If only the homemaker would read the information that comes with our products. We spend time and great effort in writing careful directions. The customer should read everything, and even read every single line that comes with a can of adhesive."

If you follow directions and take your time, you should be able to do a very good job of installing your own tile flooring.

Your dealer will be glad to give you a booklet on any of the do-it-yourself types of tile. Each will explain fully how to proceed step by step.

Be certain to tell him whether the tile is going over concrete, paint, wood, old floor coverings, or old terrazzo. He can tell you exactly how to prepare your subfloor for the new tile covering. Success depends very much on two things: the old floor underneath and your willingness to follow the manufacturer's advice for the specific tile you are using.

Natural hard-surface flooring

For the flooring of your own house, your architect or contractor will give you advice on the good or impractical points (for your particular use) of flooring materials to be used in the various areas in and around the house.

Among the rigid floorings are ceramic tile, wood, marble, flagstone, slate, brick, and terrazzo.

Ceramic tile in recent years has had a rebirth of popularity. Now this hard-surface material with its ancient history is used all over the house.

Wood is still one of the most popular of all floorings and has had many new developments in design and surface finishes.

Marble, so much the usual thing among ancient cultures and the most luxurious of floor coverings, is elegant in private homes and apartments in entranceways, halls, and bathrooms.

Flagstone can be attractive in halls and vestibules and will almost anywhere outside in areas such as the patio, terrace, and bypaths. Slate also has a practical outdoor use on the patio floor or on the terrace.

Brick has come up with a new rosy glow; some bricks present a lovely pinkish cast, a fine idea in country kitchens, dining, and living rooms, also fine in the hall, the patio, or for garden paths.

Terrazzo (which is poured concrete made with inset chips of marble) is rugged and durable, fine in any heavily trafficked area such as halls and bathrooms.

We will concentrate on the two most popular of these natural hard-surface floors, ceramic tiles and wood.

Ceramic tile

Today ceramic tile comes in more than two hundred colors, among which are golds, greens, pinks, blues, and various shades of celadon. Because of its many new designs, colors, and patterns, ceramic tile is appearing inside, outside, and all around the home. It is lovely to look at, wears well, and is easy to keep clean.

What can ceramic tile do? It can be very elegant in your entranceway by opening it out with sparkling, light colors and a smooth, fresh look. Since this is usually a heavily trafficked area, cleaning is the simplest ever.

In a dining room, in any period from contemporary to Mediterranean, you will be able to find a ceramic tile design to complement the setting. Again, in this area where there are likely to be spills of food and liquids, nothing can be damaged for more than the time it takes to wipe it up.

When shopping for tile, you will find it in three general types:

Glazed wall tile, which can also be used on the floor, is most familiar in 4¼-inch squares, but does come in other sizes and shapes. It is available in a wide range of colors, designs, and various glazes.

Ceramic mosaic tiles, made in a large assortment of colorful shapes, may be had with or without a glaze. The ceramic mosaics are often just called "floor tile," but they may be used on other surfaces. They are ideal for inside and outside the swimming pool. Since tile colors and designs are permanent, there isn't any need to worry about fading.

The unglazed ceramic mosaics come in a wide range of colors from clear, crisp tones of the porcelain variety to the warm, earthy shades of the natural clays. Glazed ceramic mosaics add many additional colors. While standard design patterns are shown everywhere, if you wish a special pattern, it will be provided on special order. For a handcrafted effect some manufacturers provide triangular shapes and tiles with irregular edges, in addition to the usual square and rectangular types. Standard mosaics are 1×1, 1×2, and 2×2 inches.

Quarry tile, a heavy-duty floor tile, traditionally available in earthen-red color, is now marketed in dozens of delightful colors, in new shapes, new sizes, and new textures.

Quarries can add warmth and color to foyers, kitchens, dining and living rooms where you may wish to have an informal, country, or

Spanish look. Outdoors in the patio, quarry tiles will stand up under heavy foot traffic, scorching sun, or rain. Colors range from near white to bluegrass green in unglazed quarries, and many of these can be varied by "fire-flashing" with subtle rainbow-hued effects. Glazed quarries provide an additional color spectrum.

Added to squares and rectangles, quarries come in geometric and other shapes to create exciting and unusually delightful flooring designs. Patterned or textured surfaces are also available, and sizes range from $2\frac{3}{4} \times 2\frac{3}{4}$ inches to 12×12 inches.

In major cities, distributors of ceramic tile have beautiful showrooms where you can see all the lovely colors, designs, and shapes of tile. Also, here you can get any information you need. If your city does not have this type of tile display and if you do not know a tile contractor where you are able to buy, look in the classified telephone directory under "Tile Contractor, Ceramic."

Before buying, go to several tile contractors to check on prices. You are buying a material that will last a lifetime, so you are making a long-range investment.

In case you are wondering if you can install ceramic tile yourself, it is not recommended. However, there is always someone who is especially handy with anything. If you are determined to do it yourself, note that there are three setting methods for installing ceramic tile: conventional cement mortar, dry-set mortar, and organic adhesive (mastic). The first two are usually recommended for wet areas such as shower enclosures. Your local tile contractor will give you detailed and explicit information.

Wood flooring

If you are adding to a room or repairing an existing floor, if it is wood you must follow the type that is there. If your present living room has oak strips and you plan an addition, use the same type and grade of oak, then sand and refinish the entire expanse. If you are replacing damaged boards, you must do the same. If the existing wood floor is in a condition so bad that it can't be saved, then nail plywood or hardboard over it and install new flooring. If you want new oak strip flooring, use plywood and nail the new strips over it. If you prefer some of the block type of wood which simulates parquet, you can install the blocks over either hardboard or plywood with mastic. Be sure that the pre-installation surface is level and securely nailed to the old floor underneath. Otherwise it will be difficult to join the tongues and grooves of the new blocks perfectly. These

blocks come in several types of hardwood—oak, walnut, cherry—and
are usually prefinished so that once they are installed all you have to
do is buff a light coat of paste wax over the surface.

These prefinished hardwood flooring blocks are nine inches or
twelve inches square with a thickness of a half or three eighths of an
inch. Each block is three veneers bonded to one another with waterproof glue, and the veneers are cross-grain laminated for high
dimensional stability. On the opposite sides of the block are tongues
and grooves, to assure interlocking and easy installation. Your best
help will come from working with a qualified wood-flooring dealer,
whether you are interested in oak strip or wood blocks. It is important that you let him know about any special conditions of your
subfloor. For the wood blocks it is essential that, in most cases, installation be on or above grade on a smooth, dry, structurally sound surface. Handy homemakers who like do-it-yourself projects can install
the blocks in mastic, but it is important to read the directions carefully and get the proper type of mastic. It is wise to use a keyhole or
some other small saw, preferably electric, because the plywood
blocks are tough. It is important to cut the blocks to fit and lay them
down in sections before setting them in permanently. It can be a
sticky, difficult business and only those with some do-it-yourself skill
should attempt this.

How to Refinish Old Wood Floors

If you have wood floors—oak, pine, or fir—and they are sound but
show their age and the wear and tear of time or are in a blond finish
popular forty years ago but dated today, don't think you have to carpet or tile over them. The patina of wood gives a marvelous, rich
look to a room and most old floors can be refinished to gleam anew.
The simplest answer, of course, is to call several flooring contractors
and get estimates. However, if you want to save dollars, you can
refinish the floors yourself. It is not the easiest and most pleasant task
in the world, but it can be done. You can rent an electric sanding machine and an auxiliary edger for scraping along baseboards and other
hard-to-reach areas. A good time for this project is over a weekend
when you get the full benefit of the rental time. The rental agency
will likely have information on the refinishing process, too.

The first step is stripping the old floor—taking out embedded tacks
and staples that will snag the sandpaper on the machine and cause delays. Protruding nails are sunk with a hammer and nail punch as part
of this step. If it is an antique floor and the expansions and contrac-

tions of decades have made wide cracks between boards, you may want to fill these. The filler compound can be a prepared plastic mix or you can make your own with sawdust of the same wood as the floor mixed with glue. It can also be colored, if necessary, to blend better with the rest of the floor. The compound must be worked into the cracks and joints well. After the filler has set hard, the surface must be sanded, either with sandpaper over a wood block or a small rotary sanding machine.

Then comes the major sanding. If the floor is in bad condition, with seams swollen and butts raised, you should run the machine diagonally across the boards, using a medium-coarse sandpaper. Then the same direction is repeated with a medium sandpaper. Finally fine sandpaper is used, going up and down in the direction of the boards. However, if the floor boards are in fair condition, start by running the sanding machine in the same direction as the boards. Use a medium-fine grade of sandpaper first and follow the wood grain. Then for a last cut, use a fine sandpaper up and down the length of the boards. If it is an oak-block floor with the units laid with grain at right angles to each other, go up and down lengthwise or across the width of the room, using medium-fine and finishing off with fine paper.

You'll have to judge the degree of coarseness necessary to remove ink stains, grease, animal urine, and other special damage. Just be sure that you don't create depressions at such spots by bearing down just there. Better to use a coarse paper over the whole expanse until the stains are removed, then finish off the whole with fine. The machines have their own sawdust bags attached, but there will be some residue, so you'll want to vacuum this thoroughly and even wipe off the final dust film with a soft cloth before applying stain. A sealer-type stain is best. To get the tone you want, try mixing small parts of medium and dark walnut, or whatever. You can test in a closet or some area that will not be seen. Then use a wide brush or roller devised for floor work.

With most stains you have to wipe off, let dry for a day and apply a second coat, wiping off again. Don't apply the stain too liberally, forming puddles, or you'll arrive at an uneven look. Wipe a section at a time promptly, since stain is a penetrating product and works quickly. For a durable surface when the stain dries, you can use liquid urethane which is a plastic sealer, transparent and hard-wearing. Apply it according to directions and let it dry thoroughly before using paste wax over the surface. To buff the wax, you can usually rent an electric buffer at the same place you rent the sander.

CARPET

The new-generation carpets called indoor/outdoor are said to go anywhere and do anything. Indoors these hard-wearing, easily maintained carpets are apt to appear any place you want to enjoy the good qualities that all carpets offer, but do not wish to expose the floor covering to excessively heavy traffic or excessive soil. Such areas are, for example, the kitchen, laundry, bath, and nursery-playroom.

Indoor space can appear to be made larger by extending it outdoors with carpet and color. To give an integrated color scheme, many manufacturers provide matching colors for indoor/outdoor carpets.

Outdoors, the carpeting adds foot comfort plus beauty to dining and relaxing in the open on a porch, terrace, patio, boat deck, at poolside, or anywhere. It covers concrete walks, barbecue pits, active play areas for children, and even makes lush and colorful lawns that do not require mowing.

When you are shopping for indoor/outdoor carpets, the label of an established brand-name manufacturer is your best guide. Established brands are backed by knowledge, skill, and integrity of carpet manufacturers who are willing to stake their reputations on the merchandise they produce for the public.

A carpet label will always give you the exact fiber content, country of origin, and usually the manufacturer's name or brand name, pattern or color designation as well. In addition to reading the label carefully when you shop, when you buy floor coverings, save the label for future reference in cleaning or repairing your carpet.

Also, be certain you understand the manufacturer's recommendations for the intended use of the carpet. It is important to know whether the carpet is labeled "for use anywhere," or "for use indoors only," or "approved for outdoor use." When specifically designed for indoor use (and so labeled) the carpet usually comes with a foam-rubber backing that gives it cushioning and makes it cling to the floor. If this same carpet is placed outdoors, the backing is subject to mildew and rot. For carpet to be used outside, it must be completely of synthetic materials (including the backing), plus other properties that you would not, as a rule, need indoors. It must be specifically made so as not to rot, mildew, shrink, or buckle, whatever the weather. You can use this (outdoor) carpet indoors, too, but you will need to forego a foam-rubber backing.

Before you buy, have in mind the areas in and around the home you wish to cover. A reputable flooring dealer will answer any questions on the choices in colors and textures, the ease of installation and ease of maintenance. The way a carpet will perform depends as much on its construction as on the fiber with which it is made. If a carpet is poorly constructed a fiber's built-in characteristics do not have a chance to perform properly.

Before carpeting any of your rooms, think about the various activities that take place in each: How much traffic is causing how much wear and tear? Ask yourself how much you entertain by giving large dinner parties in the dining room, or if the living room needs your attention, is it used only for formal entertaining, or is it used for watching television and family gatherings as well? Do your children entertain their friends and their various pets in the living room also? Jot down the answers to these questions; have them fixed in your mind before you finally go shopping.

While there are no longer any rigid rules about which type of carpeting you choose for a particular room, it does make good sense to pick the one that will give you the most for your remodeling dollars. Your carpet dealer with his vast knowledge of carpeting will help you in every way possible, but you will be able to help him if you have at your fingertips the function of each of the rooms you wish carpeted.

Your shopping venture will be much more enjoyable, and profitable for you, if you do your homework before you go.

What carpet fibers to buy

Inevitably the answer to such an important question should come from the collective knowledge of a large group of major carpet and rug manufacturers, the Carpet and Rug Institute, Inc., of Dalton, Georgia. Here's what they say:

"The answer is tough because there really is no single answer. First, there is no one carpet fiber that is best . . . superior to all of the others in every characteristic. Second, the performance of the finished carpet depends more on how the fiber is used.

"All of the major carpet fibers used today will give excellent performance when used in good, dense construction. The more fiber used and the denser it is packed in the pile, the better the carpet. On the other hand, any one of these fibers, if misused . . . put into a sparse, thin, carpet pile could produce an unsatisfactory carpet.

"It is important to remember that carpet manufacturers select the different fibers to meet the varied demands of their carpet customers.

If the demand comes in for abrasive resistance, outstanding wear . . . certain fibers will get the call. If the customers want top-notch resilience and soil resistance other fibers may be used.

"If the order is for extraordinary stain resistance and easy spot removal, then other fibers could be chosen. Still other fibers may be favored when the ladies ask for that luxurious look and opulent feel in a carpet.

"A possible cause for some of the confusion over carpet fibers that besets the homemakers today is the great number of different brand names under which the synthetic fibers are marketed. While there are many fiber trade names, there are only five basic fiber types used extensively in carpets today. They are nylon, acrylics, wool, polyester, and polypropylene.

"The variations within each fiber group are significant, as for example, the 'second-generation' nylons or the differences between continuous filament and staple forms of a fiber. There are also meaningful similarities between different fiber types. For example, wool, polyester, and acrylics have a number of properties in common.

"In abrasion resistance, nylon and polypropylene are outstanding. Though wool, acrylics, and polyesters rate somewhat lower in this regard, they will provide long-term durability when used in quality, dense constructions.

"In soil resistance, wool, acrylics, and polypropylenes score high points. The second generation nylons with new soil-concealing features rate high also.

"In stain resistance, particularly in resistance to water-soluble stains, polypropylene, nylon, acrylic, and polyester are all excellent. But remember, stains should be removed from all carpets before they have a chance to set. Most stains can be readily removed from wool carpets, also, when promptly attended to.

"In resilience, the ability of fibers to bounce back and resist crushing, wool, acrylics, and polyesters are exceptional. Polypropylenes rate lower on this score, but when used in low, dense pile surfaces and in flat needle-punch carpet, this factor is not so important.

"All carpet fibers today are mothproof. This includes wool which is permanently treated during carpet manufacturing. All man-made fibers are also resistant to mildew, which is a problem for wool only in unusually damp conditions.

"To avoid confusion when shopping, be sure to compare the carpets and not the fibers alone."

CARPET TEXTURES

You can get bored with a room that has too much of the same kinds of surfaces. Each texture has its own end use. It's very personal, this appeal of texture. You may not even know which ones you prefer until you see the various types displayed in stores. The descriptions that follow are merely to add to your before-shopping knowledge. You may like plush or velvet, with its luxuriant quality look for your more formal rooms; twists are happy in casual, rugged surroundings, and the shags will go anywhere an informal look is desired.

Some of the terms you will hear are:

Single-cut pile. Because of its velvety appearance, is often called plush or velvet.

Looped pile. The opposite of cut pile. Loops may be single level, all one height, or multilevel loops arranged to form texture patterns such as geometric designs, swirls, or circular motifs.

Sculptured. The effect is that of "highs and lows." Often created by a combination of cut and looped surface yarns sheared at different levels. In some sculptured or embossed textures, one level of looped pile is pulled down tight, with a level of cut pile suggesting a pattern.

Shags. Some have long, loose surface yarns up to three inches long; others are shorter with a twist-yarn texture. Shags are easy to care for and come in a wide range of colors.

Twists. Because the loops are twisted, the surface has a pebbly look.

CARPET TERMS

Backing yarns. The materials that form the carpet backing or foundation to which pile or face yarns are anchored. A second backing fabric may be laminated to the primary backing, and the backing coated with latex.

Broadloom. This is not a "kind" of carpet. It is a term of measurement and does not describe any special quality, style, or construction. The term refers to any carpet made in a seamless width of six feet or more, and applies to all designs and qualities.

Carved. This is the effect of a pattern in relief, creating shadowy effects by shearing the pile in high-low designs.

Density. A carpet factor which is the single best clue to quality. It refers to the closeness of construction of the surface yarns, and the best rule of thumb is "the deeper, the denser, the better." Or, the more fiber, the better quality of carpet.

Ply. This refers to individual fibers which are used to make up yarn. Three-ply yarn means each tuft is made up of three strands of yarn spun together. The number of plies used does not necessarily improve quality, it does affect texture and surface effects in a carpet.

Tufting. The construction process used for most carpets and rugs today. Pile yarns are attached to a preconstructed backing by wide multiple-needled machines.

Wilton, Axminster, and Velvet. These are types of looms on which carpet is woven. Carpets made on these looms may be described also by these terms: a Wilton carpet, a Velvet carpet, or an Axminster.

Before shopping you may wish to know how much your carpet venture is going to cost. To get an idea of how much carpet you will need, and then determine the cost, it is necessary to measure the area to be carpeted. Some stores will do the measuring job for you even before you buy, but it is best to check to see if this service is provided. For your own information, here is how the measuring task is done. Multiply the length by width of the room in feet, then divide by nine to get the square yards; for that is the way most carpets are sold. That figure, multiplied by the price per square yard, will give the approximate cost.

For example, a room that measures 12×15 has 180 square feet. This number divided by nine gives twenty square yards. If your selection is a carpet that costs ten dollars per square yard, your carpet cost will be two hundred dollars.

Before the carpet is installed, your dealer will make professional measurements of your rooms, give you the exact price of the carpet, plus the cost of installation.

An underpad of cushioning material will prolong your carpet's life by acting as a shock absorber for daily foot traffic. Also, it will add to your personal underfoot comfort. In addition, an underlay adds to the carpet's capacity to soak up noise and provides support for a taut carpet installation, that is, it prevents slipping or shifting of the carpet. There are several types, among which are felted hair, jute, foam rubber, or plastic-foam material. All are serviceable, and you can decide which is right for you with the help of your carpet salesman.

TIPS ON CARPETING STAIRS

Stairways show off so beautifully when well carpeted. While you want to pick a color you like, to help in disguising signs of constant use, it is best to select a medium shade with a tight-looped pile. Color in stair carpeting does not need to exactly match the adjoining areas if it is chosen in a harmonizing color, texture, and pattern.

Here is one place where it would be foolish to skimp on the quality of carpet, for in most homes the stairs get a lot of traffic. Also, it is important that carpet on stairways be installed securely. In addition, be certain the carpet is kept in good condition with no worn spots or loose edges to present hazards.

Use a good-quality padding under the carpet to protect it. A firm, taut padding is essential. Heavier carpet padding over the (stair) edges protects the stairs better, too.

Another suggestion: When the carpet is laid it should have an extra foot of carpet length folded under the top riser. When edges look worn, simply shift the carpet an inch or two down the stairs, and fold any excess against the lowest riser.

CHAPTER TWELVE

PAINT POINTERS

It has been said that paint is the least expensive remodeling tool at the command of the homemaker. It has many advantages: to the apartment dweller it is one thing the landlord doesn't usually object to and which you don't have to worry about leaving behind when you move; it covers a multitude of sins on bad walls and woodwork; it does magical things in changing the seeming proportions of awkward rooms when properly used; and it establishes period style instantly, if you go with color schemes strongly identified with Early American, French, English Tudor, or whatever.

There are two basic types of paint—water-based or oil-based. The former are latex or rubber content and the latter are alkyd. Within the alkyd type you will find gloss, semigloss, and flat-finish types for interior work plus eggshell enamel and satin finish varieties which give a somewhat softer, smoother appearance. For exterior, alkyd offers gloss and semigloss. In the latex category, there are flat and low-sheen types for exterior work and flat and semigloss for interior. Latex paints are thinned and brushes and rollers cleaned with water. Alkyd paints use mineral spirits for a thinner and for cleaning brushes and other utensils. Gloss and semigloss are recommended for kitchens, baths and other utilitarian rooms where walls and woodwork must sometimes be washed or scrubbed down. Flat finishes look good in living rooms, dining rooms, and bedrooms and are especially helpful in improving the looks of uneven plaster and other wall defects. Woodwork in these spaces is usually done in semigloss or satin finish. The trend is to water-based paint and in many instances oil-based paint is being phased out.

Certain types of paintbrushes and rollers are recommended for various types of paint and various surfaces to be painted. Your paint dealer or painting contractor will be able to tell you what is best for what.

As with every other part of remodeling, preparation is the way to a satisfactory job: walls should be filled and sanded after any loose plaster is removed. Woodwork should be made smooth: all old paint buildup of drips should be scraped away, cracks filled and the surfaces sanded. Greasy areas should be cleaned thoroughly with a solvent before any paint is applied.

New plaster or gypsum board walls must be coated with a primer, tinted slightly with the surface color to be applied later. That way, one final coat will usually be enough to cover, except in the case of pure white, which is one of the most difficult paints to apply for a shadow-free effect and requires two or more coats for perfection. Better to use a bone white which is the closest thing to pure white and needs only one coat over a white or light-colored surface.

Paint and the Problem Room

Paint is a valuable ally. It can seemingly correct bad proportions in a number of ways. A too-high ceiling can be "brought down" by painting it the same or darker than the walls, while, conversely, the too-low ceiling can be "raised" by painting it white or a lighter shade of the walls. A long, narrow room can be seemingly shortened by painting end walls a darker tone than the longer side walls. The minuscule room can be visually enlarged by treating walls and ceiling in the same color.

Older homes are often riddled with architectural flaws: exposed beams, posts that seem to come from nowhere, off-center windows, obtrusive radiators and air conditioners, doors located without regard to symmetry, etc. Once again, paint comes to the rescue. By painting the entire wall—door frames, beams, radiator—the same color, all the elements blend into a whole. A dark tone in a flat finish is usually the most effective camouflage in this case.

Often older homes present difficulties with too many doors and windows. In this case it helps to paint everything the color of the walls, blending woodwork, trim, and walls into one unified backdrop. Odd bays and room extensions, arbitrary divisions between areas of the same room, and overpowering stairways are often the earmarks of the late Victorian house. With these, color works its same magic, underplaying one element, emphasizing another to bring everything into harmony.

CHAPTER THIRTEEN

REMODELED FAÇADES

IF YOUR HOUSE is showing its age from the street, there is a lot that can be done relatively inexpensively to make its façade up-to-date and impressive. It is amazing what can be done to take the dated look off a house with clever new design. Here are a few ideas and your architect or designer can give you many others especially suited to your structure. The easiest and most immediate way to change the looks is with encasement, that is, building a new façade right over the existing one. In that way, front windows and the entrance can be revamped almost like erasing them. A new framework of 2×4s attached over the elderly stucco, brick, shingled, or clapboard exterior can be surfaced in modern-looking panels of plywood which comes in so many guises: grooved, battened, resawed; and many faces—fir, cedar, redwood. New anodized aluminum-framed windows can be inserted into the new surface, and an entrance detail in contemporary style can be designed.

Encasement can also be done to give a different, traditional look. For example, the suggestion of a mansard roof to the depth of the reconstructed façade, plus arched windows, shutters, and the trappings of French Country style will give a slick new appearance. English Tudor can be achieved with a half-timbered design and stucco panels on the new encasement, plus leaded windows, heavy-paneled door, and other earmarks of that style. Cape Cod or Early American effects can be created with clapboard, paneled shutters, small-paned windows, six-panel door, carriage lamps at the entry, etc. An architect or designer can be of great help in arriving at the style you want.

Lopping off an old porch is another way to a streamlined look. A new, smaller entry stoop in brick or tile and a stairway with a graceful iron railing can be created leading to a new main door chosen to complement whatever style you have chosen for the new façade. Stock doors and detailing are available in many styles—Georgian, Early American, French Country, and Spanish. New windows in compatible style—small-paned if the look is traditional, aluminum-framed solid panels if contemporary—can be added. Shutters are a nice touch if the look is period, long ones at either side of the entrance and a height scaled to the sides of the windows.

And don't forget the magic of paint. Old houses—especially fancifully detailed Victorians—can be given a whole new lease on life with clever painting. Vivid colors used in contrast and careful proportion can do a lot to capitalize on this style.

CHAPTER FOURTEEN

COMMUNICATIONS

WE LIVE in a world of communications today, so while you're remodeling you might as well consider getting as many of its benefits in your home as you can. Telephone systems, music systems and entrance-annunciator systems can always be added after remodeling, but then you have exposed wires running all over the place or you have to break into walls, which is a messy and costly business. Far better to plan the systems you want in advance. Then, when walls are opened up during the course of your home-improvement project, it is an easy matter to install what you need inexpensively and unobtrusively.

TELEPHONE

Your local telephone company can tell you of the many services available to you besides the conventional handset for incoming and outgoing calls. Today all telephones are installed with jacks in the wall or baseboard and with plugs on the instrument itself, so that you can use one handset in any room of the house where you have included a jack. You can also plug wall phones into jacks if you prefer that style of phone. You can specify a system whereby you can buzz someone in another room and talk without the inconvenience of having to travel from one part of the house to another. "Home Interphone," as it is called, consists of an annunciator at the entrance door so that you can have the security of speaking to someone before letting them in. Another convenience is "Automatic Phone," which records messages while you are away from your phone. One option with this system is a "Remote Caller" which allows you to call home and receive messages recorded during your absence. Other interesting new services offered by the telephone company include a "Call Waiting" system whereby if you are on the phone and receive another call, you hear a beep and can hold the second call until you are finished with the first. A "Call Forwarding" system permits you to leave home and have your calls forwarded to another number where you'll be. "Call Conferencing" is a new system that permits you to talk to two or more people at once. When you plan to remodel, contact your local telephone company in advance so that any of these systems can be built into your home as part of your project.

MUSIC

If you want to have music piped throughout the house with the controls at a central point, the time to plan and install such a system is during the remodeling. Speakers with volume control can be built into the wall of a given room easily and relatively inexpensively without unsightly wires showing. Speakers are best placed as high as possible in a room, and if you want stereo reception, there must be two speakers at least eight feet apart. This system provides whatever sound is relayed from the AM or FM radio, eight-track or cassette tape, or record that is being played at the central control point. If individual sound selection is desired in various rooms, then a separate music system must be installed in each. Sound quality is determined by the equipment you choose, of course, whether it be components or a unitized system. The best location for the central controls—radio, tapes, turntable—is in a room such as the study or family room that has independent access from all other rooms. The equipment and controls can be built into the wall or into a breakfront, bookcase, or some other piece of furniture.

HOME INTERCOM

Several manufacturers offer house-wide communication systems. Included are an annunciator at entrance door or doors as well as speaker boxes in individual rooms which permit talking from and to a central point, or from one room to another. There is usually one central control point, most often in the kitchen at a homemaking desk, but other control points can be included if desired. Once again, this kind of a system must be preplanned as part of the remodeling.

TELEPHONE MESSAGES

We have already noted that the telephone company offers a message service. However, there are many manufacturers which provide equipment that can be attached to the telephone system to take messages while you are out of the house. It is best to have these installed with the supervision of the telephone company, but it is not mandatory. This kind of equipment varies greatly in price and range of conveniences, so it is wise to shop around to arrive at the degree of service you require.

CHAPTER FIFTEEN

ELECTRICAL CONSIDERATIONS

WITH electrical servants the order of the day in our homes—dishwashers, laundry equipment, ovens, toasters, vacuum cleaners—it is important not to overlook the responsibility that comes with them. And that is to have your home's electrical system prepared to handle their requirements. Every elderly house, forty or more years old, may be seriously underpowered, which means simply that there is not enough available energy to handle an array of electrical appliances. The result: circuits are being overloaded; appliance motors are being overworked and worn out; aging wires may be drying out with insulation falling away so that the wires may be dangerously exposed within your walls. All this adds up to fire hazard from short-circuiting.

So safety considerations alone dictate that, as you plan your remodeling project, you must be sure to have a licensed electrical contractor examine your whole existing electrical system. Safety considerations also dictate that you not attempt to do any part of the electrical work yourself. If ever there was a project for the experienced professional, this is it. All electrical work must be done in accordance with local code requirements and must be inspected by local building department officials. Unprofessional and uninspected wiring can cancel out your fire insurance protection, so it is not only unsafe but unsound and foolish to risk an electrical fire by tinkering with the electrical system yourself or having an unlicensed amateur do so. Have the licensed contractor not only review your system and make recommendations but also develop an electrical plan for the home improvements you plan to make.

To determine whether your system has enough power to handle the upgrading you intend to do, the contractor will examine your main fuse box or circuit breaker. From the underwriter's label on the box, the contractor can tell at once if the electrical supply is inadequate. If it is, the contractor will recommend replacing your supply wires and service entrance with a new setup providing at least 150 amperes and 200 if you want air conditioning, an electric clothes dryer, electric heat, electric range. In fact, 200-ampere service is the way to go so that any electrical eventuality is foreseen. All 150-ampere service requires three-wire, 220-volt hookup to the power company's pole on the street. The contractor will get a pretty good idea of the kind of wiring he can expect to find behind the walls after examining the main box. He will know what kinds of cable are no longer permitted by local codes, what can be kept, and what must be ripped out and replaced.

The next step is to go with the contractor through each room, examining what outlets you have and what you would like to add. In fact, it is a good idea if you don't plan to use an architect to do a complete house layout of your wiring and include what you want to have. Again on graph paper draw each room to measure and mark existing fixed lights, switches, and outlet plugs. In a different color you can include fixtures, outlets or appliances you plan to add now or in the future. If you plan a future addition, tell the contractor what appliances you will require in it so that he can run a circuit near to where the addition will be. Based on this kind of information, the contractor can tell you the minimum service entrance you must have and what it will cost. To anticipate future eventualities, have the contractor install the largest capacity entrance you can afford.

Be sure to include extra circuits for parts of the remodeling that you plan to do in the future. These can be added for attic, basement, or garage. Wiring them now will save money later. Don't forget to include one or more weatherproof outdoor electrical outlets, which will permit the security of outdoor lighting, as well as the convenience of electric outdoor cooking and use of power tools for gardening and other projects. And by all means, specify a circuit breaker. A reputable contractor will likely recommend this, but if he doesn't, insist on one. It eliminates the danger of overloading of circuits because when overloading occurs, the circuit breaks and you can tell from the position of the switch in the box which outlet is involved and take the necessary action. The circuit breaker is also safe, unlike the old fuse box, which can give a shock when you examine it or replace fuses.

CHAPTER SIXTEEN

PLUMBING CONSIDERATIONS

MOST HOMEOWNERS who have lived in a house for many years tend to take the plumbing for granted. Unless there is a serious leak, a toilet that won't flush, or discolored drinking water, there is little or no thought of upgrading the water system. So when you are in the market to remodel and improve your home, that is the time to review what you have and bring the system up to date. Old, corroded pipes are a good place to start. Not only does the corrosion cut down on the rate of flow of the water, but the corroded pipes—especially the ones carrying hot water—will give a rusty brownish cast to the water, rendering it unattractive and nonpotable. Replace such pipes with long-lasting copper lines that will guarantee no leaks or rust. It may not be necessary to replace all the older pipes; the plumbing contractor will be able to advise you on this.

You will want a reputable, licensed plumber for your project. In most localities, plumbing work other than the routine maintenance of changing a washer or repairing a toilet requires a permit and a final inspection by a city official. Employing an unlicensed amateur, while not as dangerous as using an unlicensed electrician, is foolish because leaks can cause a lot of damage and mean heavy expense to repair. Review the water areas of your home with your plumbing contractor —the kitchen, baths, laundry, and wherever water outlets are needed. If you intend to install a swimming pool or a hot tub you will need his advice, too. The plumber can tell you the minimum-size requirements for new baths, the best arrangement of fixtures given the size and the window and door placement of the bath or baths you have. As we pointed out in the section on bath planning, the plumber is not usually well versed in design, but he can tell you what is practical from the standpoint of function and plumbing-code requirements. He can advise you on the size of water heater needed for the demands of your family living and he can recommend the most practical location of a new bathroom to tap into an existing vent stack for economy.

While the plumber is adding new sink, dishwasher, and automatic ice maker in your kitchen or creating a new bath in an addition, have him go over all the existing toilets, lavatories, tubs, and showers in the rest of the house for any leaks and malfunction. If you live in the country and are on your own water system, have him check the size of your storage tank and your pump. It may be that new demands will require a new, larger tank and more powerful pump. If the valves for water outlets in the garden or garage are corroded and hard to manipulate, the time to replace them is while the plumber is on hand. To repeat, a plumber's services are among the most expensive and his cost-clock starts to tick the minute he leaves his shop, so it is wise to make the most of his services while he is on the premises.

CHAPTER SEVENTEEN

HEATING AND COOLING CONSIDERATIONS

WHEN YOU PLAN your remodeling, it is wise to study the heating system you have, first to be sure it is in tip-top shape and second, to be sure it is adequate to handle the scope of the renovation you have in mind. Central heating systems which are warm air, hot water or steam burn oil or gas at very high temperatures. So if the equipment is old, the firebox may have corroded through and the motor may be on the verge of wearing out. These parts should be inspected by a heating contractor or furnace repair service. If they find things in generally good order they will at least want to clean the burner and its controls. If your system uses natural gas as a fuel, the burner is apt to be quite clean and unclogged, since natural gas is a clean-burning source of energy. A fuel-oil burner is another matter, since oil produces soot and combustion by-products, so this should be looked into. With a steam system, you should have the boiler drained to remove impurities which build up as the water boils. A hot-water system is not normally drained as a matter of course, but your heating contractor may want to do so as part of a thorough inspection.

With a forced-warm-air system, the air filter will certainly be inspected and if it is a fiber-glass disposable type it will be replaced if necessary, or if it is a permanent type, washed thoroughly. If you have an electric heating system—embedded in the ceilings of rooms or baseboards under windows—of course there are no motors to wear out and no flames to cause problems. With an electric heat pump which heats in winter and cools in summer, you essentially have a forced-air system and there is a filter to be checked and a motor to be inspected, but again, no flame to corrode a firebox.

The contractor, if you have an old-fashioned, massive-gravity warm-air furnace, will probably recommend a space-saving, compact new furnace and perimeter heating ducts under windows. This will give you a much more efficient, less energy-wasting system. If you have a gravity hot water two-pipe steam system, it will likely be recommended that you convert to forced hot water. This changeover will not be unduly expensive and you will get a more even heat promptly at the touch of the thermostat. Old, bulky, space-consuming radiators can be replaced with compact radiant hot-water baseboards which can be painted to blend with room decor. And speaking of thermostats, be sure to have the present one you have checked for accuracy. If there is a big difference in temperature between the high point when the furnace or boiler turns off and the low point when it comes on, your thermostat is defective and should be replaced.

HEATING REQUIREMENTS FOR ADDED LIVING SPACE

The foregoing presupposes that you are remodeling the living areas of the house without changing the cubic volume of space. However, if you are expanding into an unheated attic or basement or are putting on an addition to the house, you have an entirely different set of circumstances. These areas have to be heated and your heating contractor must decide whether your present system is adequate to handle the new requirements. It is most important that this be done far in advance of remodeling construction: the heating must be planned before, not after, expansion is begun. If you have already anticipated the expansion, warm-air ducts or hot-water pipes may already have been brought up to where the addition will go and have been capped off, so that the furnace or boiler is presumably sized for handling the expansion. In this case, the contractor will merely have to extend the heating system.

If this is not the case and your existing system won't handle the new demands to give the degree of comfort you want in both existing and new space, then you must do one of two things. Either the central system you have must be provided a new, larger furnace or boiler or you must plan auxiliary, separate heating for the attic, basement, garage, or addition you are remodeling. Such separate heating can take several forms. Gas-fired floor or wall heaters can be provided, thermostatically controlled. Vented and recessed or of the sealed-combustion-chamber type, these space heaters are the answer to many situations. Electric heating is another choice for added living space. There are four different types: baseboards, wall or ceiling panels, and a window-installed heat pump. All are thermostatically controlled and all have the advantage that they can be activated only when the space is being occupied so that they can be economical to operate. The heat pump, of course, has the extra advantage that it can be used in summer to cool. If the new living space is large—a huge attic or an addition of several rooms, the answer may be to install a separate forced-warm-air or hot-water system with its own compact furnace or boiler located in a closet and air ducts or baseboards planned in a perimeter layout along the outside walls and under windows.

HEATING FOR THE OLDER HOUSE

If you are remodeling a very old house, chances are that the existing heating system is totally unsatisfactory and should be replaced. In that case you will have to change the whole layout and you should study all the choices and decide what system you prefer. You will have to talk with a heating contractor and study the various systems that are available and then select on the basis of personal preference, comparative fuel cost, cleanliness and, finally, what you can afford to pay. Be sure to find a reputable contractor and rely on his knowledge and professionalism. And do not attempt to do any part of this project yourself. Like the electrical parts of the house, heating is definitely the province of the professional. And the first thing he will insist on is that the walls be thoroughly insulated and all cracks and joints sealed to keep cold air out and warmed air in. More on this subject will be found in the chapter on solar heat.

REMODELING TO INCLUDE COOLING

As with renovation for efficient heating of your home, insulation is mandatory for air-conditioning it. Without insulation of some kind in the ceiling or roof, the walls and all floors over open crawl spaces, cooled air will be dissipated. All cracks and joints must be sealed tightly to remove the escape of cooled air. If you have a forced-air heating system, most often you will be able to use the existing ducts and hook up an air-conditioning unit near the furnace plus a condensing unit outdoors and pipe cooled air to your rooms. An air-conditioning contractor can advise you whether your present ductwork is suitable and whether the registers or diffusers in your rooms are suitable. The contractor may decide that a special air cooling layout is required to conditioning your home more efficiently and economically.

If you have steam or hot water heating, then it is a whole different matter, and it is recommended that a separate system be added for cooling, to provide forced, cooled air through new ductwork to your rooms. An evaporator-blower unit will have to be added inside the structure (preferably in the attic if you have one) and a condenser added outdoors somewhere near the structure. You can choose either a gas- or oil-fired system.

Another solution, if you must build in new heating *and* cooling, is to use a heat pump which, as mentioned before, will heat in winter and cool in summer. The principle with this system is that even in the coldest air there is some heat and even in the warmest, there is some coolth. The heat pump extracts and magnifies whatever degree of coolness or warmth there is. The use of a heat pump presupposes a forced air system with ductwork and is an all electric system.

Whatever type of air conditioning you choose, it is important to zone the house with separate thermostats for various areas. In the average-size house, two zones are sufficient—one for daytime living areas, the other for nighttime sleeping areas. This will provide the comfort you need when you need it, in the most economical way.

CHAPTER EIGHTEEN

REMODELING FOR SOLAR HEAT

As we all know, the trend today is to use the rays of the sun rather than the dwindling supplies of fossil fuels to heat our homes, our water, our swimming pools. A new house, built from scratch, can be designed and constructed to function as a solar structure from the drawing board to the finished product. An existing house is a different matter, but much can be done in the course of remodeling to use the sun for heating. A new term, retrofitting, means adapting the house you have for solar heating systems, and it can be applied to many remodeling projects.

Of course, the basis of a successfully solar-heated house is the insulation in the structure. That comes first—keeping cold air out as much as possible and conversely keeping the warmed air inside with as little escape as possible. The following are insulation ideas to keep in mind as you plan home improvement. If you intend to add new windows, consider units with insulating glass—double-glazed with a pocket of air between. (Also excellent to reduce the entrance of unwanted sound.) Such windows are especially important on the north elevations of a house, where wind and cold are most prevalent, but they are useful on all elevations. Any existing wall which is opened up from the inside or outside should be insulated with fiber-glass blankets if it is not already so equipped. Any new wall should most certainly have blanket insulation stapled to the studs so that each vertical space is securely filled. Attics with open rafters should have insulating blankets added snugly between each. Where attic space does not exist—that is, the roof is too close to the ceilings—insulation of several kinds can be blown in, either through small holes drilled into the ceiling or, on the exterior, through holes drilled in the roof (later securely plugged and tarred for water-fastness).

Where existing interior walls are in bad repair and you wish to merely resurface, first add 4×8-foot sheets of rigid fiberboard which can in turn be surfaced with gypsum board and painted. These sheets are an excellent insulator. On the exterior of a house, foamed plastic boards are available for application over roofs and sidewalls. As a final coating, they must be given a weather-resistant surfacing. All cracks and openings should be sealed with caulking or other sealant material; windows and doors should be weatherstripped. In areas of extreme winter cold, storm windows and entrance doors should be provided. Remember that of all the surfaces of your house, the roof is the most vulnerable to heat loss, because warm air rises. Exterior walls—the sides of your house—are second most important and third are floors over unheated or exposed areas. The last might be in a house with a crawl space instead of a basement. One effective way to insulate in this instance is to close off the open perimeter with cement block or some other masonry material and then blow insulation in the area so created. If space permits, a carpenter can staple insulating blankets to the exposed floor joists from underneath.

Once the foregoing steps are taken to keep in the heat, what can be done to "solarize" it further? There are two important terms in the solar-heating vocabulary: passive and active. A passive system collects and stores the heat of the sun without equipment activated by mechanical energy. An active system uses specialized equipment powered by mechanical energy to gather and take the heat where it is desired. With this in mind, let's examine some ways that retrofitting can be part of your remodeling plans. A water-heating system derived from solar energy is a feasible idea. A gas or electrically powered water heater is one of the largest users of energy in a house, because it is required twelve months of the year unlike space heating. Collectors for solar-heated water can be installed on the roof or, if that is not possible, on a wall or on the ground close to the house. In one system for domestic hot water, flat plate collectors are mounted on special supports. Air is circulated by an exchange unit in which solar energy is transferred to water which is pump-circulated. The heated water is circulated into a storage tank as long as solar energy is available and until the tank temperature reaches 160° F. When a hot-water faucet is turned on, water is drawn from the conventional water heater and preheated water is drawn in from the storage tank. Essentially, then, the conventional electric or gas water heater becomes an auxiliary system which comes on only when solar-heated water is not available, thus cutting down considerably on conventional energy consumption.

If your plans include new fenestration, consider a large expanse of glass facing south. Such a window has a great deal of solar energy available to it and over a whole heating season, a glass expanse gathers more heat than it loses. If you plan an addition, a garage, a porch, or a greenhouse, retrofitting can be called into play. The unheated garage can be of help in two ways: its placement can act as a buffer to the cold air outside and the warmed air within the room adjacent to the garage; and its new roof can be used for the placement of solar collector panels. A greenhouse located on the south elevation can trap sun-heated air and transfer it through registers to the rest of the house. A glass-walled porch could act as a buffer to protect the interior of the main structure and also by leaving an existing window open to the porch, could transfer heated air to the house proper. And if your roof needs repairs, be sure to consider retrofitting in the project. An architect or roofing contractor can tell you how this can be done. In fact, an architect or structural engineer who is involved in your project will be able to suggest many ways of remodeling to include solar heat if you point him or her in that direction. Some of the energy-saving devices save you money here and now. For example, certain kinds of insulating projects are deductible on your federal income tax and an insulating company or specialist can tell you about that. The extra expense involved in retrofitting now will be more than repaid by fuel savings in the long run, to say nothing of the importance to our whole society and way of life of conserving fossil fuels.

A FINAL WORD

THE MAIN PURPOSE of this book has been to give you information to remake your home as efficiently as possible into a new vehicle for living, better suited to the lifestyle you now lead. We hope you will succeed in this. However, no book, no matter how complete or well researched, will answer every question or fulfill every need, because anything pertaining to a home is so personal that individual considerations are inevitable. So it is important to remember that there are many other sources of valuable information available to you. Building-supply dealers, homemaking centers, paint-store salesmen, vendors of electrical, plumbing, kitchen, and bath equipment can be enormously helpful. So don't be afraid to ask questions; knowledgeable people in special fields do not expect you to have answers.

Remember, too, home remodeling is an ever-changing business. There are always new materials and new ways of doing things and you'll arrive at a better house by looking and asking. Professionals in all the phases of remodeling like to show off their expertise and they will help you keep abreast of developments. Many cities have home remodeling and restoration shows where the latest equipment is presented and much can be learned from them.

Perhaps most important is to make your remodeling project a broadening experience. Use it to make yourself a richer, more informed person. Use it also to strengthen family relationships, to learn better how each family member is growing, what his or her new needs are and how your home can help them to better express themselves. You will be spending a lot of time, effort, and money, so make it a memorable experience. Take before photographs—the simplest snapshots will do—and keep an informal scrapbook of the various phases of the project and then compare the finished product. It will give you and all the members of your family an enormous sense of pride and belonging to have been involved in such an exciting undertaking.

It has been said that remodeling brings out the Pygmalion in all of us: there is something basic in human nature that loves to turn dross into gold. A successful remodeling project makes us feel more purposeful, more needed, more alive. That, if nothing else, makes all the painstaking effort, the heartaches and headaches, the aggravations, disappointments, and frustrations worth it. And make no mistake; even professional remodelers goof and often wish in retrospect they had done something differently. Everyone makes mistakes, especially the first time around. As they say, hindsight is always twenty-twenty, so don't berate yourself for what might have been better done. Make honest, well-informed decisions as you go along, and then you can live happily and comfortably with the home you love and which you have raised to a new standard of livability.

A GLOSSARY OF REMODELING TERMS

Amperes—a term to describe the amount of electrical input entering a home; 200-amp service is recommended for today's energy-equipped house.

Attic—the space between the ceiling of the uppermost room and the roof. It may have sufficient headroom to serve as living space or may be merely a crawl space, or smaller still, just an air space.

Attic vents—louvered or screened openings in the soffit or gable ends of a house to permit air circulation for dryness and summer cooling.

Baffle—an interior or exterior privacy screen

Baseboard—a piece of lumber, often a 1×4 at floor level to give a finish between wall and floor. Often given a molding to trim its upper edge.

Batten—wood strips that cover joints in exterior walls of boards or plywood, usually repeated in sequential pattern for decoration.

Beam—a basic part of structure used horizontally to support whatever is above it. Can be exposed for room decor or covered.

Bearing wall or partition—a structural element that divides areas and helps to support what is above it.

Blind-nailing—the use of headless nails that are countersunk so that they do not show. Holes are filled with putty.

Brace—an angled piece of wood or metal attached to wall or floor for strengthening the over-all structure.

Built-up roofing—a system of roof surfacing with three to five layers of asphalt felt interspersed with hot tar and finished off with gravel. A system primarily for flat roofs.

Casement—a type of window that opens out or in, hinged on a side, top or bottom. Frame of the window may be metal or wood.

Casing—moldings used to trim doors and windows.

Checking—cracks that appear in wood or painted surfaces. Usually not serious in thick wood beams. To test strength, stick an icepick into the wood and if it is mushy all through, replace the member. If paint checking is extreme, surface should be scraped and repainted.

Code—the standards formulated by a local building department and to which remodeling work must conform to be legal.

Cornice—a roof overhang provided for decoration. Combined with facia board and moldings forms the entablature of a house. Or in rooms, a decorative molding used as finish between wall and ceiling.

Cove molding—another type of wood finish between wall and ceiling, with a concave appearance.

Crawl space—a shallow area under a house, usually enclosed by a foundation wall. Or a shallow space in the attic or area above the uppermost rooms.

Cripple—a stud that does not go to full height.

Dado—the lower part of a wall often called a wainscot, commonly found in dining rooms and halls where chairs along the wall are apt to harm the plaster or paint.

Deck—a structure, usually wood, created as an outdoor extension of an indoor room, open to the sky.

Dormer—a projection in a sloping roof to form headroom and an area for a window.

Downspout—a pipe to take roof water to ground.

Drip—part of an upper exterior wood or metal structural member designed to divert water to ground.

Dry-wall—a type of interior wall surfacing, usually gypsum board.

Duct—metal tubes for taking warmed or cooled air from furnace to rooms.

Eave—the overhang of a roof.

Encasement—the creation of a new face for a house, made by covering over the existing exterior with plywood or other material.

Façade—the front or street elevation of a house.

Fascia—a board around the top of a house under the roof line, often combined with moldings.

Flashing—sheet metal used to protect a structure from water entry.

Flat paint—a type of interior wall finish that dries to a matte finish.

Flue—the space through which smoke or gas passes from interior fireplaces or furnace to outside air. Usually enclosed in a chimney which can accomodate one or several flue pipes. Flues are made of terra cotta pipe or galvanized metal.

Footing—the base for a foundation, secured below frostline. Usually concrete.

Foundation—the supporting structure of a house, under the first floor.

Framing—the skeleton of a structure, usually wood for a house but can include steel studding and beams. Houses are most often of balloon framing whereby vertical elements of bearing walls rise as studs, attached to a plate atop the foundation, to the roof plate. Platform framing is a variation in which each floor is framed separately and rests as a unit atop the lower, separately framed floor.

Furring—wood strips applied to wall or ceiling to form a base to which finish material can be attached. Useful in creating an even appearance.

Gable—the triangular section of the roof above the eave line.

Girder—main beam of wood or steel to support points of heavy load.

Gloss—a type of paint used in kitchens, baths, and other areas where a dense, wipable surface is required. Dries to a shiny look.

Grain—the pattern of wood created by the direction of fibers.

Ground—a way to make electricity safe by taking its charge to earth.

Grout—a paste made of water and powder to fill spaces between tile and other masonry.

Gutter—a metal or wood element attached below the eaves to catch rainwater and guide it to a downspout.

Gypsum board—plaster between layers of heavy paper to create a wall surfacing material. Sometimes referred to as Sheetrock which is a brand name product of United States Gypsum.

Header—a horizontal support framing a doorway, window or other opening.

Hip roof—a design which rises from the sides of a building in angled planes.

Insulation board—a rigid building board made of coarse wood fiber, found in many sizes, densities and appearances.

Jamb—the lining of head and sides of a doorway or window, usually wood.

Joist—ceiling beams, used in parallel rows to support an upper-floor structure and the ceiling of the room in question.

Landing—a break in a staircase in the form of a level platform.

Lath—a strip of wood or a metal grid onto the cracks of which wall plaster is secured.

Lintel—a horizontal piece of lumber supporting a heavy load over a door or window.

Louver—a shutterlike wood or plastic series of horizontal slats with openings between.

Lumber—boards planed and cut in a sawmill to various sizes for various structural uses.

Mantel—a shelf over a fireplace opening or an item of millwork which includes all the trim around sides and top of the fireplace. Comes in many stock sizes and period designs.

Masonry—brick, concrete block, stone, gypsum block, used together and held with mortar to create a wall.

Mastic—a viscous substance used as a bonding agent for floor tile and other material.

Millwork—items such as completed doors and windows, mantels, shutters, sidelight panels, etc., made of wood in a factory.

Molding—a wood strip, often ponderosa pine, with curved or other decorative detail for use as trim.

Mullion—a wood strip to divide a door or window into small glazed areas. Or a plastic snap-in grid to achieve a similar purpose.

Natural finish—a treatment for wood to preserve the appearance of its grain and color, using shellac, urethane, varnish, or other sealant.

Nonbearing wall—a partition to divide interior space that carries no overhead weight.

On center—or O.C., the term for the spacing of structural members, the most common being the standard width between studs in a wall—sixteen inches on center or 16" O.C.

Panel—a flat segment of wood or plywood used for interior or exterior covering. Comes in modular sizes, 4×8 feet, 4×10, 4×12, etc.

Partition—a wall to divide interior spaces.

Pitch—the slope of a roof given in inches of rise per foot of run.

Plate—horizontal wood member attached over the foundation and running the perimeter of the structure to which vertical studs are attached. The top plate is the horizontal member which tops the studs and supports the ceiling joists.

Plumb—truly in line vertically.

Ply—an increment of thickness in any multilayered building material.

Plywood—a structural material of wood, manufactured in panels, with three or more layers of wood veneer, crossgrain laminated with glue. Usually with two faces—one for a premium, finished look, the other raw. Plywood panels come in a variety of exotic woods and can be found with both faces of premium quality.

Preservative—a substance used to treat wood to render it rot- and/or termite-proof for a certain length of time. Many sizes of lumber can be found treated accordingly, pentachlorophenol being the most common preservative, factory-applied.

Primer—the first coat of paint or the paint itself used as a first coat.

Putty—a filler material made of whiting and linseed oil made into a doughlike substance. A generic term for any kind of filler material.

Quarter round—a molding that results from a circle cut into four pieces. Comes in sizes—¼″ quarter round, ½″, etc.

Radiant heating—a forced-hot-water system using baseboards, radiators, or pipes embedded in the floor. With electricity as the fuel, radiant heat can take the form of resistance ceiling coils embedded in plaster.

Rafter—a roof-supporting structural member; same as a joist.

Rail—cross member of a paneled door or of a window. Also part of a staircase.

Reflective insulation—usually aluminum foil used in walls to reduce the loss of heat or coolth across an air space.

Restoration—remodeling to preserve and enhance the architectural character of a building.

Ridge—the top edge of a gabled roof, the ridge pole being the member at the apex of the gable to which the rafters are attached.

Rise—the height of one stairway step to another. The riser is the board at the rear of each step.

Rolled roofing—an asphalt-fiber material. Comes in 36″ widths and weighs usually 45 to 90 pounds.

Sash—a frame with one or more pieces of glass. As in upper or lower sash of a double-hung window. Generically a window.

Scratch—a coat of plaster—the first rough coat to which subsequent layers are attached.

Sealer—a clear or colored liquid finish over wood.

Semigloss—a kind of paint or enamel that has a medium luster.

Shake—a thick shingle, handsplit from red cedar or other water-resistant wood.

Sheathing—a sheet of plywood or boards nailed to studs to strengthen walls and to which a finished material is attached. Or nailed to roof rafters to form the undercoat for surface roofing material. Sheathing paper, of felt or wood pulp, is applied over the plywood or boards to reduce transmission of air and moisture.

Sheet metal—used for flashing, downspouts, gutters, etc.

Shingles—an exterior building material of wood, asbestos-cement or asphalt, used over sheathing.

Shutters—louvered or paneled units used at the sides of windows and doors as decoration or movable and closable for security.

Siding—any outer exterior building material.

Sleeper—a wood member that supports a floor.

Soffit—the underside of a roof overhang.

Square—a measurement for roofing—100 square feet.

Stile—the upright framing in a door, perpendicular to the rail.

Strike plate—a metal device in a door frame which receives the latch and bolt.

Stringer—the stairway sides which support the treads and risers. Or an extra support for cross ties in a floor or ceiling.

Strip flooring—narrow boards, usually oak.

Stucco—an exterior building material, plaster with a cement base.

Stud—upright structural members, usually fir, attached to the base plate at the bottom and the top plate above.

Subfloor—plywood panels or boards forming the understructure for finished flooring.

Suspended ceiling—a system which hangs from the joists.

Threshhold—a wood strip with beveled edges which spans the flooring and door sill. Can also be metal.

Toenailing—driving a nail into wood at a slant so as to reach into another wood member.

Tongue and groove—refers to a type of milling to form male and female joinings on boards for floor, walls, siding, etc.

Tread—the flat part of a stairway, the step.

Trim—moldings and other decorative millwork to finish off openings.

Truss—a factory-made frame which serves as support for an extra-long span.

Undercoat—about the same as a primer coat.

Underlayment—any material used under a finished surface to assure an even surface. Such as hardboard under vinyl or other floor tile; rubber or felt padding under carpet, etc.

Valley—the low point where two roof slopes join.

Veneer—a thin sheet of wood resulting from the rotary cutting of a log. Three or more veneers are used to create a sheet of plywood.

Vent—a pipe or duct that conducts air in or out of a house. The vent stack is a special part of the toilet plumbing system that carries gas up through the roof to the outdoors.

Weatherstripping—metal or felt strips that seal around doors and windows to reduce entrance of cold air or moisture.

Zoning—city ordinances that ascribe legal uses to buildings in certain areas, as in zoned residential, zoned commercial, etc.

INDEX

(Page numbers in italics refer to illustrations.)